THE
PLACE
OF HOME

THE
PLACE
OF HOME
English domestic environments, 1914–2000

ALISON RAVETZ
WITH RICHARD TURKINGTON

Taylor & Francis
Taylor & Francis Group

LONDON AND NEW YORK

Published by Taylor & Francis
2 Park Square, Milton Park, Abingdon, Oxfordshire OX14 4RN
711 Third Avenue, New York, NY 10017

First issued in paperback 2011

First edition 1995

© 1995 Alison Ravetz with Richard Turkington

Typeset in 10/12½ pt Times by Cambrian Typesetters, Frimley, Surrey

This book was commissioned and edited by Alexandrine Press, Oxford

A catalogue record for this book is available from the British Library

Publisher's Note
The publisher has gone to great lengths to ensure the quality of this reprint
but points out that some imperfections in the original may be apparent

ISBN 978-0-419-17980-1 (hbk)
ISBN 978-0-415-51426-2 (pbk)

CONTENTS

ACKNOWLEDGEMENTS

Thanks are due to the Department of Social Policy and Sociology of the University of Leeds, where Alison Ravetz held an Honorary Fellowship from 1992 to 1995; to the Librarians of Pershore College of Horticulture and to Nicola Coxon, Conservation Officer, Birminham City Council for their assistance to Richard Turkington; and to Ann Rudkin and Anna Ravetz for their valuable editorial help.

We are grateful also to all those who have provided pictures for the book and in particular to the following for their kind permission to reproduce illustrations: Abbey National, Avoncroft Museum of Buildings, Birmingham City Council, Eldonian Community, English Heritage, Focus Housing Association, Peter Mitchell, *Newmarket Journal*, Town and Country Planning Association, *Yorkshire Post*. Apologies are made to any copyright holders for unintentional omissions.

Where no other source is given, illustrations are from the personal collections of Alison Ravetz and Richard Turkington.

Finally we would like to thank Steve Poolton for his skill and patience in photographing our originals from some very difficult source materials.

1

INTRODUCTION: THE CONTEXT

When this story opens the population of England numbered less than 34 millions, distributed in some seven million households and a lesser number of dwellings. Eighty years later the population size was over 46 millions, and there were nearly a million more dwellings than the nation's eighteen and a half million households. Over the middle decades of the century the population had made net gains from migration, with the consequence that by the 1990s slightly over 6 per cent belonged to ethnic minorities, the black minorities, in particular, being heavily concentrated in the big conurbations. The fraction of people who lived in the care of others, in institutions of various kinds, was tiny – less than half a per cent – and it had fallen by nearly a half since 1914.

The time span covered here, the best part of a century, was one of unparalleled economic, technical and social change. It included the two World Wars, several lesser conflicts and a 'Cold War'; and two major economic depressions, of the 1930s and the 1980s, each accompanied by mass unemployment and restructuring of industry. It also saw the full implementation of a Welfare State in the 1940s, building on more tentative attempts of the early 1900s and between the wars. Essential to this, and owing much to 'the revolutionary influence of war upon social policy' (Marwick, 1968, p. 122), was an increased role for government. In 1914, the state could not even

reliably know how much people earned; when it emerged victorious in 1945 there were very few areas of life, including the interior of the home, into which it had not intruded.

Though deep structural changes had long been under way, England in 1914 was a strongly hierarchical society. The poor were a race apart, clearly recognizable from their physique, clothing, speech and behaviour. Many lived at or little above survival level, in homes with a pre-industrial level of squalor. 'Gentility' was still recognized and, though not necessarily linked to financial wealth, it could command many privileges, including private education, service from tradesmen, and domestic servants. War hastened changes already in train. From 1921, and particularly over the period 1931–1951, those in white collar, salaried positions began to increase, so that they eventually outnumbered those in manual occupations by the mid-1970s; but their incomes fell relative to skilled manual workers. Between the wars, new industries had caused a drift to the south east, leaving residues of the unemployed in the old industrial areas. Half a century later, a new generation of 'sunrise' industries was less able to absorb large numbers, and with progressive contraction of traditional manufacturing industries there was a growing polarity between those who were unemployed or in low-paid, insecure service jobs, and those with the management and information skills relevant to a rapidly changing economy. It was now becoming a very real question whether the future economy would ever again be able to use the labour of the many unskilled people, who were now more of an 'under class' than a working class.

Between these two points lay a period of rising productivity and affluence. Rearmament had offered a way out of recession in the 1930s, and egalitarian wartime measures followed by a period of full employment brought an unprecedented class convergence. The rising cost of living was offset by rising incomes and smaller families, while increasing numbers of wives were able to make a contribution to family incomes. The proportion of married women in paid work rose from around a tenth in 1931 to over a half by the mid 1980s. With universal and free medical care, better diet, increased educational opportunities and powerful unions, these trends rapidly eliminated the old and most obvious indices of class difference: malnourished or maimed bodies, children dressed in hand-me-downs, and young mothers aged before their time. Up-to-date family housing, with all its associated possessions,

made its own contribution to the 'increasingly pervasive influence of middle-class values' (Stevenson, 1984, p. 465).

Change in the family, that 'essential glue of the social fabric' (Marwick, 1982, p. 171) was crucial to twentieth-century lives. A reduction of family size had begun as long ago as the 1870s, but at the turn of the century marriages with five or six surviving children were still normal. Average family sizes then steadily reduced, touching under two children per marriage by the mid 1930s, and again after 1972. The downward trend was interrupted only by a short boost to the birthrate after 1945, and a more sustained one between the early 1950s and 1964. This meant a significant contraction in the active period of childbearing and rearing, the period between a woman's first and last childbirth nearly halving between the 1930s and the 1970s. Working-class families continued on average to be larger than middle-class families, a difference that was discernible in council owned and owner-occupied houses. A much greater difference, however, was seen in the ethnic minorities: those of Pakistani or

There was no ambiguity as to the poor, how and where they lived. (*Source*: n.d. but 1960)

Bangladeshi origin, in particular, continuing to have families of a size not seen in the indigenous white population since Victorian times (Coleman, 1988).

Households, in distinction to families, were further diminished in size by the final disappearance of resident domestic servants after 1939, and of lodgers, who were a normal part of many households to around 1960. At the start of the century the average household size was around four and a half. From 1931 it declined sharply, to become little more than two by 1985. By mid century, nearly two thirds of households contained three people or less; but the most dramatic rise was in the single person household: a rarity before 1939, this accounted for more than a fifth of all households by 1981. A big contributing factor was the growing independence of young people; but the main cause was the changing age distribution of the population. Between 1911 and 1981, lower birth rates and increased life expectancy, particularly among women, brought about a threefold increase in the proportion of people of sixty-five and over, while the proportion of children under fifteen was reduced by one

The functions and deeper social or personal meanings of the home were established long before 1914, so that even the Blitz could not disturb this Plymouth family. (*Source*: Boyd Orr, 1943)

third. The recognition of the existence of single
people not living in families, and of the
propriety of their having homes of their own,
was an important strand in housing in the later
half of the century.

The most important steps in the creation of
the modern home had been taken long before
the start of our period: in particular, its
functional separation from commerce and
manufacture, along with its physical relocation
in the suburb, where women and children were
segregated in each other's company and away
from the formal economy (Hall, 1982; Davidoff
and Hall, 1983). From this there arose a new
kind of domestic economy: dedicated to producing, not items for sale or even items consumed
within the home, but care of children, husbands
and other family members, with accompanying
social rituals, and an elaborate care of the
home itself, in the form of housework (Davidoff,
1976). These together constituted a 'domestic
culture' which reflected dominant and deeply
held social, moral and religious values of the
time.

Although apparently segregated from industry, capitalism and the city, the role of the
home was in fact crucial to urban-industrial
society. Industrialization had brought with it
new ways of living and confusions of different
populations who lived and worked in close
proximity but who had different backgrounds,
customs, religions, skills and occupations. Social
gradations became crucially important to identity and security, most particularly at borderlines
between classes. The most important of these,
in the eyes of Victorians, was that separating
'respectability' from 'non respectability'. This
not only divided middle from working classes,
but was sensed at many levels of the social
scale where, coming from diverse origins,
respectability was 'best seen as a bundle of self-
generated habits and values derived from past
customs and present responses to living and
working conditions' (Thompson, 1988, p. 355).
One of the things that gave it great force was

Wives were the chief guardians of family respectability, and the scrubbed and whitened doorstep and
sill (as here) its most important sign. (*Source*: Allied
Iron Founders, *c.* 1954)

fear of falling victim to the harsh Victorian
Poor Law, which was 'perhaps the one big
success of the century' in impelling people
towards respectable domestic standards (*Ibid*,
1988, p. 355).

How people were housed played a critical
role here. Clearly, identity and security were
best guaranteed by one-class streets or districts,
notably the 'byelaw' suburbs of one-family
houses which became the norm for a wide
cross-section of working and middle classes in
the half century before 1914. 'Enveloped however thinly in its own privacy' (*Ibid*, 1988, p.
182), the house could show its status by
lace curtains and whitened doorstep, while a
developing technology served to 'encapsulate'
it. With its own back entrance, water supply,
privy, and clothes line, it was released from the
necessity of sharing: 'release from the necessity
of doing one's dirty washing in public was
literally the path to respectability' (*Ibid*, 1988,
p. 193).

Thus a peculiarly English atmosphere of residential repose was created. For many years respectable middle-class citizens had been passing byelaws to cleanse their streets of unwanted traders and other intruders (the 'no hawkers, no circulars' plates found on many front gates to 1950 or beyond providing a last reminder), and the result was to make the surroundings of the home mere 'waste space or connective tissue . . . sterile or anonymous' (Daunton, 1990, p. 204). In general, the street activities of earlier times, which had once engaged all classes, were progressively suppressed: fairs, public executions (the last in 1868), contests, gambling, cockfighting, unruly games, music and dancing, as well as more familial events like wakes and weddings (Stedman-Jones, 1974). Street life did continue in working-class neighbourhoods, but in emasculated form: a Lambeth man thought he could even pinpoint the ending of knees-ups and spontaneous dancing around 1900 (Harrisson and Madge, 1939). In the present century, social use of the street was increasingly reserved for special occasions – coronations or victory celebrations – and one last echo was the street parties of London squatters of the 1960s and 1970s, who occupied the last decaying remains of classic working-class neighbourhoods (Chapter 6, below).

Working-class domestic life was, nevertheless, noticeably more gregarious than that of the middle classes and, as long as it was not disturbed, it remained in many respects collective. The 'classic' slum was familiar, cosy and colourful, a village-like world of well understood 'tribal areas' only a step beyond the door of the house, itself always open but inviolate (Hoggart, 1957). The 'tribes' were not always friendly, and most had their outcasts (Roberts, 1971); but in hard times people owed much to their neighbours. This was not to be confused with personal closeness, for neighbourliness 'did not imply the intimacy of friendship' but rather 'reciprocity – looking out for one another'

'Keep off my doorstep, *please*' pleased Anne Blythe in *Housewife*, April 1946, viewing the resumption of such intrusions with alarm.

(Benson, 1989, p. 118). And for all their mutuality, since they lacked true autonomy such neighbourhoods were more vulnerable than anyone foresaw to the closure of their staple industries, the rationalization and centralization of their services – schools, shops, transport – and above all to the coup de grace of slum clearance.

There never was any precise definition of the slum, partly because of its multiple contributing factors – bad landlords, bad buildings, environmental pollution, overcrowding, feckless occupants – but partly also because its categorization changed with time. Even in Victorian society, technically substandard housing affected only a minority of English workers, who were widely admitted to be better and more cheaply housed than their European counterparts (Thompson,

Women in particular depended on mutual support in poverty. (*Source*: Allied Iron Founders, *c.* 1954)

1988). As much as anything, the term 'slum' was a label used subjectively, not only by different-class onlookers, but by those of its inhabitants who wished to distance themselves from it, both physically and socially.

Their attitudes, and the answering sympathies of those who campaigned on their behalf, provided much of the motivation of housing policy, notably after each World War when, as it were, the nation gathered its energies for an onslaught on the obsolete and disgraceful living conditions that some of its citizens had to endure. Thus in 1919 subsidized and universal council housing was introduced, with the explicit intention of extending what was then the most up-to-date and superior family housing to a select portion of the working class. By 1945 this and a widening experience of home ownership

between the wars made possible a concept of a universal domestic culture: the product of raised working-class standards and expectations and realistically lowered middle-class standards. The result was a compact and functional family home which reflected 'an increasingly common culture, balanced by the cult of domesticity and individual choice' (Stevenson, 1984, p. 381).

This encouraged, not a nuclear family home (for this had always been the norm in English history) but an increasing nuclearization of the family, with weakening of ties to the extended family and increasing absorption in the home itself. As well as removal to suburban estates, this owed much to increasing leisure and holiday time which was spent, if not on the house and garden, on holidays away from home. Among other things, the trend meant less readily available support for grandparents as they aged, and child-rearing practices without the active help, or even regular acquaintance, of grandparents, aunts or wider kin.

To a large extent the old frameworks of kin and neighbourhood were replaced by a new consumerism, made possible by rising household incomes and smaller families to keep. Mass production of goods for the home was far from new after 1914, but it grew in importance, promoted by the weekly and daily press, advertisements on hoardings and in the cinema. Goods were made more accessible by hire purchase and mail order, while new materials such as plastics made them cheaper or more versatile. The biggest stimulus of all, however, came from a domestic electrical supply, which began to be available to all classes between the wars but, like plumbing and hot water, only became universal after the Second World War (Chapter 7, below). Already before the war ended the independent research body, Political and Economic Planning, was assessing how the light engineering industries could adapt and expand into the market for household appliances when hostilities were over (PEP, 1945). What was not allowed for at this time was the phenomenal increase of family cars after 1950. These would take up space outside the home and fill much of people's leisure and holiday time, and indeed of their consciousness generally.

The other revolution in the home was the change in its leisure functions. Before 1914, leisure time was briefer but parlour games and homemade entertainment were more common: daughters, in particular, provided music, and children, party pieces. There was no precedent for broadcasting and nothing, perhaps, could match the first impact of the 'wireless' on the home in 1922, which was 'as near magic as anyone could conceive' (Stevenson, 1984, p. 431). Although listening to its only heavy and expensive set united the family, particularly in

Suburbanization and electrification changed family relationship within the home. (*Source*: Advertisement, North Metropolitan Electric Supply Company, June 1933)

the war years, this brought the world of national and international affairs into the sanctum of the home. But in the event it was television that did most to change domestic behaviour, for unlike listening to the radio, which did not have to interrupt household tasks, it commanded the whole attention. With larger and coloured screens, it obtruded into people's lives as radio had never done and soap opera neighbours became more compelling than real-life neighbours of the street.

Through the interwar years and beyond, the housewife's lighter tasks such as sewing and mending were usually described as her leisure activities. To judge from the huge growth of women's magazines and the rise of the Women's Institute after 1914, the full-time housewife between the wars took her home crafts very seriously, baking, preserving, rug making and adorning her home with many handmade items. Eventually there came a stage in the second half of the century when such skills were no longer passed down to daughters.

Their loss was partly offset by an entirely new phenomenon of home decorating and 'do-it-yourself', in which husbands usually played the leading part, and which eventually became a new, informal sector of the economy in its own right (Pahl, 1984). While this appeared to be completely individualistic, it was closely connected to the consumer industries and advertising. It was the paradoxical nature of the twentieth-century home to seem increasingly

New homes brought a new role for husbands, wives playing an ancillary part. (*Source*: *DIY Gardening Annual*, 1950)

self sufficient but in fact to be increasingly dependent on centralised utilities and services – part of a 'mass culture [that] was hard to escape' (Stevenson, 1984, p. 402).

The nature of poverty was also affected by these changes, becoming qualitatively different from what it had been before 1914. After the establishment of the Welfare State, 'primary' poverty was found only exceptionally. By the end of the century even those living on welfare benefits in unsatisfactory houses shared many of the goods of the affluent: not only three piece suites and wall-to-wall (if inferior quality) carpeting, but colour TVs and perhaps video recorders, which were now counted as basic items in the family budget, albeit to the indignation of older citizens who remembered them as luxuries. But many of the supports of the earlier phase of poverty had also disappeared: people were now less adept at making do and improvising and, above all, they lacked the neighbourhood support and solidarity of large numbers in similar deprivation. It was in many ways harder to be poor in a society where most were doing well. This applied particularly in housing, where a 'general improvement . . . made the condition of those who did not share in it the more keenly felt' (Holmans, 1987, p. 483).

Two fundamentals governed the course of housing after 1914: firstly, houses were durable and commonly outlasted human lives. The stock increased by accumulation, not normally increasing by more than two per cent a year, so that for the most part people's homes had been the homes of many others before them. This meant that houses built for one social order and scale of priorities served under greatly different social conditions, becoming part of an elaborate housing hierarchy: 'chronological strata of houses of different ages . . . extended and reinforced a social structure that was also embodied in the types and values of new houses' (Thompson, 1988, p. 187). Secondly, the cost of a new house, or the stored-up

capital value of an old one, was far beyond the means of most people, particularly when they were young and building families and so most in need of domestic space. Their only access to homes was then either by the form of interest called rent, or by borrowing for purchase, which was closely linked to earnings and taxation.

This was one of the routes through which the state was able directly to influence access to housing. In the earlier nineteenth century it was not at all obvious that the state should be involved in housing at all. To 1914, virtually all houses were built by private enterprise, as and when markets and land became available, and the bulk were rented from private landlords. The earliest direct state intervention was for public health reasons, through designation of dwellings 'unfit for human habitation', with closures and clearances. Other motives besides public health were involved, for crime and immorality were to be removed with slums, and valuable sites freed for commercial and highway uses. However, the actual amounts of slum clearance before 1914 were small and the two main campaigns were of the twentieth century. The first was in the 1930s, when the connection between bad housing and bad health was demonstrably clear; but by the time of the second, in the 1950s–1970s, it was far more tenuous, and other arguments had to be brought into play to justify the removal of so much older housing (Chapter 4, below).

The second intervention of the state, through the byelaws, was the regulation of technical standards of new house building. In effect this created the special nature of the pre-1914 terraced house, as well as influencing the quality of all housing built subsequently (Chapter 7, below). The unintended but momentous effect was 'to widen the gap between the rent-paying capacity of working class families and the economic price at which working class dwellings could be provided' (Cullingworth, 1966, p. 16); but the full consequences of this only became apparent over time, as the older stock of pre-byelaw houses was diminished through clearance.

Direct state provision and management of new houses, through subsidy to local councils, only began in 1919, and it was not arrived at without much controversy and campaigning. At first it was intended as a temporary measure only, and there are differing explanations of its real motivation (Swenarton, 1981; Daunton, 1987; Holmans, 1987). In the event, it was continued for some seventy years, during which it became the main form of rented housing, at its peak (in the 1970s) contributing nearly a third of the total housing stock.

What made it outstandingly important, and indeed made the British housing system unique, was that it worked alongside the freezing of rents of private landlords, first imposed in 1915. Again not intended as anything other than a temporary measure, rent control endured in one form or another for half a century, and then continued to influence subsequent rent regimes. Control was one of the main reasons for the decline of landlordism, changing as it did the balance of power between landlord and tenant 'decisively in favour of the latter' (Benson, 1989, p. 84). This was masked from the perception of many onlookers, however, because of the poor quality of the stock in question and the comparative poverty of many of its tenants, which conspired to make land-lords' rapacity, rather than the system, seem the root of the problem. In contrast, council housing at its best offered the most advanced kind of suburban family dwellings, albeit these embodied many assumptions about patterns of family and domestic life that were strongly reinforced by housing managers using a range of sanctions.

The regulation of land for housing was another and entirely twentieth-century means of state intervention in housing. For centuries, upper class suburbanization had caused the spread of cities and engulfment of villages.

With population growth and developing public transport, lower class suburbanization also escalated, and the diffusion of automobiles between the wars threatened to remove all practical barriers to commuter suburbs. At the same time there was a growing concern for countryside preservation, particularly among urban-based amenity groups seeking to preserve access to unspoilt countryside. The earliest steps towards state control over housing land were taken in 1909, when, however, they were more to do with the planning, rather than placing, of new suburbs. Between the wars state control over land development increased, but was still very limited by the powers of private land owners. The 1930s, however, saw the beginning of control of ribbon development around London, with the establishment of a 'green belt'. Planners' powers were finally transformed by the 1947 Town and Country Planning Act, which obliged all developers to conform to a development plan, without any right of compensation.

The thinking behind these statutory plans was crucial to the future location of housing. They invariably defined the urban structure in terms of concentric rings of decreasing residential densities, and marked out permitted land uses according to a principle of functional separation, most particularly of residential areas from industry and commerce. To a large extent this simply confirmed the *status quo*: the post-1919, low-density suburban estates, council owned or private, were judged to need nothing more than protection, while the definition of town centres as mainly non-residential agreed with their existing land prices and rents. With the established public health machinery there was no obstacle, when it was propitious, to removing any old, substandard housing they might have.

The more problematic areas, however, were the inner rings around centres, and the countryside. In 1947 it was envisaged that the former would be redeveloped largely as council housing

After the war, the old environment would be entirely replaced by clean, modern, low-density towns and cities, through Town and Country Planning. (Bournville Village Trust, *c.* 1946)

estates. To an extent they were, but large parts were left declining and neglected, trapped between high-value city centre stores and offices and the prosperous suburbs, and gouged by the new highways linking suburbs to centres. In rural areas the planning presumption was at first against new building of any kind, except in the strictly government controlled new and expanded towns; but population growth made it impossible to adhere to this, particularly in England's southern regions. New private housing estates were therefore conceded around many country towns and designated villages; but as far as possible remoter rural land and,

above all, the green belts now established round all major cities were treated as sacrosanct. Thus land policies achieved 'the containment of urban England': 'a uniquely British form of urbanisation' (McKay and Cox, 1979, p. 39; Hall *et al.*, 1973). It prevented the endless sprawl of low-density housing over the face of the land, but at the cost of scarcity prices for homes in the countryside, with a consequent housing problem for young or low-paid rural workers: a problem that was exacerbated by the unhindered conversion of many village houses to second homes. It also made it impossible for cities to find land for populations displaced by slum clearance, with the consequence that rebuilding often took the form of high-rise family flats (Chapter 3, below).

Amendment of this situation by the latter part of the century was at best partial. At the risk of alienating some of their natural supporters Conservative governments continued to resist demands for new houses in rural areas, even in the form of well designed new villages. They offered some cash grants for reintroducing middle-class housing in city centres, where it was placed in recognizable enclaves, sometimes enclosed by walls, and preferably with a natural attraction like a river or waterside, to tempt back buyers.

Together, these policy interventions created a hybrid system that regulated rather than replaced a free market in housing. This was somewhat masked by a public debate that was dominated by two apparently opposite and irreconcileable philosophies. That of the left favoured state housing for all, as a subsidized social service, while that of the right opposed indiscriminate state provision and would only as a last resort subsidize such people as were not provided for in the market. However, once it overcame its initial resistance, the Labour Party concurred in the rise to dominance of owner occupation after the 1950s. The privileged position of this tenure then relegated council housing to the position of a 'second estate': a complementary but inevitably inferior tenure.

Under the hybrid system neither party had the will or ability to follow its stated goals to their logical end. Regulation rather than revolution might have obvious benefits, not least of reflecting a broad social consensus; but this was on the whole an inefficient way of developing a national housing system over a period of great social change. In particular, it 'prevented debate on housing from focusing on such fundamental questions as access to housing, the extent of inequality in housing, and the effects of policy on occupational and residential mobility' (MacKay and Cox, 1979, p. 153).

One might add that neither was it particularly well designed for the maintenance of the housing stock or its technical efficiency and innovation.

The chosen route for addressing housing problems meant others that were not followed. One might have been subsidy of private developers, which was tried for only a few brief years in the 1920s. Another and more likely route would have been state reliance on the voluntary housing trusts which were becoming active providers of housing for the urban poor from the 1860s. Despite being included in every measure for public housing, they were not called upon to play an active role until 1964, when the Housing Corporation was set up to encourage them and channel special housing association subsidies. Even then, their role was not significant until 1974, when they were charged with housing single people and other special kinds of household not normally offered council housing. Again, it was not until the 1980s that they were charged with the provision of the 'social housing' which was to replace council housing, but this policy was vitiated by the fact that as yet their contribution was little more than two per cent of the entire housing stock.

There was never any serious suggestion of the state making direct payments to those in housing need, to enable them to find their own accommodation in a freely operating market. Under rent control, the subsidy of private tenants came out of landlords' pockets, through frozen rents, while under council housing the state subsidy was attached to the properties occupied so that, although it was pooled between properties of different qualities, it was limited to those selected as tenants.

Dependance on council housing as the main channel of housing reform owed much to the strong English tradition of model villages built by great industrialists, a tradition in which it seemed more acceptable to replace slums by 'ideal' dwellings than to use any more direct wealth redistribution. 'Bad housing is highly visible, and its power to shock correspondingly great . . . Such conditions offended against widespread sentiment about fairness and human dignity, even if the inequalities of income and wealth from which they sprang were regarded as being part of the natural order of things' (Holmans, 1987, p. 14).

Clearly, there were inherent dangers in such an approach. Official criteria of housing standards, and the standards of domestic behaviour these entailed, were dictated by upper-class and expert opinion, so imposing values that were not necessarily valid for everyone. The fact that they also made housing more costly left people with little freedom to decide on a different allocation of their own resources. This was not too serious as long as the pre-1914 houses could cater for those excluded or dissenting from such 'reform'; but as the older houses diminished in number they were less and less able to fill this role. Above all, the fact that the whole housing system was increasingly constrained by policy made it particularly vulnerable to public expenditure cuts, and to the changes of direction that frequently accompanied changes of political control.

Thus the last policy phase of the century, of an extreme right Conservative government, did attempt to put all housing on a free market footing, as part of its wider programme of reforming and reducing the welfare state. In principle, this might have addressed some of the weaknesses of a hybrid, public-private system, for instance by really transferring public subsidy from dwellings to people through the 'housing benefit' introduced in 1982–83. But the by now severe reduction of council-owned stock was not adequately compensated by growth in other rented housing, and housing benefit levels were cut rather than raised as rents rose with inflation. At the same time, increased reliance on home ownership at a time of high unemployment and welfare cuts accentuated some of the latent problems of this

tenure. It had doubled since the Second World War, overtaking private rented housing by 1961, and it now accommodated about two thirds of all households. Long acknowledged by both left and right as the main prop of a 'property-owning democracy' (the phrase first used by Anthony Eden in 1946), it had enjoyed a privileged status, both ideologically and through the tax system. It was so extolled, indeed, that there grew up the idea that 'home' in its truest sense could only be achieved in a house owned by the family occupying it (Saunders, 1990). This of course did violence to the long history of the cult of domesticity, but by the end of the century it had arguably become true. However, like most privileges, home ownership was best enjoyed by a minority. Once it had become the overwhelmingly majority tenure the government was no longer prepared to subsidize it so generously as before, while a disastrous fall in house prices in the late 1980s created a seriously deprived category of home owner, with a debt far greater than the market value of the home, unable to sell, and on occasion repossessed by the building society and rendered homeless.

These have been the main strands in the course of housing in the twentieth century. The most elusive player in the drama has been the user, in whose interests houses were built and policy devised. Unlike other groups, users did not have a corporate voice but entered the housing system individually, often from a position of weakness. There has been a largely undocumented but nevertheless searing collective experience of being without a home throughout the century: the experience of those who, at various times and places, tramped the streets knowing that their children, skin colour, or obvious poverty would slam doors against them. But for the majority – and notwithstanding a deterioration for some of the middle classes in the middle years of the century – this was a period of rising technical standards and satisfaction (Burnett, 1986; GHS,

1971–94). There were, however, minorities whose situation became more difficult as general standards rose. The demise of sharing and lodging, for instance, produced 'an all-or-nothing contrast between a separate house and nothing at all' (Holmans, 1987, p. 482).

Taking the users' experience into account is essential if we are to see the house or dwelling not just as a material object but as that infinitely more complex thing, a home. The crucial gap between the two is well illustrated by the furnished 'show house', which fools no one that it is a real home, however artfully a copy of the local paper is arranged on the coffee table. Like many ordinary things, the evolution of the home turns out to be a large and mysterious subject, the evidence for which lies largely in a huge body of journalistic,

biographical and oral material which is beyond the scope of the present book to explore. Here we can only draw on the evidence of the main canon of housing literature: in addition to many valuable sociological and ethnographic studies and the small field of environmental psychology, this includes user studies in some abundance. These do however have limitations, in being confined mostly to public sector housing, and framed within technical parameters that fail to do justice to that part of users' experience and attitudes that is governed by intangibles, such as economic or even symbolic considerations.

Two unique and especially valuable texts need special mention: the *Mass Observation Enquiry into People's Homes* of 1943 and a later compilation of official user studies (Hole

New houses — pleasantly built and situated — make happy, healthy citizens who are better fitted to make their contribution to motherhood, industry, and community living.

The 'house' of the developer becomes the 'home' of the family. (*Source*: City of Leicester, *c.* 1946)

and Attenburrow, 1966). With a small number of other outstanding reports and research studies, these are referred to so often that, for readers' convenience, they are listed and briefly described below. With other scattered sources, they suggest some of the historical shifts in people's relationships to their homes that are further explored in the last chapter of this book. At all times, the vast majority of people had little or no influence over the types and basic technicalities of their homes, but they showed infinite ingenuity in making secure spaces for themselves, even in the unlikeliest circumstances: whether it was the rough sleeper's cardboard box, the single armchair appropriated by an old person in an institution, the dosser's 'large rhododendron bush' (NAB, 1966), or the amazing use of a string of other people's homes by a 'resident vagrant' in a block of London flats (Parker, 1983).

The bulk of scholarship on housing is concerned with housing policy, with smaller amounts falling within urban sociology, architectural history, economics, and interdisciplinary women's studies. The present work is deeply indebted to all of these, most particularly the long, careful, and well reported research studies of urban sociologists and ethnographers from the 1930s to the 1960s. This is, however, neither a study in policy nor the contribution of housing to the social system, but a history of the home as it has evolved and been experienced since 1914. Other than John Burnett's classic work of 1986, there has been surprisingly little systematic historical study of the twentieth-century home. Besides looking at a narrower time span, the present work differs from his in looking at the whole range of housing options available at any one time. It therefore includes, among other things, institutional housing and the changing use of houses surviving from earlier periods – and in these respects it resembles the work of Shaw in 1985. The social range included is intended to cover the great majority of the population, from the very poor, homeless and institutionalized, to the generality of families and households in what would today be recognized as 'ordinary' homes. This presents no problem for most of the period. In the later decades of the century there was an increase in second homes, holiday homes and luxury homes, the last likely to be protected by

Spoilt for choice? What was on offer was the accumulation of several generations' homes and there could be a problem of affordability. Leeds, 1995.

electronic security devices and to have large grounds, swimming pools, saunas, and other luxuries not experienced by 'ordinary' people. Even these homes, however, derived from the general evolution, and while they may have set trends that others would later follow, no attempt is made to elaborate on them here.

A NOTE ON SOURCES

There are surprisingly few comprehensive and accessible documentary sources for the history of the twentieth-century home. For the convenience of readers, those that are most often referred to are listed below, according to the way they are referenced in the text.

Tudor Walters, 1918

Report of the Committee appointed by the President of the Local Government Board to consider questions of building construction in connection with the provision of dwellings for the working classes, chaired by Sir John Tudor Walters. [Local Government Boards for England, Wales and Scotland. Cd. 9191. London: HMSO.] This set standards, with plans, for the earliest subsidized council houses and estates.

Mass Observation, 1943

An Enquiry into People's Homes. A Report prepared by MO for the Advertising Service Guild, the fourth of the 'Change' Wartime Surveys. [London: Murray.] Mass Observation, described as an independent, scientific, fact-finding body, interviewed 1200 people in 1941–42 in eleven places throughout England, selected to give a representative cross-section of working-class settlement and dwelling types, including pre-1914 houses, old and new flats, garden city settlements and recently built suburban council estates.

Dudley, 1944

Design of Dwellings. Report of the Design of Dwellings Sub-committee of the Central Hous-

ing Advisory Committee and Study Group of the Ministry of Town and Country Planning, chaired by the Earl of Dudley. [London: HMSO.] This set the standards for new, postwar council housing and estates.

Pleydell-Bouverie, n.d.

Daily Mail Book of Post-war Homes based on the ideas and opinions of the Women of Britain, complied by Mrs. M. Pleydell-Bouverie. Undated, but 1944. [London: Daily Mail Ideal Home Exhibition Department.]

PEP, 1945

The Market for Household Appliances. A study of the market for household appliances produced by the light engineering industries before the war; the design of the appliances then available; and the market as it may exist in the next ten years. [London: PEP.] PEP is described as an independent non-party research organization preparing fact-finding reports and broadsheets.

Housing Manual, 1949

[Ministry of Health. London: HMSO.] This set out in text and pictures the applications of the Dudley Report.

Chapman, 1955

The Home and Social Status, by Dennis Chapman. [London: Routledge & Kegan Paul.] Based on interviews and observation of 275 families living in five different types of house in Liverpool in 1950, to illustrate the 'place, material culture, behaviour and attitudes of . . . urban families and to relate this to social differentiation'.

Parker Morris, 1961

Homes for Today and Tomorrow. Report of a committee chaired by Sir Parker Morris at request of the Central Housing Advisory Committee. [Ministry of Housing and Local Government. London: HMSO.] The brief was to consider and make recommendations for standards of design and equipment for family housing in public and private sectors.

Townsend, 1962
The Last Refuge: a survey of residential institutions and homes for the aged in England and Wales by Peter Townsend. [London: Routledge & Kegan Paul.] Based on visits to 173 institutions and interviews with 489 elderly residents.

Hole and Attenburrow, 1966
Houses and People: a review of user studies at the Building Research Station. [London: Ministry of Technology.] The user studies included surveys involving nearly 4000 people, mainly in London and the south of England, and in conurbations. They were weighted towards larger households and the families interviewed were considered to be fairly typical of those on housing estates and in New Towns.

2

THE SUBURBAN HOME

THE SUBURBAN HOME IN ITS CONTEXT

Perhaps more than anything else, the suburban home and the suburb typify the twentieth century. Not that they were entirely new, for the process of suburbanization had been going on for centuries, driven by the urge of the wealthy to live away from crowded and polluted urban centres. But after 1918 suburbanization developed with new momentum because it was catering for new or redefined social classes, with what were effectively new tenures in distinctive dwellings and estates. These served, on the one hand, a new category of home owners, and, on the other, a new category of tenant who rented, now, not from private landlords but local authorities. Both groups were in a sense 'new citizens' between whom, at the outset, there might be little social or financial difference (Mowat, 1955, p. 230).

The prototype of the twentieth-century suburb was the low-density estate of detached villas set in parkland, which was being offered by speculative builders for the moneyed classes from around 1800. This in its turn owed much of its inspiration to the country house of the landed gentry, set in a carefully contrived landscape, which was much admired, painted and held up as an ideal through society at large. Buttressing this veneration was an idealized rural past which had more to do with an imaginary arcadia than historical reality. Nevertheless it was important for the diffusion of a humbler suburbia which eventually evolved into simple, tree-lined or grass-verged streets of semi-detached houses on small plots.

This distinctive house type, a departure from the terraced house used for centuries in both towns and villages, was nearly as old as the parkland suburb itself. Early examples were little more than truncated portions of terraces but the type quickly developed its own character. Having space to spread it did so horizontally rather than vertically, so that basements or cellars became inessential. Space at the side allowed either 'front' or 'back' doors to be placed there. As a block, the pair of houses provided a neat compromise between economy and ability to make an impression. Both houses benefited from the shared roof and party wall while looking like a grander house, and this effect could be enhanced by pushing one or both front doors to the side. But when the respective owners redecorated their property, they seldom scrupled to do so individualistically, often in flagrant contradiction of the style or colours chosen by their neighbour.

There were a number of architectural idioms for the semi-detached house to be placed in. The classical 'Georgian' style, which had lasted from the seventeenth to the nineteenth century, was that which least appealed, since it represented what by definition the semi was seeking to replace, the traditional terrace of houses. Victorian Gothic, which challenged the classical in the 'Battle of Styles', waged over much of the nineteenth century, had more to offer, since it was an explicit reaction against industrialism in favour of an idealized medieval culture. It was, indeed, chosen for many nineteenth-century suburbs, but by 1914 it was too identified with long terraces of high-density, 'byelaw' housing to have much appeal. A likelier style was that called, inaccurately, Queen Anne: a highly decorative mélange of different materials and details and some affinities with the Gothic, which was widely used in the second half of the nineteenth century. It achieved one of its most successful expressions in the west London estate of Bedford Park, whose tree-lined roads and red-brick houses, with gables and bay windows but without basements, were regarded as remarkable in their own time and widely copied in the twentieth century. The success of Bedford Park helped to consolidate the semi as 'the standard unit of middle-class speculative development' (Edwards, 1981, p. 63).

Suburban style continued to evolve within the general movement of the 'Domestic Revival', a late nineteenth-century expression of medievalism promoted through William Morris and the Arts and Crafts movement and used in the domestic architecture for wealthy clients of Philip Webb and C.F.A. Voysey, as well as Normal Shaw, the designer of Bedford Park. With their traditional materials, plunging roofs, small-paned casements, decorative chimney stacks, and general air of sitting naturally in the surrounding earth, their houses owed much to an English domestic vernacular, particularly the stone-roofed Cotswold farmhouse and the timber-framed yeoman's hall of the north west. These had been favourite subjects of architects, on their 'scrambles' or sketching tours and widely published in art books down to the 1920s. A whole gallery of vernacular styles was used at the model village of Port Sunlight. This, with other model industrial villages – notably George Cadbury's Bournville, Joseph Rowntree's New Earswick and Sir James Reckitt's Garden Suburb at Hull – translated the Domestic Revival into modest houses for factory workers, supervisors and professional people.

The style thus established seemed the natural choice for the first Garden City, founded at Letchworth shortly after 1900. By now, most housing reformers, including those in the Labour movement, assumed that any state sponsored housing for the working classes should follow the same model. Two particularly

This architect's impression for the 'proposed house' of Mr Field of Kingston Road, Bridlington, symbolizes domestic privacy through the domestic vernacular; c. 1931.

influential figures in bringing this about were Joseph Rowntree (whose research foundation played an enduringly important role in housing policy and practice) and Raymond Unwin, designer of New Earswick and co-designer of Letchworth, who established himself as the country's first housing professional, in distinction to philanthropist. In his early career Unwin had translated his William Morris brand of socialism into a prescription for the ideal modern house for the working man and his family (Parker and Unwin, 1901; Unwin, 1902). Early in the First World War he entered the Ministry of Munition, (where Rowntree also served) and later, after serving as the only architect on the Tudor Walters Committee, he worked in the housing and planning section of the Ministry of Health. Meanwhile garden city design had been used by Councils in London and Sheffield for unsubsidized working-class housing, as well as at the unashamedly medievalizing Well Hall estate at Eltham, built for workers in the nearby armaments factory.

In the early stages of suburbanization it was possible to find rural tranquillity within a short walk of an urban centre. As urban scale increased, suburban development was pushed further and further out, so that for any who could not afford their own private transport some form of public transport became essential. In the first place this meant the railway, and many of the suburbs established by 1900 had a railway station or London underground station as their starting point. Trams and more particularly petrol buses, which could vary their routes to penetrate any area, further extended suburban scale. Eventually the private motor car was to liberate suburban development from public transport altogether; but although car ownership grew rapidly among new home owners in the 1930s, the car was used, then, more for leisure than commuting, so that suburbs remained dependent on railways or, in London, overground extensions of the 'tube'.

Up to 1914, suburbanization was not particu-

larly associated with home ownership. The predominant tenure at this time was renting from private landlords and new suburban houses, even expensive detached villas, were built as much for rent as for owner occupation. This changed rapidly after later 1920s, when the numbers built for home owners began to exceed those built for rent, eventually out-numbering them by some three to one by 1939. Suburban was inevitably more expensive than urban living, not only because of the capital costs of new building but because of travel expenses and higher charges of services generally in new areas. These considerations did not affect the wealthy, for whom the detached villa set in its own grounds continued to be built, but they did present problems to people climbing up the social scale, whether as home owners struggling to give their children a middle-class start in life, or council tenants acquiring self-contained homes for the first time. The less affluent home owners were helped by the state subsidy available from 1923–29 for small houses built for sale, by a large fall in building costs and house prices in the 1930s, as well as by a streamlining and cheapening of mortgage facilities from building societies in the 1930s.

The help given to council tenants was through a joint central and local government subsidy of building costs, and through measures to bridge the gap between rents and incomes. The rents of new council houses on the earliest estates might be double or triple what people had been used to paying to private landlords, and many of their tenants, in any case, had not previously been paying rent but sharing with relatives. Councils were concerned to select tenants who could pay and did not hesitate to evict for rent arrears. Many of their early tenants, therefore, were salaried workers not greatly different in their social origins from the new home owners. But although owning one's home had hidden expenses, it also offered the chance to build up a capital stake that was not available to the tenant, unless, as might be the case after 1923, his council allowed him to purchase his home as a sitting tenant. Thus the two suburban tenures not only came to reflect social class but offered a new and housing-related criterion of social class. It is not surprising, therefore, that the distinctive types and styles of houses in either tenure became the object of intense public interest and debate.

THE SPECULATIVE SUBURBAN HOUSE

The main concern of the speculative builders, who towards 1939 were increasingly dominated by large 'volume' builders, was to sell houses as fast as possible in order to release their tied-up capital. While they served all sectors of the market, the group mainly targeted was the small family with a modest middle-class income, for whom they built mainly three-bedroom semis on a variety of plot sizes. The other popular dwelling was the bungalow. Anglo-Indian in origin, this had been widely used in 'arcadian' suburbs at the turn of the century, when its symbolic associations were with leisure, freedom and an upper-calss bohemianism (King, 1984). The bungalow, often in fact a 'chalet' with one or two rooms in the roof, now appealed for economic reasons – the 1923 Ideal Homes Exhibition, for instance, displayed a 'bungalow town' of labour-saving, low-cost homes; but before long it acquired an explicit association with the elderly, particularly when it was located at the seaside or in other favourite retirement areas (Karn, 1977).

The speculative builder dressed up his products in such a way as he supposed would best attract buyers. With the whole range of styles to draw upon, he eschewed the neo-Georgian, among other reasons because it was now associated with council housing; and he was too penny-pinching to indulge in full-blown Queen Anne. After an experimental period, when styles chosen were similar to those used before 1914, his obvious choice was

A prominent feature of suburban estates, the bungalow ideally has a room in the roof. Leeds, 1955.

from the domestic vernacular. This allowed him to use pebble-dash walls (which gave savings on facing bricks), two-storey front bay windows and tacked-on 'half-timbering' – all, in fact, features that had begun to appear by 1914 but from which there now emerged the mock Tudor or 'Jacobethan' style, in which symbolism rather than architectural purity was the important thing. The basis of this symbolism was that social ambition that had always been the driving force of suburbans, great and small:

The home of the average business and professional man is indeed his castle. It is the lair in which the British lion rears his young. However small a part he may play on the world's stage, yet on his home boards he may roar as he will. Opening that front door with his latch-key, he steps at once from the ranks of the driven multitude to the position of lordship. Naturally he loves his home and he wants it to bear the mark of his individual taste. His wife manages it for him with little and often inefficient help. (A Layman, 1927, pp. 10–11)

The symbolism of the new house bolstered this search for status: the panelled entrance hall, stained glass windows and the non-functional chain-link front garden fence were reminders of the landed gentry. These were reinforced by some of the interior ornaments: the fire irons, brass warming pans and cauldrons, wall mounted swords, often miniaturized to suggest their owners' mastery over the past (Barrett and Phillips, 1987). Another message was escape and freedom: the 'rising sun' so often adorning garden gates and front door window panels; other stained glass motifs such as galleons under full sail; cliffs, seagulls and light houses. The ultimate goal of such freedom was depicted by the humble cot nestling in its dell. The messages were driven home by the advertising literature of large developers which lured visitors out on free trips to see the exciting new show houses which, it was made clear, were for new model families where father was out at work all day and mother was a fulltime and enthusiastic housewife, looking after their one or two children.

The naming of estates, roads or individual houses, made a big contribution to suburban status. Royal names were not such automatic choices as in the earlier eras of Brunswick, Hanover and Balmoral; but any aristocratic connection, especially that of the original owner of the land, could be exploited. So could any natural feature or village association: according to the Halifax Building Society, 'The Cottage' and 'Rose Cottage' (with 'The Bungalow') were still the most popular house names in the 1990s. Street names making use of 'Gardens', 'Grange', 'Grove' and 'View', as well as the ubiquitous 'Park', established the right pedigree in the eyes of builders and buyers, who named their own homes to commemorate important events in their lives, not least their pride of possession and reaching the stage of 'Dunroamin'. The important royal connection was preserved through the Daily Mail's annual Ideal Homes Exhibition: Queen Mary's dollshouse, designed by the eminent architect Lutyens, was exhibited in 1925. In 1932 Princess Elizabeth's miniature cottage, with thatch and electricity, was shown in a 'Tudor Village' set round a green, complete with pump, stocks and town [sic] crier. The 1937 exhibition had a series of replica rooms of

kings and queens of England, and in 1935 some 200,000 people traipsed through a demonstration 'King's House' which was erected the following year in Surrey.

In the last resort suburban status was protected by having suitable neighbours. In previous centuries new suburban enclaves were often provided with gates and porters' lodges. Now the main mechanism for keeping out undesirables was price: estate agents were expected, and expected themselves, to steer away prospective purchasers who would not 'fit', even if they had the money. Failing this, owners would even club together to buy a vacant house, to ensure that it did not fall into the wrong hands (Chapman, 1955).

The lack of architectural purity of the new suburban house, its confusing combination of individualism and conservatism, and its endless, petty variations on a basic monotony that was 'at once elaborate and mean' (Edwards, 1981, p. 128), brought only contempt from the more avant garde architects and planners. It is not true, as is often stated, that architects were uninvolved in its creation, for developers frequently made a selling point of their 'architect designed' houses; but their habit was either to employ jobbing architects, or to buy architectural plans which could be used repeatedly on any site. By now a new, twentieth-century 'battle of the styles' was raging, where the high moral ground was taken by advocates of modern architectural purism who took their inspiration from the turn-of-the-century Italian Futurists, from the Bauhaus of the Weimar Republic, and from the manifestoes of le Corbusier and other architects subscribing to the CIAM (Congrès Internationaux d'Architecture Moderne) and the 1933 Athens Charter. The basic principle of 'Modern Movement' design was to let a rationally thought-out and functional interior express itself in the building form, without recourse to any applied ornament or style. This had, in fact been the principle followed by Unwin in his plan for the ideal working man's cottage, but its exponents now were prepared to adopt a much more radical building technology, using steel frames, concrete, glass curtain walls and flat roofs. They also took a more summary approach to the house interior, which they tried as far as possible to make open-plan, with even fewer concessions to traditional room divisions and functions than Unwin had wished to make.

The new style appealed little to suburban house builders, who were convinced of their customers' innate conservatism. Before 1939, therefore, other than a few blocks of 'progressive' working-class flats, it was used only in a number of one-off houses commissioned by wealthy clients (Yorke, 1937). An unconvincing attempt to apply it to the mass housing market was made in the 1934 Ideal Homes' 'Village of Tomorrow' whose houses had rendered walls, strip windows and flat roofs. This was merely modernistic rather than an authentic application of Modern Movement principles and some of its features, without any underlying change in construction, were briefly taken up by some developers. They also created the 'moderne', whose somewhat raffish looking houses with pitched, often green-tiled roofs and metal window frames wrapped round corners were judged particularly suitable to seaside and similar locations. Mainstream developers proceeded in happy disregard of such ideological experiments and imitations; their conventional products gave rise to a good half century of savage architectural criticism which viewed the speculative semi and its suburb as blots on the landscape (Sharp, 1932; Edwards, 1981). In the same spirit the designers of the 1951 Festival of Britain built 'Gremlin Grange', a mock-up of a crazily leaning, jerry-built semi intended as an object lesson in both bad design and bad building. Jerry building had long been associated by the public with speculative housing, although, as time was to prove, it was not typical of the sector as a whole, apart from a few notorious cases. This

Buying the 'moderne' look. (*Source*: Letchworth Urban District Council, *c.* 1934)

was eventually acknowledged in a dissenting tradition of architectural criticism which saw the semi as not only soundly built but a valid expression of cultural values that did, after all, give pleasure to a large majority (Richards, 1946, 1973; Jackson, 1973; Oliver *et al.*, 1982; Barrett and Phillips, 1987).

THE SUBURBAN COUNCIL HOUSE

This gulf between the suburban vernacular and architectural purism proved to be of crucial importance for the suburban council house. The earliest examples of this followed the model village and garden city tradition: a tradition where ideal standards for working-class homes rather than any consideration of market appeal were the main consideration.

The introduction of subsidy for such houses had been preceded by many years of debate about the best way to address working-class housing problems, and the building of some unsubsidized schemes, notably by London County Council. Most local authorities had never previously been either housing developers or landlords and they embarked upon what at the time was regarded as a daring, but temporary, social experiment with varying degrees of enthusiasm and trepidation. For guidance as to house plans they had the Tudor Walters Report and a 1919 Manual of the Local Government Board, the former a compromise between Unwin's principles and the government's insistence on 'economy and despatch' in this new state undertaking (Tudor Walters, 1918, title page). In the event most authorities were not backward in using their own variants of recommended plans, although these were closely scrutinized by Regional Housing Commissioners. Even so, now as later, the financial and other constraints within which council housing had to operate ensured that its products were, like speculative houses, uniform in type and style, with little in the way

of local materials or other differences to distinguish them.

Since the Housing Commissioners were obsessed with economy, their preference was for terraced houses rather than semis, and for a flat-fronted, neo-Georgian style without such unnecessary details as fussy roofs, projections and mouldings, which would add to costs. Certain cities, including Sheffield, Liverpool and Manchester, did opt for this style, using it on huge estates that were as much exercises in formal town planning as housing. But the style more generally used was a form of the domestic vernacular in which, under the generous Addison Act subsidy, the Commissioners were unable altogether to block the introduction of gables, interesting roof lines, front ground-floor bay windows and items derived from the garden city tradition. The mock Tudor or Jacobethan style was rarely used by local authorities and even when they did lean towards it they eschewed all the symbolic fripperies of the speculative semi. They laid more emphasis on function than decoration, and in spite of all advice to the contrary they did succeed in adopting some of Unwin's most cherished

HERE ARE TWO ROADS
GIVEN FREE CHOICE . . . IN WHICH WOULD YOU PREFER TO LIVE?

This was a fair question, given the social and design idealism of early council housing. (*Source*: Ministry of Health, 1938)

principles. These included a shallow, wide-fronted house plan designed to bring as much sunshine as possible into the interior, and a design rationale which worked from the inside out, rather than subordinating room orientation and quality to the facade. Some houses, in consequence, had their chief rooms at the rear rather than the front, or had relatively un-important – for instance larder – windows, or even sections of blank wall, on the face presented to the street.

That this was a new design logic was some-thing that was at first widely appreciated. It was not only the immense leap in working-class housing standards brought by this, but its modernity and architectural quality that struck contemporaries. This was at a time when the inflation of the early 1920s was severely hampering speculative house building for sale and when a subsidy to private builders (operative from 1923 to 1929) required them to work to the same standards as the public sector. It is not surprising, therefore, that architect-designed houses for the Ministry of Health won prizes at the 1920 Ideal Homes Exhibition, or that state subsidized houses were seen as a worthy model for all to follow (Architectural Press, 1924).

Such general esteem, however, was brought to an end by severe reductions in both subsidy and specifications which led to the sorts of economy previously urged by the Housing Commissioners, but now for nakedly utilitarian rather than valid architectural or functional reasons. The new houses, now more often rule-of-thumb products of municipal engineers and surveyors than of independent architects, became smaller, narrower, built in longer terraces and at higher densities. Bay windows, hot water systems and even bathrooms (which were now in theory obligatory) were often sacrificed. The gross floor areas specified for subsidized houses built under the 1923 Chamberlain Act seemed to preclude a parlour, the principal criterion of housing

status at this time (p. 156 below); and although some of the space lost was restored with the 1924 Wheatley Act subsidies, many fewer parlour houses were built from now on.

The justification of the cuts was the need to keep rents within the reach of working-class tenants at a time of national economic crisis; but contemporary opinion recognized them as a retreat from the visionary, Tudor Walters goal to 'housing for the poor' (Swenarton, 1981, p. 161). It was a retreat that became even more apparent in the slum clearances of the 1930s, when some authorities built still more basic dwellings (particularly flats) for people dislodged from slum homes. They also re-housed them on existing estates where their lower – or at any rate different – domestic standards offended established residents and might convert the estates into targets of general public abuse.

The suburban council house now being built had few stylistic pretensions of any kind, although it still betrayed its original garden city inspiration, remaining a self-contained, two-storey, single-family 'cottage' set in its own gardens. Moreover even when policies and subsidies were inauspicious some authorities still managed to find ways of maintaining space and architectural standards through clever use of rent rebates or an admixture of superior, unsubsidized houses, so that some excellent houses were built even in the difficult 1930s (Finnigan, 1984; McKenna, 1991). The speculative house, meanwhile, had developed its own unmistakeable appearance – an appear-ance that most took for an obvious superiority of design as well as social standing. By the later 1930s it was overwhelmingly important to the new home owner that his 'sham Tudor' home should look 'so different from the decent exterior of the council house that the casual observer must see at a glance that its owner is *not* living in a council house' – even at the sacrifice of the latter's frequent 'pleasant and simple designs' (Betham (ed.), n.d. p. 33).

SUBURBAN ESTATES BETWEEN THE WARS

Only the merest generalities are known about the overall qualities of speculative estates, since their range was huge and detailed local studies are lacking. In addition to large developments around rail bridgeheads there were undoubtedly many small infillings and roundings off of existing built-up areas, as well as the notorious 'ribbon development' along highways, one or two lots deep and parasitic on existing roads and infrastructure. Estates were built at all densities, from two or three houses per acre upwards, although they are presumed mainly to have conformed to the Tudor Walters norm of twelve per acre used on council estates. All new estates, private or public, observed strict rules as to roads and frontages. The 'building line' of older 'byelaw' housing was extended to new suburbs in 1925 and the '70 ft rule' between facing houses developed for high-density urban conditions, was observed. Another requirement was the 'splayed corner', the site left vacant at road junctions to give sight lines for traffic. With urban-scale road widths and footpaths and gaps between pairs of houses this contributed to the suburban 'leakage of space' that architects found so distressing (Edwards, 1981). Where design standards were high, empty corners could be filled with specially designed houses or short terraces set diagonally, as happened on some better planned council estates. Private developers seldom bothered to design any of their houses to fit the site, or indeed to lay out house plots to suit the convenience or privacy of their owners.

Public estates tended to be on cheap, peripheral land and large in size to achieve economies of scale. Like those of the private sector their designers were given to geometric, often concentric, road layouts which made best sense when seen from the air (or on the drawing board) but were labyrinthine and confusing on the ground. In general, they were provided with more shared open space as well as larger gardens than speculators' medium price developments. Some of the open space came from the custom of setting houses round hollow squares whose interiors were intended for play areas. More came from large 'circuses' or traffic roundabouts, and the use of semi-circular or rectangular grassed bays of houses set back from the road. These were elaborations of the cul de sac, used by Raymond Unwin in his garden city designs to economize on made-up road costs, and widely adopted on council estates to overcome some of the rigid highway requirements. In practice, these generous areas of green were of little practical use, although their explicit symbolism was the ever popular 'village green'. The grass verges found on many council estates and the more expensive private ones were more functional, serving as dog runs and convenient channels for water, gas and cables. In private estates they were often planted with shrubs and trees which

The 'village' remained a perennial ideal, whether for council housing or (as here) up-market owner occupation. (*Source*: Advertisement for a Bovis development, 1955)

provided screens for the houses, but all too often such planting replaced any existing trees on the site – although it was generally admitted that local authorities were lesser offenders than private developers in this respect.

The most obvious difference in layouts of public and private estates, however, was that the latter were planned with the car in mind. Once the semi had ousted the terraced house, plots could contain side 'drives', at the rear of which, behind the building line, owners were expected to erect garages at their own convenience. No comparable facility was provided on council estates, where it did not matter that the majority of houses were terraced, for people able to afford a car were not expected to become tenants.

The convenience and quality of estate life, in either sector, depended largely on location, which in turn was closely related to size and tenure. When estates were accessible to urban centres or established suburbs, their transport, shops and other services could be used. To develop its own range of services, including shops, surgeries and schools, a suburb needed a population of critical size and economic buoyancy. The most successful were likely to be those developments where a shopping parade or 'broadway' could be encouraged or perhaps even built by the house builders themselves, hinged not only around public transport but a large multiple store like Woolworths, to entice other traders. The classic, private, outer London suburb developed a distinctive environment and culture of its own: its railway station with coalyard sidings and platform bookstall; its high street with gleaming Odeon, wedding photographers and dainty tea shop; its daily and weekly rhythms of alternating bustle and sleepy tranquillity (Richards, 1946).

In such respects, the large, isolated council estate on an unfashionable side of town could not compete. Here a small parade of tenanted lock-up shops was limited to the four or five basic trades, with perhaps a branch of the local

Co-op. The only public house was likely to be a large, impersonal 'road house' placed where it might catch passing trade, rather than providing a cosy 'local', while some councils insisted on their estates remaining 'dry' altogether. On certain notoriously huge estates built beyond city boundaries – London County Council's Dagenham or Manchester's Wythenshawe – residents had to wait years or decades to be supplied with adequate public transport, shops and places of entertainment. Straddling different local government and parliamentary boundaries, their populations were effectively disfranchised. Even their children went unschooled for several years, until the state education system caught up with their needs.

The vibrant private estate and the peripheral council estate represented extremes, and quite possibly the majority of suburbans lived somewhere in between, enjoying the novelty of a suburban lifestyle, whether as tenants or home owners. This included a string of tradesmen who came to attend to the wants of the housewife throughout the day (Jennings and Madge, 1937). Both owners and tenants revelled in finding themselves 'almost in the country' and both proudly entertained friends and relatives who came out specially to see and admire (Mass Observation, 1943). The general public also came, not only to see the tempting show houses for sale but also the new council estates, which were judged worthy of a special expedition (McKenna, 1991).

Since the whole point of suburban living was taken to be the separation of jobs and home only rare attempts were made, in either sector, to introduce industry, although eventually a maturing suburb generated many jobs of its own. For council tenants the point was reinforced by tenancy regulations which prohibited the operation of any trade from the home. Even the taking of lodgers required special permission, although this was usually granted, provided that it did not entail overcrowding and a higher rent was paid. For those in employment, therefore, the working day was extended by a more, or less, lengthy journey to work, while home life revolved around the two-generation family. Numerous studies confirmed that contacts with the extended family were less frequent than before, and increasingly they depended on the telephone, if this could be afforded. Shared enthusiasm for the new home brought husbands and wives into a new relationship, which was buttressed by friendly exchanges and domestic rivalries with neighbours. While this applied in both private and public sectors, it was clear that those who were able to afford new things for the house and garden, and eventually above all to buy a car, could develop into more complete and enthusiastic suburbans than those whose incomes were stretched to the limit to cover this new way of life.

The social life of the middle-class suburb revolved largely around the church, the parent-teacher association, the tennis and cricket clubs, and women's groups. Full participation required not only some surplus income but a degree of leisure and certain social skills that excluded working-class suburbans, or made them feel excluded (Willmott and Young, 1960). Those tenants who came from a background of overcrowding and poverty were wary of strangers and reluctant to ask neighbours or other 'outsiders' over their thresholds. In any case, they were likely to work more hours, have longer journeys to work, and larger families to care for, than most home owners. Council estates did eventually develop their own social and cultural life, but it might take many years to emerge. In their early years housing managers and community workers placed much reliance on formal community associations, the size of whose membership was then taken as a yardstick of an estate's social success. Such associations did form and last on many estates well into the 1960s, when they were displaced largely by spread of TV

and commercialized leisure. But in practice they appealed only to a minority of residents so that those who kept them going tended to work themselves to exhaustion with little thanks. At their foundation, or indeed at any juncture which outsiders judged to be critical, invasions of professionals and volunteers who worked but did not live on estates would try to address their perceived social needs (Young, 1934). Local churches were a steadier and more enduring influence, acting as welfare and social centres. The cultural activities that commonly arose on council estates – pigeon fancying, credit clubs, bingo, girls' bands with majorettes – were of a special nature and reflected 'a divergence as much as a congruence' when compared to the suburbs of home owners (Daunton, 1990, p. 241).

Not all of this was widely apparent by 1939, when both private and public estates were relatively new, and each represented a minority tenure. A growing consciousness of their respective differences was, however, already showing in patterns of territorial behaviour. The best known, though not the only example of its kind, was provided by the Cutteslowe Walls of 1934 in North Oxford. These were high brick walls topped with iron spikes, erected as a barrier across two residential roads which linked a new private (mainly rented) estate and a new council estate. The developer who took this summary action to protect his investment in effect walled in a population of council tenants. Pulled down but re-erected once before 1939, the walls remained in position for twenty-five years (Collison, 1963).

Less well known is the fact that early council tenants could also, on occasion, resent the arrival of a speculative estate which they feared might detract from their own well-planned environment (Dresser, 1984). The commoner occurrence was the development of social hierarchies within council estates, both through a general mixture of people from different districts, and more particularly through the arrival of batches of new tenants from the slums. This was to prove of lasting significance, not only for the social development of such estates but for the whole housing system; for it encouraged the more upwardly mobile public-sector tenants not to regard their house as a permanent home but rather as a stepping stone to another tenancy on a superior estate or, better still, to home ownership. Not all who wished achieved either of these moves and there were yet to come in the postwar years fresh waves of first-time council tenants, many of whom regarded renting from the council as superior to home ownership (Donnison, 1961; Zweig, 1961). But by 1939 the stigma already being attached to council estates would ensure that in future the main desire line would operate in one direction only, from the public to the private suburbs.

THE POSTWAR FAMILY HOUSE

After six years of hardship and hope deferred, a home in which to restart normal life was the first of most people's priorities. Years of debate and polemic in film, press, radio, official propaganda and Forces education, with countless opinion surveys, had somehow conveyed the impression that once peace broke out British society – so powerful in winning a war – would be able to create the quantity and quality of homes and environments that people wanted. Although there was a significant swing towards flats, the overwhelming preference of the majority remained the suburban cottage. Under the Town and Country Planning Act of 1947 house building, with all other forms of development, was constrained by development control and the statutory development plan. The old powers for slum clearance were now augmented by 'Comprehensive Development Areas' and it was widely accepted that eventually all residential environments would in turn be pulled down and rebuilt on the best approved lines. It was in this mood of optimism that the

Dudley Committee was briefed in spring 1942 'to make recommendations as to the design, planning, layout, standards of construction and equipment of dwellings *for the people throughout the country*' (Dudley, 1944, para. 1, Itals added).

The revival of public housing fell to the Labour cabinet's most radical member, Aneurin Bevan, as Minister of Health, who had two principal goals. The first was to restore its original purpose of providing the optimum dwelling, rather than a barely adequate derivative for people cleared from slums. The second was to make it available to all members of society, so going much further than public sector housing had ever tried to go before. It was intended, now, to become the normal housing provision, mixed with only a very limited amount of owner occupation. To that end subsidies were increased, the rents and rights of private landlords further restricted, while the Housing Act of 1949 made the symbolic stand of removing the thirty-year-old limitation of subsidized housing to working-class tenants. For a few years there was effectively no competition from private house builders since a system of building licenses gave priority to the public sector. Such houses as were built independently were typically one-offs, built in stages so that they could be enlarged as licenses and materials became available. Far more people than previously, especially newly married couples, were forced to look to councils for their homes; but in the prevailing housing shortage this was all too often in vain.

Like the Tudor Walters Committee before it, the Dudley Committee sought to establish not only the best standards for the present but for some time into the future. It considered the now apparent shortcomings of Tudor Walters dwellings and estates, as well as the technical and social changes that had since occurred, particularly as these related to housewives. Illustrations of how its principles should be applied, together with examples of best practice from various parts of the country, were gathered in an official 1949 Housing Manual. This showed a preference for semis over terraced houses, and the semis now had an ample provision of outhouses and stores which were set under a roof linking them to the main body of the house. They had an increased floor area, fitted kitchen worktops and, if intended for five people or more, a downstairs WC. An estate was no longer to consist exclusively of two and three bedroom family houses but to have a mixture of types to accommodate a normal, mixed population. Therefore it was thought appropriate to include some three-storey houses, bungalows for the elderly, flats, maisonettes and hostels for retired and single working people.

The classic example of such a mixed estate was Lansbury, rebuilt after bombing and used as a 'living architecture' exhibition in the 1951 Festival of Britain. Designed by the LCC as a 'town within a town' to cater for three old East London communities, Lansbury had a mixture of dwellings for about 1,500 people, with shops, an openair market, pubs, churches, schools, a park and exhibition centre. Although the circumstances of Lansbury were unique, it demonstrated an important shift in thinking about the modern family house: whereas previously it would unquestionably have been placed in a family-based suburb, it was now found appropriate for a mixed inner urban neighbourhood. The implication was that the quality of domestic life might in future depend not so much on a suburban setting as the type and quality of the home itself.

The further evolution of the postwar house arose as much as anything from innovations in building technology which had been greatly hastened by wartime shortages, substitutions, innovations and the rationalization of materials and labour to speed the building process. This resulted in both stylistic and internal change; only those houses in rural areas, it was suggested, should retain traditional room arrangements and a vernacular style (Housing Manual, 1949). The new council house became little more than a box with a pitched but shallow roof, simple chimney, and no protruding sections other than, at most, a glazed porch (but more often a plain slab canopy over the front door). As wood was now scarce, door and window frames were reduced to minimal dimensions but glazed areas were enlarged. Windows were no longer deeply recessed and outer doors often had glazed top and bottom panels.

The simplicity of the facade was such as to seem almost without style. However, it owed more to the domestic vernacular than the white concrete and flat roofs of modernism, and there were some who even saw in it an updating of Georgian classicism. Its plainness might be softened by tile hanging and weatherboarding, elements borrowed from the Scandinavian countries which had developed their own interpretations of modernism between the wars. These interpretations were now given circulation in Britain through the 1951 Festival.

Bevan clung tenaciously to his high standards for space and fittings, determined that his council houses should serve far into the future, in spite of the slow progress of his housing programme, the rising discontent of the homeless, and even the alarm of his own colleagues. While heavy odds of postwar reconstruction and economic crisis were against him, the fact remains that the succeeding Conservative government won credit for a great new house building drive in numbers that could, however, only be achieved at the expense of standards. In Harold Macmillan's 'People's House' economies came from exploiting the single living room already adapted for functional reasons in Dudley ground plans, eliminating utility and store rooms and a second WC, and even, in some four-bedroom house plans, reverting to a ground-floor bathroom.

By 1959, when the Parker Morris Committee was appointed, these lowered standards were blatantly at variance with rising living standards and expectations and its Report marked the last attempt to put the public sector in the vanguard of design. Its recommendations were intended to apply both to public and private sectors, as well as to housing associations, and it was therefore not inappropriate that a house incorporating them was shown at the Ideal Homes Exhibition in 1962. In the event, those recommendations that related to space were adopted and made mandatory in the public sector between 1969 and 1981. They were never made in any way obligatory for the private sector.

As their primary concern was the house interior the Parker Morris Committee were little concerned with style, leaving it to arise from the internal plan, according to the best principles of modern architecture. This most naturally resulted in a deep terraced house, which might be staggered with its neighbours to give more privacy to back gardens. Ideally the narrow facade was without ornament, its ribbon windows and flats roofs simply reflecting the interior organization of space. This could also be met in a number of unconventional building types and shapes, including three-storey houses, houses with monopitch roofs, 'back-to-front' and 'upside down' houses where the normal relationships of fronts and backs, living and sleeping levels, were reversed. Indeed, the house no longer needed to be a freestanding building at all but could be incorporated in large blocks of flats and maisonettes.

Such innovations were strongly associated with the spread of industrialized building at this time. Various forms of modularized and factory-made building systems, using panels of reinforced concrete and synthetic materials, had been applied to council housing from the 1920s. Mandatory Parker Morris standards, which were coupled to a 'Housing Cost Yardstick' introduced in 1967, and the need for fast and expanded housing programmes now further encouraged its use, so that it accounted for over forty per cent of public sector completions in 1970 (Crawford, 1973). Many of these were high-rise flats built for slum clearance, but they also included houses. The most remarkable of these were to be found in the new towns, which functioned now, as earlier, as design laboratories. In the 1940s new town estates had strongly reflected their garden city origins. Now some of those in Milton Keynes and contemporary new towns would not have looked amiss in projects of the Bauhaus or le

Parker Morris applied in the New Town. Netherfields, Milton Keynes in the 1970s.

Corbusier. Like high-rise flats, they were apt to win awards, which was a reflection of the degree to which they were 'judged by architects for architects' (Scoffham, 1984, p. 177). For, whatever the merits of their internal appointments, the style of their houses disagreed with popular taste (Morton, 1994). This was a very different situation from that between the wars, when the Tudor Walters house represented a style and image that were universally accepted as the best society could offer.

The speculative housing market had meanwhile more than revived during the 1950s. Once licenses were lifted there was a rush to build, in many cases to plans held since before the war. But as developers had to work under the same technological constraints as local authorities, they began to build to higher densities and their estates tended to resemble the contemporary public sector, with a mixture of dwelling types and sizes. House size and internal layouts were also similar, but there was a rising demand for detached houses, which were brought within the reach of more home buyers by greatly reducing plot sizes.

'Get the Abbey Habit'. The 'umbrella couple', Abbey National's symbol since 1948, have periodically been given new clothes and are still evolving.

This gave rise to closely spaced houses with narrow passages rather than driveways between, and the variant of 'link' houses where car ports, rather than garages, bridged the space between separate dwellings. These changes altered the balance of house types, so that by 1991 there were roughly two-thirds as many detached houses as semis. These, though far less commonly used than between the wars, reappeared in the form of two extremely small houses disguised to look like one reasonably sized detached house. The terraced house (at 1991 roughly equal in numbers to the semi) had reappeared in the 1960s under the new designation of 'town house'. There was also the possibility of using the courtyard or patio house, found in Europe from the late 1920s. Estates of such houses could increase density without loss of privacy, for houses could be staggered so that the side wall of one gave seclusion to its neighbour's courtyard. But they were also deeply contrary to the English tradition of the public street, presenting an 'alien casbah' that for the most part only council and housing association architects had the nerve to attempt (Scoffham 1984, p. 99).

After an early postwar convergence, the private sector needed to reassert its stylistic difference from public housing. It went through a sequence of styles, which included the 'ranch house' borrowed from the USA, sometimes built on 'split levels' and notable for its large areas of picture window. By the end of the century there had been a veritable parade of styles, many of them no more than skin deep, but all expressing a yearning for past history. They included a new version of the perennial Jacobethan, now associated with the upper rather than the lower end of the market, and yet another revival of Georgian, which benefited from 'kits of parts' such as fibreglass porticos and all-in-one front doors and fanlights, often flanked by replica carriage lamps. These could easily be applied to the new box-shaped houses, as well as to older houses of any

The 'Jacobethan' house never lost its appeal. Lower Earley, Berkshire, 1995.

period. The latest stage in the stylistic cavalcade was a 1980s Victorian revival, with highly coloured, polychrome brickwork, decorative fenestration, porches and barge boards.

The only well known attempt to use an authentically modern style in private housing was the Span estates designed by Eric Lyons. The largest of these was New Ash Green in Kent, developed in the face of many obstacles from planners and building societies in the 1960s, and eventually completed conventionally by a volume builder. The original houses had an open ground floor plan with room dividers. The main living area at the rear was separated from a private back garden by a glass wall and the service side of the house faced shared landscaped space and walkways leading to a well serviced 'town centre', the 'front door' being situated in a ground floor, flat-roofed extension. The estate succeeded because it appealed to a particular kind of professional, often an architect, who 'prefers to buy roses from the florist rather than to grow them himself, and who does not require a greenhouse, a workshop or an outdoor run for a boxer dog' (Edwards, 1981, pp. 178–9); but its main distinction, almost unique in speculative

housing, was to create a mechanism for the collective management of the well designed common spaces.

Within all the styles was a generic small house, whose main real difference from its public sector counterpart was an emphasis on appearance at the expense of function and rationality. Each sector needed to make its products more affordable to its client population, but whereas in the public sector priorities could be professionally determined, its need to be different from the public sector meant that external appearance took priority in private housebuilding (Burnett, 1986). The size of the house was, like the plot it sat on, affected by rising land and other costs from the 1960s. Although not constrained by Parker Morris standards, many developers did for a while compete with those of space, but later abandoned them. From 1967 they could voluntarily adopt the code of the National Housebuilders' Registration Council; but unlike Parker Morris this was a minimum rather than an optimum standard. Even with it, kitchen and garden areas, storage space and, above all, the third bedroom were commonly sacrificed to keep prices down. The ultimate extreme was the deceptively advertized and presented studio flat which, with other varieties of 'starter home', successive governments urged developers to build from 1975 on. Intended for first time buyers, these were little more than double bedsitting rooms whose purchase price included furnishings and white goods, which quickly lost value and made it difficult for owners to resell (Goodchild and Furbey, 1986). The small starter house made sense only as a first step on the home ownership ladder and was not designed for long-term or normal family use. This became obvious whenever it or even superior speculative houses remained unsold and were taken over by councils or housing associations for homeless families. What had been a viable living environment for a fully employed and childless couple who ran a car proved very inadequate for a family with children, living at best on one income and at worst on social security benefits.

Council housing reached its peak in the mid-1970s, when localized surpluses of dwellings gave prospective tenants the confidence to refuse undesirable properties and local housing departments' control over their own revenues was greater than it was ever to be again. This had both positive and adverse effects on the quality of their housing. The more progressive councils, notably the Greater London Council (the successor of the LCC), increasingly consulted their tenants, devolving some management and even design decisions to them. There was active discussion of councils becoming general housing 'enablers', with powers to operate in all tenures. Among other things they were being encouraged by Whitehall to build unsubsidized houses for sale, to approximately the same standards as their rented stock. But there was also growing awareness of the unpopularity of particular dwellings and estates, especially high-rise flats, and, aided by the counter pull of owner occupation, this attached indiscriminately to the public sector as a whole. Already under the 1974–79 Labour

government, councils were instructed not to impede private developers whose standards dipped far below Parker Morris; and from 1981, under the succeeding Conservative government, any new council houses had to conform to private sector standards. In effect this marked another downward 'people's house' revision; but this was not now for the purpose of expanding the public sector but rather in the interests of its rapid contraction.

What was to prove a penultimate chapter in the century's evolution of the small family house originated spontaneously in the early 1960s, in a new domestic vernacular. It was encouraged partly by practical considerations, such as an increasing need for developers and housing associations – and later housing co-operatives – to fit estates into small, tight sites, and a growing concern with energy saving, after the profligate assumptions of Parker Morris design. It was also fuelled by the historic anti-suburbanism of architectural critics who since the 1950s had inveighed against the degradation of historic 'townscapes' into 'sub-topia', largely through the onslaught of the motor car (Nairn, 1956). It was argued that much of this was due to the unthinking transfer of highway rules to all environments, even when it was quite unnecessary for every house curtilage to have direct access to public streets that were planned indiscriminately for any through traffic.

The Essex Design Guide of 1973 crystallized such concerns (Essex County Council, 1973). It sought to establish rules of good practice for private house builders working in its sensitive rural areas, so as to halt the relentless spread of identical, low-density suburban estates with urban road widths, pavements and street lighting, regardless of context. With an official design bulletin on roads in residential areas (DoE and Department of Transport, 1977) this and design guides of other authorities helped to spread the new idiom that was already emerging in both rural and urban areas. In it,

The mews court became the idiom of the later twentieth century, both on private housing association and rehabilitated council estates. Leeds Partnership Homes, 1994.

houses were clustered in culs de sac or court-yards where the customary 70 ft distance between frontages might be reduced by more than two thirds and where the building line effectively disappeared, as front gardens were eliminated and house walls formed the road edge. This was no longer a road in the conventional sense, as what had previously been taken as rigid rules for road widths, turning and passing spaces and footpaths were relaxed. The entry and speed of cars was controlled by constricted entries, special paving materials and other visual signs, so that vehicles and pedestrians, notably playing children, were able to share the same space. Car standing bays as close as possible to houses usually replaced garages or garage blocks, even in private developments. With plentiful tree and shrub planting, especially on the housing association estates, this amounted to a revolutionary replacement of the individualistic, road-dominated, older suburban environment (Edwards, 1981).

There were a number of features of these mews developments, as they were often called, that appealed to the public. They presented an image of security and cosiness that was particularly important when, for instance, housing co-operatives were able to commission their own small estates, or when groups of 'refugees'

from large, impersonal council estates won the right to design their own replacement dwellings. The small, clustered houses with pitched roofs and porches presented a 'villagey' image, which was being given added credence through the growing fashion for second homes (typically in humble village cottages), the conversion of real stable mews into some of London's most expensive and sought-after housing, and the growth after 1967 of Conservation Areas with conversion, rather than demolition, of older houses.

A great diversity of dwellings sizes and types could be fitted into the small islands and odd spaces that were generated. As in traditional villages, the high densities gave rise to short terraces, houses abutting one another at various angles, and blank walls that could be used as a device to increase privacy or screen environmental nuisances such as major roads. The variety of dwellings naturally catered for the mixed population that was thought to be desirable. Notwithstanding all these advantages, the new vernacular house provoked much hostility from architects, rather as the suburban semi half a century before. In particular they criticized the Essex Design Guide for presuming to lay down a blueprint for schemes that, ideally, should always be individually designed for every site, and they had only contempt for the low quality 'Noddy' or 'Toy Town' houses offered for sale. This, then, was a further chapter in the divergence of architectural and popular taste, for the small, cottage-like house in a courtyard setting became increasingly accepted as the desirable home of the later twentieth century. The only sign that this, in its turn, would be replaced by another idiom was the return, in the 1990s, of the conventional street lined with terraced houses, sometimes in conscious imitation of the classical Georgian terrace (Gray, 1994).

POSTWAR ESTATES AND SUBURBS

It was a basic tenet of the postwar town and country planning system that urban centres should be surrounded by zones of decreasing residential densities. Even the heart of the city centre was expected to have some residential building, although this was long delayed because when redevelopment did at last begin, in the late 1950s, escalating site values usually precluded domestic property. Private developers, for preference, continued as always to build family houses on virgin sites, and only when the supply of such sites was exhausted did they turn to more central sites and a wider range of household types. Public estates, intended from the start for mixed populations, were now governed by a new measure of density: no longer houses but people or 'bedspaces' per acre, according to the zone that they were in. In the innermost one it might be as many as 120 persons, or over twenty houses, per acre according to the Dudley Report, and higher than this in some plans of the 1940s (Scoffham, 1984). This opened the way to high density coupled to low- or mixed-rise housing, in contrast to the uniform 'twelve to the acre' of Tudor Walters estates.

The theory on which public estate layout was now based was no longer the garden city-suburb but the 'neighbourhood unit', a concept of American sociologists and planners that took its original inspiration from the English garden city in the early 1900s. Its appeal was that it offered a physical framework for mixed and balanced populations: one felt to be applicable both on virgin land – as in new suburbs, council estates and new towns – and in old, inner-urban environments in need of total redevelopment. The neighbourhood unit was first put into operation in the 1920s in an unfinished scheme at Radburn, New Jersey. Here houses were arranged in 'superblocks' bounded by a perimeter road, from which a series of culs de sac gave access to service courts and the service side of houses. Their other side faced across back gardens to a common green 'spine' or park. Along this went a pedestrian way which safely traversed the encircling road by means of under or overpasses.

From their inception in the 1940s British new towns laid out their estates in 'neighbourhoods' but the application of Radburn principles, though mentioned favourably in the Dudley Report, waited unitl the 1950s to be generally applied in council housing. This was partly because the separation of cars and people did not seem so urgent in Britain, where the imminent explosion of car ownership was not anticipated. It is also partly explained by an engrained conservatism concerning house fronts and backs which gave rise to an 'overriding' expectation that the front door would face a public highway (Scoffham, 1984, p. 43). When eventually Radburn planning was widely adopted it was in a hybrid form where houses were arranged in short rows accessed by public footpaths both front and back. The car was taken along a short cul de sac to the garage court or block, which might be located out of sight of and at a short distance from the house. Thus cars and other vehicles were unable to drive up to the front door. Endlessly stamped over wide landscapes, these 'Radburn type' rather than true Radburn layouts were confusing both to residents and visitors. Emergency

Radburn-type layouts breached the accepted codes of propriety. Cars could not be brought up to the front door, and as this no longer faced a proper street it might be confused with the back or service quarters of the house. These occupiers have done their best by replacing the Council's stock pattern door with a neo-Georgian version. Leeds, 1995.

vehicles were unable to find addresses and children ran riot in garage courts. In effect, they condemned their residents to endure high-density living while being surrounded by plentiful open spaces of uncertain and possibly sinister function.

The apparent design clarity of neighbourhood unit planning was often contradicted by social realities. Radburn type layouts were arranged to allow children to walk to school without having to cross roads, and the school was presumed to be the unifying factor for a neighbourhood of five to ten thousand people. But housing and education were not necessarily coordinated – they might even fall within different administrative authorities – nor were the realities of tenant selection and mobility or the implications of ageing populations taken into account. The lack of privacy to both fronts and backs of houses (particularly as this affected back gardens) and the distance of the car from the home caused frequent management problems. Such layouts were never used by private developers, although they might make

limited use of the cul de sac to bring the car to the 'service' side of the house. Thus Radburn or Radburn type estates were instantly identifiable as council housing.

The fallacy in neighbourhood unit planning was to confuse physical layouts with social structures. As a design device it was a convenient way of drafting a plan for a specified population size, but this could not of itself cause a raw estate to develop into a self-sustaining and vibrant community. Private developers proceeded more pragmatically to meet the demand for new homes, having no need to create new neighbourhoods or communities, other than as superficial advertising devices. Their estates ate into the countryside, particularly in the south and home counties where pressures were greatest. An archetypal example was Lower Earley near Reading, where 6,500 homes for nearly 20,000 people were served by a giant supermarket and leisure centre (Boseley, 1988).

Where demand existed, houses had only to be built to be sold as fast as possible and there

The late twentieth-century suburb depended more on ownership of one if not two cars than location or community services. Lower Earley in 'Silicon Valley', 1995, reportedly the largest housing estate in Europe, was built with singularly few of the latter.

was scarcely a fraction of instances where residents could influence the character of their own homes, still less their surroundings. Even to new towns, with their highly developed public relations management, people came, as always, to an 'instant environment, designed by architects and managements to be complete as soon as built, functionally and visually. There is little scope for do-it-yourself activities on the part of the inhabitants, enabling them to achieve a sense of unity, because unity of a different kind has already been imposed from outside (Richards, 1973, pp. 6–7).

Whatever individuals may have felt in taking up possession of a new home, the fact was that by now the collective excitement of becoming a suburban pioneer had dissipated, as was recognized by J.M. Richards when he came to revise his classic book (*Ibid*, 1973). A recognizable and cohesive suburb no longer represented the lifestyle of the later twentieth century. Living patterns were now more centralized and so, in a general sense, more urbanized. Journeys to work, to education, entertain-

ment, shops and services necessarily increased in length, and the growing frequency of holidays – many of them abroad – weakened ties to the home environment. Quality of life more and more depended on use of a car, and it is not surprising that the proportion of income spent on motoring and fares was not much less than that spent on housing, or that in absolute terms it rose steadily (Regional Trends, 1975; 1993). Private transport gave access to all services, which if they were not available locally could easily be sought farther afield. Its growing importance even changed the conventional relationships between housing tenures and locations, for a suburban but car-less home owner might be environmentally less privileged than a car-owning council tenant (Ambrose, 1974; Boseley, 1988).

Planning theory incorporated these changes by presuming that ideally people would live simultaneously at a local and a wider metropolitan (or even international) level (Hall, 1963). The purest expression of this in practical terms was the new town of Milton Keynes, founded in 1967 for a population of 250,000. Its discrete and visually distinctive housing estates (many of them using the mews idiom) were clustered around existing villages or natural features and set within open landscapes, with the intention of providing 'areas of identity' that owed more to a 'romantic desire for traditional identification' than any social reality (Scoffham, 1984, pp. 170, 183). At the same time its whole land surface was overlaid with a grid of fast highways which linked all its 'villages' to one large and well served town centre. Any citizens without private transport were dependent on inadequate county bus services and, although underpasses were provided, setting out to walk from one part of the town to another was something not lightly to be undertaken.

In residential environments in general, those members of society with most wealth and choice assembled their homes and surroundings from the best that was on offer, new or old. Ideally this might include a family home in a country mansion or converted barn, a *pied-à-terre* in the city, and one or more holiday homes in this country or abroad. Linkages were provided by at least two cars per household and fast access to airports and motorways. The majority who were unable to afford such an 'exurban' lifestyle continued to live in what were still described as suburbs, although it is uncertain how much of the integrity of the interwar suburb, with its sense of escaping town life to be 'almost in the country', remained.

Physically, it is true, such suburbs remained surprisingly intact for half a century. Few demolitions occurred and house plots were seldom redeveloped. The houses still mainly served the nuclear family rather than any replacement population, for house extensions were considerably more common than subdivision into flats. Many such extensions were to create a 'granny flat', but perhaps as often

they provided an extra bedroom or games room for the two generation family. It was the low-density, Edwardian or Victorian suburbs where most physical change took place, for as well as house conversions their large gardens were often sold off for small enclaves of council or housing association dwellings, frequently flats, around the inevitable cul de sac or mews court (Larkham, 1992).

Tenure diversification also occurred on suburban council estates, partly through the tenants' right to buy introduced in 1980 and more systematically through new building, conversion and purchase of their stock by housing associations, co-operatives and private developers. Thus the monolithic suburban council estate began to be broken down, largely as a policy response to the problems identified with the 'peripheral estate'. Official remedies were mainly environmental rather than social or economic: demolitions, conversions, improvements to houses and environment; but on some estates tenants worked hard to set up new industries and social initiatives such as crèches. Tenants and managements came together through tenant consultation and management boards which were encouraged, among others, by the Department of Environment in its Priority Estates Project, begun in 1979 and continued through the 1980s as Estate Action (Power, 1987a).

Whether tenure diversification and tenants' purchase of their own homes achieved any of the hoped-for effects is still, in the 1990s, unclear. Many tenants exercising the 'right to buy' evidently stayed put (Forrest and Murie, 1990), but others, offered a portable discount, used it to move away. The broader context of council housing was its 'residualization'. By the end of the 1980s, when it still comprised more than a fifth of the total housing stock, it had been reduced in size by roughly a quarter, having lost many or most of its best houses in the best locations; and these were not being

It was important for tenants using the 'Right to Buy' their homes to make them look as much like owner-occupied houses and as little like council houses as possible. Leeds, 1995.

replaced. Movement into and within the sector was therefore greatly constricted, and this at a time of rising numbers of homeless families with a statutory claim for rehousing on their councils. It was also a period of rising unemployment so that, on many estates, those living on welfare benefits greatly outnumbered those in work and earning. In particular, the overwhelming majority of their young people began what was apparently going to be a lifetime on the dole as soon as they left school. Thus estates were at risk of social ghettoization, both of their populations relative to the rest of society, and internally, when the homeless (and particularly single parent families) were clustered in the least desirable, once hard-to-let dwellings. In such circumstances it was difficult for estates, whether or not physically improved, to maintain their equilibrium – still less to avoid the vortex of mass unemployment, poverty, drug trafficking and youth lawlessness (Campbell, 1993). With problems of such magnitude the council estate was no longer, as it had once been, simply a poorer suburb in a society where the majority were travelling towards suburban affluence; rather, it had become a reservoir of deprivation in a society whose mainstream mobility and affluence threw its problems into sharper relief.

3

FLATS AND MAISONETTES

THE ORIGINS OF THE ENGLISH FLAT

The long and intricate history of the house
reflects its close relationship with English
culture; the much shorter history of the flat, on
the other hand, reflects how far it was alien in
the English scene, always second best to the
house and allowable only in exceptional circumstances. The purpose-built flat, and still
more the maisonette, were minority dwellings,
which together comprised seven per cent of the
housing stock in 1964 and only twice that
amount by 1990. Converted flats and 'rooms'
in houses contributed a further five per cent at
the latter date. While these were mainly in the
private sector, purpose-built flats and maisonettes were disproportionately represented in
the public sector, where they made up over a
third of council owned stock in 1990 (GHS,
1971, 1990).

Unlike Scotland and many European countries, England had no native tradition of flats
or tenements in large blocks. Its only indigenous
flats were the Tyneside flats and the East
London 'half houses' (also sometimes called
maisonettes) which were built in large numbers
from the 1870s and 1890s respectively. These
looked like ordinary terraced houses, except
that they had two front doors. Inside were two
self-contained dwellings each with access to its
own separate backyard or garden, and they
were looked on as house substitutes rather
than flats in the normal sense. The other

situation where flats occurred was so common
as to find little mention in the records. This was
the flat over the shop, in the upper storeys of
shopping parades that were built in large
numbers for the expanding suburbs from the
1890s onwards.

'Walk-up' blocks of purpose-built flats, five
or six storeys high, originated in the 1840s as
'model dwellings' for the working classes (Tarn,
1971, 1973). The earliest examples resembled
the upper-class urban terrace in height and
general appearance. Internally, their self-
contained dwellings were designed to high
standards in order to set a precedent for more
general application. When, however, housing
trusts, railway companies and other bodies
followed the example on a large scale in
London, they dropped standards to reduce
costs and bring a return of around five per
cent. The self-contained dwelling was usually
replaced by a suite of rooms sharing sets of
sculleries and WCs on common landings. The
external appearance of these 'Buildings', as
they were commonly termed, was determined
by their mode of access, either by internal
staircases or open galleries with rows of front
doors on each level. The two uppermost
storeys often accommodated a maisonette with
its upper floor set in a mansard roof.

The largest estates, such as those of the
Peabody Trust, had massive blocks facing
inwards round bleak courtyards, to facilitate
the monitoring of all comings and goings by the

janitors. Their barrack-like appearance and authoritarian management gave them a notoriety that was reinforced by a reputation for overcrowding and unhealthiness. This was at odds with the social composition of some estates, at least in their early years, which was dominated by white collar or skilled workers, rather than the poor. Rents were high and tenancy regulations banned lodgers and the taking in of work like laundry, which were important to the poor. Nevertheless the negative image endured, with lasting effects on the history of the twentieth-century flat (Ravetz, 1974*a*).

By 1914 certain recurring patterns had become firmly attached to the use of multi-storey dwellings. They were an inevitable corollary of slum clearance, since it was taken for granted that only they could supply enough accommodation for the numbers of people displaced. Thus from the 1890s when the LCC and a few other local authorities started to build on cleared sites, like the housing trusts before them they built tenements. Such building was also often used as an occasion to carry out road improvements and town planning. The LCC's Boundary Street and Millbank estates were designed with impressive boulevards and at Boundary Street these converged on a small central park with parades and a bandstand. The mostly white-collar population of tenants here reflected the costs of such ambitious planning. This reflected a gap between slum incomes and multi-storey redevelopment that would be repeated many times during the twentieth century.

Purpose-built middle-class flats (called 'Mansions' rather than 'Buildings') followed some years behind working-class tenements. It was not until the 1870s that they began to be

London's early council walk-up flats were in the tradition of the nineteenth-century housing trust 'tenements', but more humane. (*Source*: LCC, 1931)

built in numbers large enough to attract general notice, and this was almost exclusively in London. One of their claims was to reduce the need for domestic servants, although they were in fact often provided with small, cramped servants' quarters. Planned without any garden or open space, their back rooms overlooked narrow light wells; but they had the luxury of hydraulic lifts and, since their management was supposedly for the benefit rather than disciplining of their tenants, their janitors could be treated as servants rather than supervisors (Jones, 1988). After 1900, Mansions began to compare badly with suburban homes for families and any new blocks more often took the form of 'Chambers' for professional men and women. These might still provide a room for a single servant but they were also sometimes designed with 'small continental kitchens' complemented by common dining rooms – a trend that was disapprovingly associated with the growing independence of the modern young woman (Muthesius, 1979).

MIDDLE-CLASS FLATS AFTER 1914

The building of flats for sale or private renting resumed in the 1920s. In the 1930s they were regarded as a popular form of investment and large numbers were built (Betham, n.d.). Although marketed as luxurious and labour-saving, this was a cliché that could mask abominably low standards of space and planning (Lancaster, 1960). The distribution of such flats was uneven. They were still found mostly in London, in both central and outer districts, but they were also built in the older suburbs of provincial cities and, most particularly, in seaside resorts, where they catered for a growing demand for retirement homes.

Estates of such flats were mainly small, consisting at most of a few three- or four-storey blocks set in maintained grounds. Their construction was usually conventional but, as in contemporary council flats, a modernistic style

Flats for the middle or upper classes were felt to pose a special challenge. (*Source*: Heath Robinson, *c.* 1930)

was often used, particularly at the seaside, where white, rendered walls, flat roofs and ribbon windows lent an ocean liner symbolism. Only exceptionally, however, was an authentic modern style used, as in the celebrated Lawn Road and High Point flats at Hampstead, both of the 1930s and by masters of the Modern Movement. The second phase of the latter, eight storeys in height, incorporated many luxury and collective features, but it provoked much opposition from the local planners. The nearest parallel the private sector had to the large estate of council flats was Dolphin Square in Westminster (1938), which covered 7½ acres and was intended to have 1,310 dwellings in a range of sizes up to five bedrooms, with servants' accommodation. The estate incorporated shops, a social centre, restaurant and health club and was for upper income groups, including many government ministers and MPs.

When middle-class flats began to be built again after the war, it was for both rent and sale. At first they were marketed as small family homes, but increasingly they became reserved for single, childless or retired people. In this guise middle-class flats continued to make unobtrusive contributions to the housing stock down to the present day. They were supplemented by flats in large, converted mansions, which had a particular appeal to affluent older people who, with the proceeds of an ordinary family house, could thus live in more gracious surroundings than they had ever previously done.

FLATS FOR SPECIAL GROUPS

Flats for special social categories had a long background history in housing and welfare: the special needs of single working women, for example, were recognized by early housing reformers and religious bodies, finding expression in the YWCA (founded 1855) and the hostels for young women workers found in most industrialists' model villages and garden city settlements. The special needs of women arose from the fact that, historically, they had no legal or financial identity outside the family and marriage; but single people in general, as we shall see in Chapter 5, had to struggle to achieve their own homes. This applied still more to the aged, unless they were wealthy enough to maintain a house, or lived in their children's home. In the 1930s the per capita

slum clearance subsidy encouraged some more enlightened councils to build bungalows or small flats for the elderly, and from 1946 a special subsidy for one-bedroom dwellings was available. This survived the abolition of the general housing subsidy in the 1950s, so that to some extent these groups were singled out for special treatment; but in practice, most authorities only recognized the claim of the aged and took no responsibility for single people who were catered for, if at all, by housing associations.

The Dudley Report of 1944 anticipated that, after the war, more old people than ever before would want to maintain their own homes, and it envisaged purpose-built small dwellings on every street, as well as residential Homes under the care of wardens. A halfway stage between independent living and residential care was suggested by the Nuffield Foundation in 1947, and the first scheme to provide this, in the following year, looked very much like a set of ancient almshouses, with two-storey cottages set round a court where a central refectory occupied the position normally allotted to a chapel (*Housing Manual*, 1949).

What came to be termed sheltered housing began to evolve from this and from the growing custom of providing bungalows or flatlets for the more active elderly in the grounds of residential institutions (Sumner and Smith, 1969). A more deliberate step was a Stevenage scheme of 1962 for single old people and couples, who shared a warden, common room, baths and laundry, but had their own WCs, kitchens and emergency alarm bells (MHLG, 1966a). There followed a rapid growth of such schemes, which were at first designed to the recommended size of around thirty units and later to considerably larger sizes. By the later 1970s sheltered housing was divided into two categories, for the active and non-active elderly respectively. The former were provided with self-contained flats or bungalows, often for couples and with gardens. The latter had self-contained dwellings in blocks with warden service, common rooms, guest rooms and laundries. In many respects sheltered housing operated no differently from other wardened hostels with self-contained accommodation for people with disabilities of various kinds. Perhaps its main difference was the emergency alarms installed at various points inside the dwelling. The term itself seems to have been reserved exclusively for the elderly.

The main obstacle in the way of purpose-built housing for single people was the high cost of kitchen, bathroom and utilities in relation to living area. Economies could be made either by reduced living space or shared sanitary facilities. Thus instead of a bedroom, many old people's flatlets were given a 'bed recess', a narrow, usually windowless, alcove screened only by a curtain (see p. 85, below), which proved so unpopular that the Parker Morris Report recommended its discontinuation. The 1962 Stevenage scheme made savings by shared refrigerators as well as shared bathrooms. Later sheltered flatlets were usually self-contained, with their own front door, small cooking corner, shower and WC. In their effort to cater for other single people, many housing associations provided 'cluster' flats: these were bedsitting rooms which shared kitchens and sanitary facilities. In practice this degree of sharing created problems, the most visible sign of which was the range of padlocked food lockers in the 'common' kitchens.

Sheltered housing further developed into large complexes with a range of facilities that could serve a neighbourhood-wide population of older people. In the 1980s it also assumed a new role of catering for the very old and frail elderly in 'extra care' schemes. While they could not be designated as such for funding reasons, these in effect operated as nursing homes, providing residents with meals, laundry, bathing and round-the-clock personal care.

Applicants for either sheltered or single-person flats had to satisfy councils' and housing associations' quite rigorous criteria of need and in the 1980s only some five per cent of the relevant age group were estimated to be in sheltered housing. By way of criticism it was argued that the subsidy given to it was mis-directed, in as much as the amenities provided were not fully utilized, while any practical advantages arising from concentrating services on one site were offset by the obvious disadvantage of ghettoizing the elderly. As it was established that old people generally preferred to remain in their own homes, it was there that public resources should be concentrated (Butler et al., 1979).

Housing associations tended to interpret the housing needs of elderly applicants in social as much as financial terms, and their residents noticeably included more of the better off than council-owned schemes. The difference became accentuated when in the 1980s they were compelled to levy higher charges or take loans from any residents with independent means. They had for some years operated leasehold schemes under which 70 per cent of the equity in the flat was sold to entrants. This was imitated by private developers, who also built sheltered housing for outright sale, to supply the growing market of old people. In this manner sheltered flats began to bridge the divide between renting and owning (sometimes in the same scheme) and so to break free from the welfare connotations of such provision.

Perhaps the most forceful criticism of sheltered housing was that few if any of its early residents chose for themselves this unfamiliar and indeed previously unknown form of housing, which rather was chosen for them by doctors or relatives. With the exception of any of the men who had been in the armed forces, residents could not have had any previous experience of collective or institutional living, and it was daunting, in old age, to have to learn the complexities of its group politics and unfamiliar environments. In common with other old people in 'residential care', many residents feared eviction in case of illness or incapacity. Their legal status was that of licensee rather than tenant, and they had no legal entitlement to their own homes, even though these were self contained. Among other things, this drew into question the role of the warden. Initially intended to be simply a 'good neighbour', the warden increasingly became a manager, if not something akin to a nursing home director, with considerable power over residents' lives. In practice, the day-to-day running of sheltered housing schemes was sensible and humane, but the underlying issues were a legacy of its 'welfare' origins.

COUNCIL FLATS TO 1939

Both councils and housing trusts continued to build tenement blocks for families after as before 1914, sometimes with continuity on the same estate. But in general the balance of opinion was against flats. Like the garden city movement, the Tudor Walters Committee was hostile, discussing them only to dismiss them as unsuitable for English families; and the only flats given official support at this time were conversions of larger houses. Many councils, however, started to use their housing subsidies

for cottage flats. These were really an updated version of the 'half house': in effect a pair of 'semis' each containing upper and lower flats, and as their rents were lower than whole houses demand for them was high. It was not until the withdrawal of the general subsidy in 1933 that councils were driven to apply the per capita subsidy for slum clearance of the 1930 Housing Act to multi-storey flats. London, Liverpool and Manchester, in particular, rebuilt large parts of their inner areas with walk-up blocks, usually of the gallery access type.

There were huge misgivings about such dwellings. Mass Observation thought 'no subject in the whole field of social science arouses fiercer controversy than the time-honoured argument of houses *versus* flats' (Mass Observation, 1943, p. 46); and this 'keen controversy' (Dudley, 1944, p. 12) was probed in almost every housing text and opinion survey of the time, with many references to the unpopular older tenements and doubts that any flats, however modern, could be proper homes for English families. Their use, however, was indicated by all the earlier constraints, including the need to rehouse as many people as possible on cleared sites, and the need of manual workers to live close to their city centre jobs.

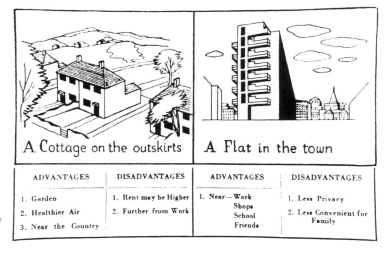

The pros and cons of houses and flats were endlessly debated. (*Source*: British Way and Purpose, 1944)

To these were added recent experience of outlying council estates, which made a centrally located flat seem 'a lesser evil than a cottage twelve miles away' (Thomas, 1935, p. 11). Multi-storey estates were again used as occasions to improve highways and embellish towns; but to overcome engrained prejudices against them, fresh arguments for flats were needed, which were supplied from a number of new perspectives (Ravetz, 1974a).

One came from the rather unexpected quarter of the garden city movement, inimical though this was to any form of high-density development. It now conceded that high flats in town centres would help prevent suburban sprawl, particularly ribbon development; and so began the Faustian bargain where the typical 'urban containment' of English planning was bought at the expense of workers living in flats (Hall et al., 1973). Another new argument came from the writings of le Corbusier and projects for workers' flats of the Bauhaus School, some of

whose members fled to England in the 1930s. Towers sixty storeys high were a feature of le Corbusier's proposed 'Ville Contemporaine' for three million people in 1922, and long, unbroken twelve-storey slabs framed the centre of his proposed Ville Radieuse of 1933. In the event only fractions of his concepts were built, in a handful of *unités d'habitation* – single slabs combining apartments with urban facilities – of which that at Marseilles of 1952 is the best known; but the concepts had an incalculable influence on the idea of flats as a modern and desirable form of housing.

The aesthetics of modern movement flats, like its houses, derived from new building technology. Above five or six storeys heights could only be achieved by means of a frame structure. Walls then became non-loadbearing and, if desired, they could be of glass, to enable sunlight and long distance views to be maximized. Le Corbusier thought in terms of the dweller looking outwards into the public

Early post-war acceptance of le Corbusier's vision created the climate for high-rise flats, but without their intended infrastructure. (*Source*: Ministry of War Transport, 1946)

realm, rather than how the public realm related to the dweller. Indeed, since ideally his apartments were placed far above the ground, they did not meaningfully relate to publicly used space at all. A childless professional with international rather than local affiliations, he conceived his ideal city in abstract, almost sculptural, terms; but English councillors and municipal architects, faced with the problem of rehousing large populations on restricted sites, found the terms seductive.

A final stimulus towards acceptance of modern flats arose from their association with socialist reconstruction. English councillors and architects looked for inspiration not to the home of the skyscraper, the USA, which had no social housing programme at this time, but to cities in France, Austria, Germany, Holland, Czechoslovakia: wherever multistorey dwellings had been used in postwar recovery. They did not need to be socialists themselves to be

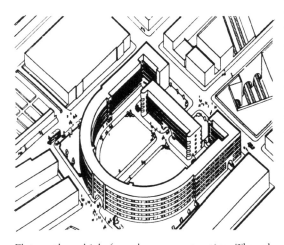

Flats as the vehicle for urban reconstruction. Though lacking the comprehensive social services of Quarry Hill or Kensal House, large walk-up flats estates were used for the wholesale redevelopment of Liverpool city centre in the 1930s. The 'Bull Ring', St Andrews Gardens, Liverpool (now a listed building being renovated for use by students and nurses). (*Source*: Council for Research on Housing Construction, 1934)

influenced by the ambitious scale of what they saw. Some came away unconvinced that flats would work in their own cities, but those already persuaded of the inevitability of flats embraced it as a model. They were particularly impressed with the provision of common nurseries, laundries, playgrounds, gardens – some of the things, in fact, previously provided in English tenements, but without éclat and with little present awareness. With ever-present and luxuriantly planted window boxes, such things symbolized a new kind of residential environment, at the opposite pole to individualistic English suburbia. At the same time, it was agreed that English self-containedness and high internal standards, much above those on the Continent, should not be sacrificed, and in fact London and several other authorities had introduced larger and better appointed flats, with staircase access, after 1933. The combination of external and internal improvements strained resources, however, and when it came to a choice between them it was almost a foregone conclusion that interior provision should win.

The estate that adhered most closely to the European model was Quarry Hill Flats in Leeds, opened in 1938 and for long regarded as an architectural and social showpiece. It borrowed its prefabricated building system from France but modelled its layout and social amenities on Vienna, forever afterwards suffering a dual reputation as the pinnacle of modern working-class housing and a hopelessly extravagant 'red' estate. As construction was cut short by the war, its intended community centre (with tennis courts and bowling greens borrowed straight from the garden city) was never in fact provided, and this had a damaging effect on its short and contentious history (Ravetz, 1974b). The only other example that came near it in community provision was Kensal House, a small, all-gas estate of the Gas Light and Coke Company in Kensington. Designed in an authentic modern movement style (whereas the Quarry Hill estate was merely modernistic) it was described as an 'urban village' with kindergarten, club rooms, stage, allotments and other social innovations (Ascot, 1938). Other than the innovative Ossulston estate at Euston, which was planned too early to be influenced by European example and shorn of most of its innovative features (Pepper, 1981), interwar council flats were, in most cases, little more than stacked dwellings with a bare playground, a common laundry room and odd shrubbery or lawn.

Such were the provisions intended to overcome the inherent unsuitability of flats for families. There was a continuing assumption that flat dwellers would have 'more of a 'community sense' than those living in houses' (MHLG, 1952), but a surprising absence of reference to experience. For instance, no one was concerned to assess life in the pre-1914

A high-rise estate that paid more than lip service to community needs was Park Hill in Sheffield, with around 1000 homes, completed in 1960. It was outstandingly more successful than its younger neighbour, Hyde Park flats, still functioning intact in 1995, when most of Hyde Park has been demolished. (*Source*: City of Sheffield, 1955)

tenements, whose outstanding practical problems were noise and an overabundance of children. Astutely commenting on the apparent success of European flats, a rare research study noted that, in contrast to Britain, there was in Europe 'no feeling that a scheme when once completed can look after itself as far as general beauty of upkeep is concerned' (Manchester University Settlement, 1932, p. 23); but the implied warning went unheeded.

The fact was that large flatted estates with high densities of children were now inevitable; and there were many, particularly members of church congregations and women's organizations, who were prepared to accept this as the price for staying in their own neighbourhoods, rather than being removed to remote public suburbs. The new, improved flats were regarded as 'labour-saving' and particularly well received. In the event, some estates of flats became well integrated into their neighbourhoods and communities, the principal preconditions apparently being a central location (Vereker et al., 1961; Ravetz, 1974b); but where blocks of flats were built in suburbs they could develop into beleaguered islands with problems of every kind (White, 1946).

COUNCIL FLATS AFTER 1945

Between the Dudley Report, which thought flats should not be family homes, and the Housing Manual of 1949 there was a change in official opinion. In the Manual, at any rate the lower floors of blocks of flats, with maisonettes, were unambiguously considered to be family dwellings, with a place in mixed developments of houses and bungalows, even on the urban outskirts. Most authorities still preferred to build houses, and when they built flats it was either to use up prewar plans or for non-family use. Apart from one or two isolated experiments, Quarry Hill Flats had been the only interwar council estate to have passenger lifts, which were financed out of an extra few pence on rents. Although there were still fears of ignorant council tenants abusing such advanced technology, it was now accepted that blocks over three storeys high must have lifts (Dudley, 1944). This at first limited some flats to three storeys but the introduction of a special lift subsidy in 1946 opened the way to high-rise building. Even then, most provincial authorities refrained from building higher until they were constrained to do so by a repetition of the situation of 1933: the withdrawal of the general subsidy used for suburban houses and the introduction (in 1956) of a special subsidy for flats (Cooney, 1974).

The conventional interwar limits of five to six storeys were breached first in London, where blocks were taken to eight storeys (a height previously reached only on the Quarry Hill estate), then to eleven, which proved a terminus until more sophisticated lift and water technologies, as well as appropriate building systems, encouraged building higher. The highest tower blocks in Britain were Glasgow's 31-storey Red Road Flats. In England, even in the most active period of high-rise building between 1958 and 1968, the majority of blocks did not exceed fifteen storeys; but the weighting of the subsidy to increase progressively with height encouraged authorities to go as high as possible, and around 1965 there was a burst of building above fifteen storeys (Cooney, 1974; Dunleavy, 1981).

There yet remained some urban authorities who refrained from building high-rise family flats altogether, doubtless to their own great relief when these later became totally discredited. Formally, the decision to build them was the product of many compelling factors, although it must be said that it was often opposed at local level by both councillors, officers and electors (Dunleavy, 1981). Most major cities and in particular the inner London boroughs, desperate to clear their waiting lists and lacking new building land, built high flats in profusion down to 1968. In this year the collapse of the Ronan Point tower in Newham provided a symbolic end to a programme that was already faltering through the ending of subsidy and a growing sense of unease. Some of the London boroughs were then left with 50 per cent or more of their stock in the form of high flats, and this proportion might later increase, as their stock of houses was sold off under the 'right to buy'. By 1991, when all purpose-built flats made up some 15 per cent of the national housing stock, the 400,000 flats of

Early post-war technology and finance made increased height possible. Lidgett Towers, Leeds. (*Source*: Opening commemoration booklet, 1957)

six storeys or above constituted only a little over 2 per cent, and less than half of these were in blocks of twelve or more storeys (DoE, 1993).

THE HIGH-RISE ESTATE

In this manner, after a delay of one or two generations, the multi-level city heralded at the turn of the century, began to take shape. For the most part its translation into conventional British council housing was a travesty of what the architectural visionaries had had in mind and only a very few examples stood out from the general debasement. Such classic cases included Ernö Goldfinger's Trellick Tower in west London, proposed for listing by English Heritage in the 1990s and fiercely defended by some of its occupants; and the renowned Alton West estate at Roehampton, which owed much of its quality to the parkland in which it was set (Scoffham, 1984). In mundane practice, the simple and sometimes elegant freestanding tower was elaborated into the cruciform, T or

Realization of the modernist ideal: Trellick Tower, Kensal Green, London by Ernö Goldfinger, 1969–72. Noisy lifts and services are in the semi-detached tower. (*Source*: English Heritage)

Y-shaped 'point' block, while the slab could become a building raised above ground on legs or *pilotis*, as le Corbusier had advocated; but instead of being used for flowing green space as he had envisaged, the ground level had to be allotted to stores and carparks. The slab placed on a podium could be developed into a deck access complex. No use was made of flat roofs and entrances to buildings that might house hundreds or thousands were small and mean.

More importantly than their lack of architectural quality, most high-rise estates made little if any physical link with their surroundings, but they stood in isolation, neither containing urban amenities within themselves (as was the case with le Corbusier's 'Unités') nor having around them anything more than council estates normally provided. On urban sites they mostly occupied tight plots where any surrounding space was appropriated by road access and car parking. But in the interests of mixed development and what was often described as 'architectural emphasis', they were also sometimes placed in suburbs or on the edges of towns, where there was no apparent reason to save land and where tightly crammed dwellings contrasted oddly with liberal amounts of 'public open space' within the estate. Large deck-access estates became, in effect, labyrinths impenetrable to outsiders, the invariable telltale being a profusion of direction signs with arrows pointing to block names or flat numbers divided into 'odds' and 'evens'; for as in Radburn layouts, the absence of streets made addresses impossible to find by any ordinary logic.

The alien nature of estate architecture increased with their scale. Before 1939, most flatted estates contained a few hundred dwellings or less. In its Quarry Hill Flats, with around 900 dwellings, Leeds had boasted the largest such estate in Europe; but after the war, the Aylesbury estate in Southwark housed 8,000 people in over 2,400 units, in blocks up to a third of a mile long. Some of the large

central London estates were, it is true, endowed with shops, cinemas and other amenities which could be used by a wider public. The outstanding but untypical example of this was The Barbican in the City of London, built for over 2,000 high-income council tenants and incorporating the London Museum, a public day school, church and theatre. The far commoner case, however, was the estate that looked spuriously self-sufficient and repelling to outsiders. Broadwater Farm, made notorious in the 1980s by a youth riot and murder, provided an example: its gleaming white, deck-access complex placed without any relation to the surrounding north London streets, where it appeared to have landed like a capsule from outer space. Indeed, it was often the designers' purpose to make such estates look as different as possible from normal environments, as in the notorious Southgate estate at Runcorn new town, endowed by Sir James Stirling with coloured plastic ('legoland') cladding and large, round, 'porthole' windows (Morton, 1994).

LIVING IN FLATS

In the second half of the century flats became an established form of housing for the single and the elderly, though still not entirely without some taint of welfare origins. If not as terminal, they were still likely to be treated as only temporary homes. But outside a small luxury market, family flats were almost exclusively council owned, and held in low esteem. Like some of the peripheral council estates, they easily developed into reservoirs of people living on welfare payments and with larger than average amounts of unemployment, of large families, and perhaps drug traffickers. It was hard to remember that in their opening years many such estates operated well, with tenants who were appreciative of them (Morton, 1994). In prewar walk-up flats, the ideal situation found in Kensal House might be thought overdrawn, were it not for many

The peak of urbanity in architectural drawings, vast multi-level estates become labyrinthine and menacing in reality. (*Source*: GLC, 1967)

similar accounts from other estates: 'each balcony has its tenants leaning elbows on the rail, smoking, gossiping, happy, like a group of cottagers perched above each other on a steep cliff' (Ascot, 1938, p. 62). It was evidently possible for something like this to occur even on a large, postwar London estate of maisonettes and high flats: 'If it's someone's birthday on your landing, we always have a bit of a sing song along the balcony. If it's a wedding or a funeral, everyone turns up and cleans the landings and the stairs because there'll be visitors coming . . . and that's why I say I wouldn't want to live nowhere else' (Parker, 1983, p. 70).

But increasingly the legacy of the high-rise boom was the estate that failed to stabilize

socially and seemed to be a disaster from the beginning. This applied to the architecturally pretentious, deck-access estates of Southgate, just mentioned, to the system-built, deck-access estates of the 'YDG' type in Leeds, Hull and Sheffield, and to Hulme in central Manchester – this last the product of a long planning history which dated back to the 1930s, when local people had fought off slum clearance and redevelopment (Ravetz, 1992; Hulme Study, 1990, Spring, 1994).

Yet in terms of dwelling interiors, the technical standards of flats were often high, and to a large degree successful. Even councils' early walk-up flats, although cramped and sometimes lacking bathrooms, improved on the earlier tenements by being self-contained.

In the 1930s a number of authorities used the 'improved' flat with superior internal standards, notably staircase access and individual balconies (Ravetz, 1974*a*). The Quarry Hill Flats, in particular, with their first use of a waterborne system of refuse disposal and other features, represented the most advanced living standards of their time (Ravetz, 1974*b*). High internal standards continued to be applied after 1945, making it possible for the Parker Morris Report to refer to 'standards which before the war were scarcely dreamt of for anything but the luxury market' (Parker Morris, 1961, para. 117). This no doubt accounts for the high levels of satisfaction that residents of flats commonly reported, even on estates that were otherwise regarded as failures (MHLG, 1970*c*; GHS, 1990; Morton, 1994). Maisonettes shared such standards and at first were felt to have particular advantages in being cheaper to build than houses, making rents lower, while it was

possible for them to have individual gardens, at front or back. Their popularity did not last, however, and they soon became 'possibly the most unpopular type of council dwelling of all' (Power, 1987*b*, p. 54). The reasons for this are not entirely clear, but an important factor was doubtless the alternate layering of living rooms and bedrooms, which made maisonettes even noisier than flats.

While both flats and maisonettes benefited from Parker Morris space standards and fittings – which could even include such things as refrigerators and wallpaper – there was no effective attempt to address the practical problems of vertical living. Postwar high-rise dwellings were built with an apparently total absence of inquiry into the operation of existing walk-up flats. The introduction of lifts, while seeming a self-evident improvement, enabled architects and managers to imagine that they were replacing conventional with 'vertical' streets or 'streets in the air' without any serious consideration as to the practicalities involved. Normal practice was to provide pairs of lifts which stopped on alternate floors. Economies and minimal technical standards resulted in slow speeds with frequent breakdowns, which were not only frustrating but provided maximal opportunities for vandalism, graffiti and use of lifts as urinals. The confined space of the lift had to be shared with people from different floors who were not neighbours in any meaningful sense. When lifts broke down, dingy and menacing staircases had to be used. It is not surprising therefore, that flats on the first floor were most in demand. The top floor was the favourite of people who felt able to trade problems with lifts for peace and long distance views; but those on the ground floor moved away whenever they could, because of noise and general disturbance (Ravetz, 1971; Parker, 1983).

The Garchey system of refuse disposal, first used in Leeds in the 1930s utilized in London and Sheffield after the war. (*Source*: Elek, 1946)

Deck access design tried to address some of these problems. Sited at strategic deck and bridge crossings, their lifts could be fewer in

Typical postwar maisonette
blocks. Leeds, 1995.

The street in air is no substitute
for a playground. YDG deck
access flats: Hull, 1976.

number but larger and more efficient, while
the decks themselves were intended to provide
opportunities for socializing, thus restoring the
friendly, busy atmosphere of the neighbourhood
street, without its traffic noise and danger
(Smithson, 1967). In reality, decks involved a
superfluity of hard-to-maintain stairs, passages,
landings and illumination; far from being convivial, they were cold, draughty and menacing
places where the prudent did not linger (Morton,
1994).

The main victims of living off the ground
were children, with their mothers. The high-
level playgrounds provided on some of the

larger estates were soon closed for safety
reasons; but nationwide there were in most
years one or two fatalities of children falling
from windows and balconies. Once let outside
to play it was impossible for parents to control,
or indeed even to see their children, many of
whom got up to ingenious games which easily
developed into vandalism (Parker, 1983). One
consequence was that children old enough to
play outside were kept inside the home, where
parents desperately tried to keep them quiet
for fear of annoying the neighbours (Stewart,
1970).

A home in a high flat thus brought a special

kind of 'encapsulation', where 'to reach one's own floor, to step out onto a long, empty corridor or a small, empty landing, to be faced with closed doors and to have this happen *time after time* can give an impression of being alone in an unfriendly world. To look out of a twentieth-storey window at a miniature world peopled by midgets is to look on a planet of which one has no "natural" experience . . . even to hear noises from other flats, while seeing no one, can contribute to an eerie sense of loneliness' (*Ibid*, 1970, p. 8). Inward-looking people who mainly saw the home as a refuge may not have minded, indeed may even have enjoyed, such detachment; but it could not be maintained in families with children without giving rise to health and stress problems.

Daily problems of domestic living were intensified as the scale and height of flats increased. They included the disposal of refuse, which was compounded by its changing nature (Chapter 7, below) and an inexplicable habit among some tenants of discarding unwanted appliances by lobbing them over balconies (Holme, 1985). But the most serious problem of all was universally agreed to be noise. Flats had more contiguous neighbours than houses with in addition all the noises generated by the block: lifts, plumbing, people tramping along access balconies, and in the case of deck-access blocks decks that ran above the ceilings of inhabited rooms, often bedrooms. Bare concrete stairwells and open courtyards compounded the problem, particularly of noisy play.

Problems of security also affected flats more than houses. In the early years of high rise building, no security devices were provided on block entrances, so that anyone could enter and wander round unchallenged. Intercom systems began to be fitted in the 1970s but these could not be used on deck-access estates where decks had the function of through streets. Yet these were not streets in any ordinary sense: in particular they were not overlooked by windows, as streets of houses would be, and the rows of front doors along them could belong to dwellings on three different levels. This exemplified a special phenomenon of high-rise estates: unfamiliar kinds of space which were neither public nor private, and which lacked any defined function. At the same time, the important buffer space between the home and the public street, traditionally provided by the front garden, was absent.

The new high-rise environments, therefore, lacked cultural roots or social consensus as to their proper use. Successful usage would have required much cooperation and control, particularly over children. This had in fact often been achieved in the interwar walk-up flats which had resident caretakers whose authority was not questioned; but on postwar high-rise estates, which in any case had more complex layouts, problems were critically increased when for reasons of economy one council after another took the step of replacing resident caretakers by mobile teams of cleaners. The problem of children was addressed by a policy decision to remove them from high blocks, or at least from higher floors; but at best this was only partially successful (GHS, 1977) and it was a policy that could not always be maintained under pressures of family growth and housing demand.

All the inherent problems of high-rise living were intensified by the adoption of industrialized system building in the 1960s (Dunleavy, 1981). The amount of heating needed in high blocks, which were quickly chilled by high winds, had always been underestimated; but poorly designed and hastily erected blocks using patent, prefabricated systems had their own inherent heating problems, as well as dampness, condensation, fire risk and noise. All gas heating systems installed in them were banned after the collapse of Ronan Point in a gas explosion in 1968 and the electrical systems that replaced them were often ineffective, expensive to use, often not allowing the user to control use from within the home. It was not uncommon for the cost of heating to rise to as much or even more than the rent itself, and in consequence many tenants were disconnected from the supply, or cut themselves off. They then resorted to portable paraffin heaters which created further problems of condensation and mould growth. For many years, the response of housing managers was to deny the existence of the problems or else to blame them on the tenants, who were given spurious advice which included leaving windows open in all seasons, avoidance of vapour-producing activities such as boiling kettles or even 'deep breathing'. The problems were in reality so serious that they eventually led to a tenants' 'dampness campaign' which later developed into a national movement, the National Tower Blocks Network (Community Links, 1988).

In due course the problems of high flats, and of system building in particular, became too obvious to be officially ignored and, some years after the Ronan Point disaster, blocks here and there began to be deliberately demolished. Less desperate measures included the 'lopping' of upper storeys, a device particularly useful for converting blocks of maisonettes into conventional houses, and the reroofing and recladding of blocks, to provide both better insulation and a more attractive appearance. Blocks were also divided into separate layers allotted to different populations (Institute of Housing, 1983). Such initiatives showed that under certain circumstances high-rise housing could operate successfully: it served well as sheltered housing, for instance, and when sold off and converted, as up-market, owner-occupied homes. But radical transformations were also possible without turning out the original population, as the experience of the Priority Estates Projects and numerous other cases of estates improved through tenant consultation showed (Power, 1987a; Thompson, 1985; Owens, 1987a; NHTCP, 1987). Nor was it always necessary to carry out major structural

The direct method of solving high-rise problems: demolition in Sandwell, West Midlands.

work: estates could be changed from 'hard-to-let' to much-in-demand through intensive management (Morton, 1994), through the introduction of such apparently simple things as carpeted and well-lit entrance halls, or the use of 'concierges', who more than covered their wages by the consequent reduction of vandalism and unlet flats (Brent Community Law Centre, n.d.).

The essence of the problem of council flats was that, unlike the English house, their use by families was not rooted in a long, evolutionary process. In addition, they were the products of monolithic and large-scale design which gave little scope for the users to modify through their ordinary domestic behaviour. Besides

A subtler solution was found in re-roofing, recladding, refenestration, redivision of internal space and possibly re-allocation to different social groups. The ownership could also be changed. Belle Isle, Leeds 1995, 'before and after'.

fatally underestimating repairs and maintenance, such design was inflexible, cowing even its housing managers. On the deck access estate of Hunslet Grange in Leeds, for example, the local managers found that small children who ran along decks got lost and could not find their way home, because the long rows of white-painted front doors were all identical. The estate's architect, however, refused to agree to a variation of colours on the grounds that this would destroy the 'visual unity' of his architectural design.

The result was that this most expensive and difficult to live in of all housing was assigned to some of the poorest and largest families in society. This was partially mitigated in the early stages by the fact that the first residents were likely to be local people who appreciated having up-to-date housing standards in their own neighbourhoods. But on outlying high-rise estates, and increasingly on all of them over time, tenant populations became both more heterogeneous and more deprived. Thus a fatal combination of environmental with adverse social factors accelerated obsolescence, to the extent that many estates, both of pre- and postwar flats, had a shorter life than houses – much shorter, in fact, than many of the postwar prefabs whose planned life was only ten years (Chapter 6, below). In the case of the Quarry Hill Flats the life was only around thirty-five years, but Southgate and Hunslet

Grange lasted for little over fifteen. In effect the estates of council flats degenerated into new and in a sense purpose-built slums, a situation without precedent since some of the worst workers' housing of the industrial revolution.

While equally serious problems could be found on peripheral council estates, high flats were less amenable to physical change and more visible to the general public, with whom their over-ambitious and failed utopianism brought the whole idea of public housing into disrepute. As we have seen, their contribution to the housing stock as a whole was only small, but nevertheless flats and maisonettes made up over a third of all council housing in 1991. About a fifth of the 170,000 high-rise (12-storey and above) and over 30 per cent of the walk-up flats fell into the worst 10 per cent of the English housing stock (DoE, 1993).

It was an open question how far into the future flats could continue to serve as family homes. The Priority Estates and other initiatives demonstrated that those schemes of improvement which worked best were the product of joint physical and managerial change, with partial demolition, separation of different household types, perhaps some diversification of tenure, and tenant management. The re-allocation of neglected and vandalized spaces could give residents more control over and pride in their environments, as well as protecting these from abuse by outsiders, notably commuters using them as carparks. But ultimately the degree to which estates could be converted into 'normal' residential environments was probably limited, not least because any scheme of improvement demanded high levels of commitment to collective action. Many residents gave this gladly at times of crisis or when there was a real prospect of change; but it was unclear how far such a level of commitment would be sustained, or need to be sustained, into the future.

There were also physical barriers to enabling estates of flats to function like houses and it is notable that, when given the choice, residents re-designed their homes in the form of houses, usually of the mews court variety (Morton, 1994). Any reshaping of high-rise layouts was usually on the principle of 'defensible space', a concept derived from a study of criminal behaviour and resident reactions to it on several multi-storey New York estates (Newman, 1972). It confusingly involved two distinct strands of meaning: the first was that personal proprietorship, like that offered in conventional houses with front gardens, enabled residents to recognise and repel intruders, who would therefore be less likely to encroach in the first place. The second was that public places, and particularly the ordinary street, were naturally and informally 'policed' by a large variety of legitimate users (Jacobs, 1961).

While changes to estates could sometimes give them a physical resemblance to ordinary streets, they could not provide the shops and other attractions to encourage a general public to use them, and what appeared to be a more obvious way of protecting them from abuse was to break them down into smaller units. On deck-access estates this was achieved by dismantling the bridges between blocks, so that access to any block became exclusive to its residents, on a larger scale but similar to the mews court or cul-de-sac. This was the strategy of the DICE experiment which arose from a detailed survey of physical conditions in some 4,000 high blocks (Coleman, 1985). Convinced that this showed that not only vandalism and other abuse, but family and social breakdown, were directly caused by high-rise layouts, its author deliberately excluded from her experiment 'any other innovation, such as security devices, new estate office, or concierge systems', so relying on design modifications alone (Coleman, n.d., p. 15).

At the time of writing, the results of this experiment are unknown, and they would in any case take a considerable time to manifest.

It is clear, however, that they will withdraw the estates concerned still further from the public domain, rather than reintegrating them with this. In this connection it is interesting that on the redeveloping Hulme estate a minority of residents were seeking to recreate something like the street decks, which they had adapted to their own way of life, while the majority were insisting that any new houses should be on old fashioned corridor streets rather than the segregated and isolating cul-de-sac: 'the idea of defensible space is anathema to people in Hulme' (Spring, 1994, p. 46). The DICE experiment, however, reflected the more conventional approach, which sought security in the manner of upper-class home owners who retreat behind security fences, rather than through return to a public domain whose use is governed by unwritten codes. It seems likely, therefore, that this and similar 'improvements' will increase rather than otherwise the vulnerability of multi-storey estates to outsiders and criminals (Hillier, 1988). While perhaps prolonging the useful life of flats as dwellings, they will extend their use as 'unnatural' residential environments, so reinforcing their peculiarities and divergence from the English house tradition.

4

THE SURVIVAL OF
THE PRE-1914 HOUSE

THE ENGLISH TERRACED HOUSE

The dwelling that seemed particularly English to foreign contemporaries was the terraced house in which the huge majority of people made their homes in 1914. From time immemorial it had been used wherever street frontage was valuable, as in countless towns and villages, and it took fresh inspiration from the formal urban terrace, imported to London from Italy in the 1630s, which became the universal mode of urban house development for the next three centuries.

The terraced house was designed to be inhabited by servants and 'family', who together formed one household, a fact that amazed Europeans accustomed to all classes, including servants, having their own separate quarters in different levels of apartment blocks. For one observer, at least, the English custom of living in houses was a 'higher form of life', part of 'an ancient culture that can look back over a long evolution' (Muthesius, 1979, pp. 9, 69).

Codes governing the construction of London houses did in fact go back for centuries. A particularly important one was the London Building Act of 1774 which governed minimum wall thicknesses and other standards for all subsequent housing. It was several further generations before nationwide standards began to be set under the 1848 Public Health and 1858 Local Government Acts, and eventually under the Model Byelaws arising from the 1875 Public Health Act. The Act of 1858 was important for defining the standard street width of new developments as 36 ft. Under the Model Byelaws there had to be a minimum open area of 150 ft^2 (disregarding privies) at the rear of houses, and the distance to the next building was required to be not less than its height. This was to prove 'perhaps the most crucial regulation of all as regards the plan of the house' (Muthesius, 1982, p. 35).

Meanwhile a number of larger local authorities had from the 1840s been instituting their own building codes, so that within a general uniformity houses built under the byelaws had many variations of plan and layout. The use of houses for shops and small business premises added further diversity to streets that were otherwise long and monotonous. The codes ensured that from now on houses were solidly built with adequate drainage, natural light and ventilation. Above all 'they could no longer be built haphazardly in courts and alleys' (Gaskell, 1987, p. 51). Incidentally, with some partial exceptions like the city of Hull, local applications of the byelaws ruled out the traditional and almost universal arrangement of English towns, where rows of houses were laid out along narrow pedestrian lanes at right angles to their high streets.

The byelaw terrace at its dreariest: Alliance Street, Stockton. (*Source*: Allied Iron Founders, *c.* 1954)

The façades of byelaw houses often mimicked the grand terrace whose central house or group of houses was distinguished by a pediment or other special features. Thus even the humblest byelaw houses might have classical door frames and bands of ornamental bricks or decorative window openings, while the usual manner of adding onto terraces by twos and threes lent further stylistic variety. When fashions changed, elements of the Gothic, Queen Anne or English domestic styles could be applied, without any change in the underlying form.

Constrained though it was by these byelaws and a rigid building line or front boundary, the terraced house had a surprising flexibility. It could be one or more storeys in height, with or without a basement and attic, and one or two rooms deep. It could be extended by a back projection, which in turn could contain one or more rooms and be one or more storeys high. For the inhabitants the most crucial point was whether or not the house was a 'through' house, that is, whether it had windows and doors both front and back. Under the Model Byelaws the prescribed open area at the rear ensured this, but the 'back to back', which continued to be built in many northern towns until finally outlawed in 1909 (and in Leeds till 1937), shared a wall with the house at its rear. Like many much older rural and urban cottages, therefore, it could be only one room deep.

A depth of two rooms allowed a functional and symbolic separation between house front and back. A further critical distinction was whether or not the ground floor accommodated a 'hall'; for even if this were no more than a narrow passage, it separated the front door from the front room of the house, which could then become a parlour, a room crucial to social status. A hall passage could also give independent access to the rear room and, if it also contained the staircase, to the upper level of the house. This then enabled the rear room to develop its own exclusive functions.

In grander terraced houses of the aristocracy, who used them for a limited season to parade social status and search for marriage partners, the most important room was that above the front entrance. The largest room in the house, this extended the full width of the frontage and could also be amalgamated with a rear room by means of folding doors, to give the maximum space for entertaining. A wide entrance hall, approached from the street by a short flight of steps, served as a buffer zone where servants could process callers. The hierarchies of servants worked in basements and slept in attics, which were often hidden behind ornate parapets. They serviced the house using their own independent circulation systems: a front entrance approached from the 'area' steps and an internal servants' staircase. Below this social level, there were infinite gradations in design and use of houses, as well as the size and composition of their households. One very important change that occurred with little or no record was the translation of the first floor '(with)drawing room' to the ground-floor front parlour – a change that was fully completed by the great burst of housebuilding in the later nineteenth century (Muthesius, 1982).

THE SOCIAL FUNCTION OF TERRACED HOUSING: CONTROL OF PRIVATE RENTING

The huge variety of households and house plans of different times and places makes it difficult for the present generation to form an accurate idea of the use of the pre-1914 housing stock. Developers put up houses both for rent and for sale, and although the conventional estimate of home ownership in 1914 is around ten per cent, it is clear that in many streets and districts it was much higher (Thompson, 1988). Most byelaw housing was built in what were, in fact, the new suburbs of their day, as family homes of white collar or skilled manual workers. Unless there was some prohibiting covenant, houses could also be used commercially, notably for the ubiquitous 'corner shops' of working-class streets, while grander residential terraces were often eventually converted into high street shops or offices.

As towns and cities continued to expand, restrictive covenants were all that protected respectable houses from social decline. The new byelaw standards in effect made it impossible to construct houses specifically for occupation by the poor. The options left for them, therefore, were to continue to live, as ever, in older dwellings, in increasingly overcrowded conditions; to stay with other families, as either lodgers or boarders; to resort to common lodging houses where beds were paid for nightly or even hourly; or to become workhouse paupers or vagrants. It was the possibility of being reduced to that most hated symbol of poverty, the workhouse, that made people set so much store on maintaining their own independent homes.

Thus whole streets and districts of once genteel family homes became 'rooming house' and common lodging house areas, where families might have only part of a room to live in. Figures are hard to come by because the Census had no mechanism for accurately distinguishing separate households in shared dwellings; but a 1887 report to Parliament estimated that 5 per cent of a large London sample of households with an employed head (and therefore not the poorest) had less than one room to live in, while over a fifth had only one room. The situation appeared to be little improved by

the time of the 1911 Census, and it was the
realization that the housing shortage was affect-
ing even respectable people who were able and
willing to pay that persuaded many of the need
for a state subsidy for housing.

Yet for all its abuses it could be said that the
pre-1914 housing stock was socially versatile. It
accommodated a wide band of social classes,
including the poorest, and its system of leases –
weekly ones for working-class tenants and
longer, tradeable ones for middle-class tenants
– was felt to allow mobility. Such a combination
of dwelling type, tenure and function was
never to occur again after 1914, and eventually
the competition of new suburban housing, both
public and private, ensured its demise as
normal family housing.

The starting point was the freezing of rents
in 1915. Though intended as a strictly temporary,
emergency measure, rent control of landlord-
owned houses lasted in one form or another for
half a century – and indeed longer, in the case
of existing tenancies. The long-term effect was
to give tenants artificially low (that is, below
market level) rents at landlords' expense, and
hence to contribute to underinvestment and
deterioration of the stock, while the rapid
contraction of the stock after 1955 eventually
froze mobility. In 1947 the Labour government
tilted the balance further towards tenants by
instituting rent tribunals and security of tenure,
allowing (in 1949) only a limited increase of
rents frozen since 1939. From this time, older
patterns of working-class renting, which had
included periodic rent strikes and legal dispossession by landlords at a week's notice,
effectively   disappeared   (Stevenson,   1984;
Holmans, 1987). This is not, of course, to say
that tenant hardship also disappeared, but it
became more confined to stress areas and
minority groups, such as immigrants, rather
than being a collective working-class experience. Among the practices that eventually died
out was the old tradition of working-class
mothers seeking out and 'bespeaking' tenancies

for their married children (Young and Willmott,
1957; Mogey, 1956).

This destructive treatment of a part of the
housing system that had a valid function –
indeed, one that was arguably indispensable –
seems to call for an explanation. The Labour
Party and all on the political left had an
ingrained loathing of any system that made
private profit out of people's homes, a feeling
that the deteriorating quality of the houses
seemed further to justify. The acceptance of
rent control by Conservatives is more puzzling,
and may be explained in the first place by
panic about Clydeside rent strikes spreading
Bolshevik revolution in 1915 (Swenarton, 1981).
Deeper structural reasons can be found in
changing financial and tax systems, and the fact
that landlords enjoyed little political patronage,
and so were treated as expendable (Holmans,
1987; Daunton, 1987). The one subsidy given
for building new houses for rent, though
actively used, lasted six years only, from 1923.
Falling building costs brought a further brief
revival of private building for rent in the 1930s;
but with the exception of high-rent flats, little if
any private housing for rent was built after
1945.

Conservative governments made three
attempts to revive private renting through rent
policy, but only the third, in the 1980s, looked
as though it might succeed to any appreciable
extent. The 1957 Rent Act had sanctioned
large rent rises in controlled tenancies and
lifted control from all houses on change of
tenancy. As a result rents rose sharply in stress
areas and, even more importantly, decontrolled
tenants lost the security of tenure which they
had enjoyed for upwards of eighteen years.
The Act was found to be unsuccessful in
increasing the supply of rented housing, for in
spite of higher rents, it was more profitable for
landlords to sell out to owner occupiers,
particularly the new 'gentrifiers' of inner
London. For unscrupulous landlords in stress
areas, of whom the notorious Peter Rachman

was one, the Act provided both incentive and means to harass and dislodge tenants (Kemp, 1992).

Protest about the Act paved the way to Labour's Fair Rent system of 1965, which reintroduced security of tenure and protection against eviction, with a regulated rent that lasted to 1988 (and longer in the case of existing tenancies). The 'fair rent' of this system was defined somewhat idealistically as a 'non-scarcity market rent' intended to provide 'a lasting foundation for a better relationship between landlord and tenant' (Cullingworth, 1979, p. 68). At first applied only to un-controlled and new tenancies, it was eventually to include all tenancies, and it was hoped that the majority of rents would be fixed by agreement between landlord and tenant. This was a 'big gamble' but one that in the event paid off, as only a minority of cases went to arbitration (*Ibid*, 1979, p. 68).

One feature of the new system, very important to thousands of people, was the exclusion of furnished property. Landlords were quick to exploit this by installing any few miserable sticks of 'furniture' and legally charging an extortionate rent. Furnished tenants were also at first barred from receiving the rent allowance available to all other tenants and they were not fully included in the fair rent system until 1974.

Though fair rents were on the whole accept-able to tenants, they only increased the determination of many landlords 'to have nothing more to do with letting' (Francis Report, 1971, p. 97). The shortlived Conservat-ive Housing Finance Act of 1972, and the phasing of rent rises and other changes made to fair rents during the 1980s, attempted to redress the balance in favour of landlords. The whole system was itself replaced in the Housing Act 1988, which established new kinds of 'assured' and 'shorthold' tenancies with market rents supposedly freely negotiated between tenant and landlord. Any gap between these and the capacity of tenants to pay was to be met by a direct personal subsidy, housing benefit, from 1982. The danger in this was that, unless it was limited in some way, it constituted an open invitation to landlords to raise rents to any level. The next few years, therefore, saw a series of exclusions from this benefit, for instance, among young people and students, and a widening of the gap between incomes and eligibility. By the 1990s there were ceilings set on rents to be covered by benefit, with the result that in areas of high demand landlords charged two rents: one paid in full by benefit, and the other a 'top up' paid by the tenants themselves.

Again, the expressed purpose of rent reform was to bring more property and landlords onto the market. New tax incentives encouraged company landlords, and from the later 1980s there was in addition a small, unplanned growth of renting by home owners unable to sell their houses. Informed opinion considered, however, that the measures came too late to restore a market that had been steadily eroding for most of the century, so that it now formed well under 10 per cent of the total (Whitehead and Kleinman, 1989). Since the home owner enjoying generous tax subsidies could always outbid the capacity of tenants to pay rent, the system was so structured that no significant renewal of rented housing could take place (Holmans, 1987).

This was becoming belatedly recognized in the 1990s, when the home owner's tax relief was being progressively reduced, and there was growing recognition, even in Labour circles, of the fiscal discrimination against private land-lords, who were not allowed to discount their losses in the same way as other businesses. The fact remained that for some eighty years this had been a malfunctioning part of the housing system, where the short-term gain of protected rents had been bought at the price of a deteriorating and depleting stock. It less and less served families, even as a stepping stone to their first suburban homes, and increasingly catered for one and two-person households, especially old people, who found themselves trapped in this tenure; but whereas their entrapment had once been an unintended effect of rent control, it was now more and more due to an absolute shortage of any other similar property to move to. The other kind of tenant of the private landlord was a young, mobile and well paid person able to pay high rents and not intending to stay long. Both extremes were catered for, haphazardly, in a sector that was more of a historical survival than an efficient part of a modern housing system.

UNCROWDING THE SLUMS

The urban slums were a growing concern from the early nineteenth century, although the less publicized rural slums might be as bad or worse. English housing law offered no exact definition of the slum and perhaps this is not surprising since it must have seemed self-evident what and where it was: the 'insanitary area', unsewered and unplumbed, the district with every imaginable degree of 'overcrowding, dirt, squalor and crime' (Burnett, 1986, p. 175). Its denizens were commonly looked on as a breed apart, creating the very slum conditions that respectable people feared but seldom experienced, and this attitude survived well into the twentieth century (Martin, 1935).

Early perceptions of the slum stressed its physical and social isolation: it was found in the oldest and most congested urban areas, in pockets that could be clearly mapped and so, in theory, excised. From the 1880s there occurred a critical change in public attitudes, as it was recognized that unfitness and overcrowding affected not only pockets but large urban tracts where 'decent' people had no alternative but to live (Garside, 1990). This change was reinforced by the new suburban housing standards after 1919, which made it seem increasingly scandalous for modern families to live in Victorian

conditions. As the oldest and worst of these were removed, the criteria of slums were themselves revised upwards so that ultimately more and more, particularly after 1950, the term was applied to sound byelaw houses that only a short time before had been acceptable family homes.

Local authority powers to deal with slums accumulated from the middle of the nineteenth century, as public health rather than housing measures. They began with the power to order the improvement of houses 'unfit for human habitation', or to put closing orders on them in default; and they progressed to the demolition of such houses if landlords failed to remedy them. When a piecemeal approach proved inadequate, whole 'insanitary areas' could be declared. These powers were repeated in every later housing Act including that of 1919, but by this time, apart from some notable schemes in London and a few other major cities, little area clearance had been done. The procedures were slow and expensive because of the multitude of small businesses as well as house owners who had to be compensated; and another restraint was the realization that, without any replacement housing, clearance might actually increase overcrowding in adjacent districts.

In 1919 there were some potentially important changes. The cost of clearance was reduced by the end of the 'solatium': the extra 10 per cent paid above market value to compensate for compulsory purchase; and councils were empowered to buy houses for conversion into working-class flats, or to make loans to private owners to do so. Neither change had any noticeable impact but some authorities carried out considerable amounts of 'reconditioning' in the 1920s (Bowley, 1945). In general at this time, the emphasis was on building new suburban houses rather than dealing with the slums, on the plea that this indirectly benefited the people living in slums by creating vacancies and so 'uncrowding' them. The flaw in the argument was that few early council tenants in fact came from the slums, and many had previously lived with parents, so that giving them houses did not create any additional vacancies. It was, however, true in the long run that the suburban exodus began significantly to empty cities by 1939 (Young and Willmott, 1957).

The first postwar Census in 1921 reflected the concern of the times with housing shortage rather than housing conditions. It attempted more seriously than before to assess the quantity of shared and overcrowded accommodation: a task previously impossible because earlier censuses had not distinguished between separate households under one roof, even in blocks of flats. Further difficulties arose from confusion between shared houses, overcrowding, and lodgers. The last formed a normal part of innumerable households but potentially vitiated the ideal of one dwelling to one family. How far lodgers were a legitimate part of the family home continued to exercise minds, and the next Census settled on their 'complementary and mutually satisfactory demands not conflicting in any way with accepted canons of decent housing' (Census, 1935, p. xl). There was a distinction to be made between lodgers and boarders. From 1951, the former were treated as separate households, and therefore potential causes of multiple occupation; but the latter, who ate with the family, were considered an integral part of it. In reality, both types of lodger were by now a dying breed.

In 1921, a fifth of English families shared dwellings, including 6 per cent who lived three or more to a dwelling – and the 1951 Census later argued that this was an underestimate. Matters were worse than they had been in 1911, and the next ten years brought only slight improvement. The shortfall of accommodation was at its worst around 1925 (Holmans, 1987). The first significant change was noted in 1951, when 13–14 per cent of households lived two or more to a dwelling, including 4 per cent who

lived at levels of three or more. The authors of the housing report of this Census warned against too optimistic an interpretation of this, as it was partly due to the many house 'conversions' of varying quality which had been done since 1931 (Census, 1956). Thereafter there was a rapid fall in sharing: in specific locations it could still be as bad as in the previous century (59 per cent of households in the London Borough of Islington shared in 1961, for example) but throughout the country as a whole only 6 per cent of households shared houses at this date. Over the next twenty years a broad equality between dwellings and households was reached, and by the last decade of the century there was a surplus of dwellings, even though there were simultaneously some hundreds of thousands of homeless households (Social Trends, 1993).

As family use and sharing reduced in quantity, overcrowding began to be thought of in terms of multiple occupancy. Under the Housing Act 1961 councils could insist on sufficient sinks, baths, cookers and means of fire escape or, in default, provide these themselves and charge the owners, or in extreme cases temporarily take over the management. But the powers were discretionary and depended on councils being willing and able to fund the costs. Many did not intervene while others with strict policies of control at one period failed to maintain them at another. In a 1991 sample, two-thirds of councils declined to carry out inspections of multi-occupied houses, partly because they were afraid of having to produce improvement grants to rectify any faults found. The failure to inspect such houses contributed to a high frequency of fires, in which 150 people were said to die annually (Cook, 1991).

By definition, sharing and multiple occupancy implied no radical alteration of a house designed for single family occupation. In a description of 1939, 'the house now occupied by four, five or six families is left exactly as it was when built for the occupation of one: sanitation, bathroom (if it exists at all), water supply, are all the same as were provided in 1840 for the single family' (Spring Rice, 1939, p. 136). Extra cookers were sometimes installed on landings, but until gas and electric heaters were available, people had to cook on open grates. In erstwhile bedrooms these had never been intended for regular use, let alone cooking, while attics and basements might have no grate at all.

Among a number of examples in a 1938 Social Survey of Merseyside were an eight-roomed house with two parlours, one kitchen and five bedrooms, containing six households of fourteen people; and a ten-roomed house with two parlours, one kitchen, six bedrooms and one attic, containing eight households of twenty-five people. In both cases the occupants shared one tap. The first house had one WC and the second house two (Jones, 1934). Where upper rooms were used as family dwellings in this way, all water, coal and slops had to be carried up and down stairs; even the baby's pram had to be so hauled, to avoid cluttering up 'the dark and gloomy, but once dignified "hall" ' (Spring Rice, 1939, p. 137).

'Overcrowding' referred to the density of people within the dwelling and though it often arose from sharing it could also exist within a single family. The large size of many Victorian families would inevitably make them seem crowded by present-day standards, and over-crowding of bedrooms was a frequently ex-pressed concern of housing reformers, who worried about incest and sexual immorality. Under the 1851 Lodging Houses Act the sexes were expected to be segregated and councils were given the right of entry and search, although in England matters were never appar-ently taken to the extreme of Glasgow where, under the 1862 Police Act, buildings were 'ticketed' with their permitted numbers and raided in the middle of the night. The Housing Act 1919 fixed the maximum numbers of each sex, and under the Act of 1930 rent books were to have permitted numbers inscribed. Sanctions

against landlords who broke these rules included prosecution, but councils rarely resorted to this for fear of incurring responsibility for rehousing any people dislodged.

It was not until 1935 that overcrowding was given a technical definition and made a statutory offence, under the Housing Act of that year, which also provided a subsidy for its relief. Technically, overcrowding occurred when two or more persons occupied a 'habitable room', and the definition of this excluded bathrooms and sculleries but included living rooms and kitchens, even though, unlike Scotland, there was no English tradition of using such rooms for sleeping. No two adults of the opposite sex who were not married were expected to sleep in the same room. In the definition of 'persons', children under ten years counted as half, and babies of less than a year did not count at all. (By this token, neither of the Merseyside houses mentioned above would have been technically overcrowded.)

The crude measure of two persons per room, which originated in standards for workhouses and barracks, was in itself a great advance on actual conditions in many Victorian slums, where it was not difficult to find eight or more persons sharing a room. Although overall levels fell, most cities between the wars had districts notorious for their overcrowding. Thus a survey of 1936 showed nearly 11 per cent of households in Newcastle on Tyne living in overcrowded conditions, even measured by a higher 'bedroom standard' which some local authorities were beginning to use, where living rooms were excluded from the calculation (Bournville Village Trust, 1941). It was a sign of change that the measure of two people per room was last used in the 1951 Census, when only a fraction over one per cent fell into this category. The next Census found it more appropriate to adopt the measure of one person per room. This then included some ten per cent, but this proportion fell to under 3½ per cent by 1981. Overcrowding was still mainly concentrated in older houses in inner areas, particularly among certain immigrant groups who financed their own home ownership by taking in lodgers or sharing with extended families (Social Trends, 1993). But the general shift in pre-1914 houses from family to single-person use meant that overcrowding was reduced: for even houses in multiple occupation were normally divided into bedsits for single occupants.

UNFIT FOR HUMAN HABITATION

The progress made with sharing and over-crowding threw into sharper relief the old issue of 'unfitness'. Like the slum itself, this was undefined, and it proved difficult to arrive at a technical definition. Indeed, at first there was no felt need for one: for should unfit or insanitary houses require more than common

sense to identify them, there were the disease and mortality statistics kept by the Medical Officers of large authorities to settle the matter. The Housing Act of 1936 was still concerned with cellar dwellings, unacceptably low ceilings, unsafe, unlit, undrained and unventilated accommodation: that is, with levels of squalor that required no elaborate code for their identification.

Until 1954 the responsibilities of local authorities were somewhat vaguely defined as 'having regard' to sanitary defects, disrepair, and how far dwellings fell short of 'the general standard of housing accommodation for working classes in the district' (Ministry of Health, 1946, para. 7). The last clause helped to perpetuate unequal standards in different parts of the country, and in 1946 the government's Central Housing Advisory Committee proposed that this should be remedied by adopting an eight-point standard

The 'slum' was almost infinitely variable: a court of Birmingham back-to-backs built in 1870 which had gardens and wash houses. (*Source*: Bournville Village Trust, 1941)

first mooted by the Ministry of Health in 1919, to be augmented by a further eight points as soon as conditions permitted. Together, the sixteen points included a hot water supply, internal or 'otherwise readily accessible' WC, a copper for laundry, 'preferably in a separate room', and artificial lighting and heating in each habitable room (*Ibid*, 1946, para. 17). The standards were not intended to be luxurious but 'essential to comfortable domestic life' (*Ibid*, 1946, para. 18).

A modified eight-point code was eventually adopted under the 1957 Housing Act. This covered: repair, stability, freedom from damp, natural lighting, ventilation, water supply, drainage and sanitary conveniences, and facilities for storage, preparation and cooking of food, with waste water disposal. This still left the overall inadequacy of some dwellings to be addressed, and accordingly 'bad internal arrangement' was added to the criteria of unfitness in 1969. This remained the basis of all official judgments and estimates until a new 'fitness standard' of 1989, which added heating and hot water supply to the established list of points.

When a local authority took action it was on the grounds that 'the house shall be deemed to be unfit for human habitation if and only if it is so far defective in one or more of the said matters that it is not reasonably suitable for occupation in that condition' (Housing Act 1957, para. 4). The reasonableness or otherwise related to the estimated expense of making the house fit, and in practice different authorities used different yardsticks, broadly based on the ratio of improvement cost to the resulting market value of the house. The public health inspectors responsible for classifying houses were backed up by the full weight of their councils and their professional institutions; yet the whole area was subjective and disputatious. 'In every one of the eight matters listed a judgment is necessary on the seriousness of the defects' (Cullingworth, 1966, p. 179).

It might be expected that owners of houses, whether owner occupiers or landlords, would sometimes disagree that their houses were unfit to live in; and still more that owners of 'fit' houses (which could be included when thought necessary for the rational redevelopment of an area) would object to compulsory purchase. In such cases there was machinery for appeal and a public hearing, which was conducted like a court of law and found intimidating by many of the appellants. After a hearing, the presiding inspector made his report to the Minister, whose decision was final. The essence of the procedure concerned the degree to which public health powers could overrule property rights, rather than the wishes of residents. Mere tenants, therefore, had no statutory right of appeal. Their rights as 'non-statutory objectors' were eventually conceded by some councils, although always at the latters' discretion (Gibson and Langstaff, 1982).

The bulk of action against the slums used clearance rather than closure and dealt with areas rather than individual houses. The two main campaigns took place in the five years from 1933 and the twenty years from 1955, on each occasion receiving special impetus from withdrawal of the general subsidy used for new suburban housing. By 1939 over a third of a million dwellings had been cleared (equivalent to about 3 per cent of the housing stock at the time), and as early as 1935 the progress made was felt to be so encouraging that in the view of the Census, 'the clearance of the slums and the restoration of pre-war sufficiency . . . should be accomplished well in advance of the termination of the 1931–41 decennium (Census, 1935, p. lxi).

Events were, of course, to prove otherwise. Councils were not again obliged to produce estimates and plans for clearance until 1954. There followed what amounted to a crusade against the slums conducted with 'almost religious fervour' (Cullingworth, 1979, p. 83). Although individual clearance areas were

'Unfit for human habitation'?
(*Source*: Fenter, n.d. but 1960)

The Copec Adventure anti-
slum campaign. (*Source*:
Fenter, n.d. but 1960)

normally no more than a few hundred houses, once the machinery was in motion so many areas were dealt with at once that they merged into huge tracts of land. Authorities varied in the zeal with which they estimated their unfitness problem, but some large cities proposed to include a third or more of their entire housing stock in programmes of demolition. Even allowing for underestimations and the progress-ive obsolescence of these now ageing houses, the rolling clearance programmes illustrated the rising standards applied to the slums. During the 1930s about two thirds of an estimated 472,000 unfit houses were demol-ished. In 1955, new estimates were over 800,000, and they trebled again between 1960 and 1967, when half a million houses were removed (Rollett, 1972).

Reactions to clearance on this scale depended on the period, the housing status of those affected, and what compensation – financial or other – they were offered. Money compensation for a fit house was at full market value, but this was not likely to be high, given the slum status of the area. 'Unfit' houses, which did not legally count as dwellings, were at first compensated at site value only. In most cases this was a derisory amount, even after small adjustments were made to take into account any money spent on maintenance. The special claims of owner occupiers were recognized in 1956, when they were given full market value, whether or not their houses were 'fit'. Even this, however, was not usually sufficient for

A council flat was a price often willingly paid in order to have a new home in the old neighbourhood: Manchester. (*Source*: McAllister & McAllister, 1945)

purchase of another home. The alternative offered was a council tenancy, but this was not available to all: lodgers were often in question, and councils did not normally rehouse single people or those who had moved into an area after its declaration for clearance. While many gladly accepted the move into council housing, others did so only with great reluctance, or found their own accommodation. The costs of enforced removal were met only by a discretionary allowance and after 1973 – when the whole process was in any case drawing to a close – by a Home Loss Payment for 'the special hardship of compulsory dispossession of a home' (DoE, 1972, para. 36).

The attitudes, generally, of people in clearance areas changed over time. In the 1930s there were already strong protests from landlords and home owners, and sometimes even from tenants, who feared being moved to distant suburban estates and strongly objected to being displaced from their own convenient and deeply rooted neighbourhoods. It was the strength of such feelings, as we have seen, that often persuaded people to opt for council flats in their own district. But on the whole concerted opposition from tenants was not found at this time, for those struggling to bring up families in shared houses were usually only too relieved to be moved to a new council dwelling.

In the second half of the century the situation was very different. Through modernization, conversion to owner occupation and reduction of sharing, the older stock was converging in many respects to suburban standards, while it was increasingly valued by those non-family households who were not being catered for elsewhere. Public scepticism towards slum clearance was encouraged by the anomalies and backtracking of housing policies. The Leeds back-to-back house provides a clear example: in the 1930s a Labour council was pledged to eradicate it, and did in fact demolish many of the oldest, pre-byelaw examples. Administrations of the 1950s and 1960s adopted a policy of giving improvement grants to the byelaw back-to-backs, improved some itself, and opened them as show houses. Within a decade, they again decided that all back-to-backs were by definition 'unfit'; but only a little later one small area was preserved as a pilot improvement scheme for the Department of Environment (Gibson and Langstaff, 1982).

Throughout the 1970s, residents in a string of Leeds neighbourhoods fought against the blanket demolition of back-to-backs, as well as 'through' byelaw houses, arguing that they were not unfit slums but useful low-cost houses suitable for the elderly and people with little means (*Ibid*, 1982; McKie, 1971; 1974). The underlying issue now was not so much public health as who prescribed domestic standards. The health officials who surveyed and condemned unfit houses were serenely confident of acting for the benefit of society, and especially for future generations, while residents, lacking any special technical expertise, were concerned with their personal autonomy. The experience of a particular residents' association in Leeds illustrates the mutual incomprehensibility of the two sides. Having persuaded the city's Chief Environmental Health Officer to view some condemned houses with them, they came to one where a basement room, although unoccupied, caused the house to be classified as unfit. Asked if he would accept a written guarantee from the owner to brick up the room, the officer replied with some indignation that it was not his business to tell people what they should do with their own homes.

Once an area was 'declared', although it might be many years before its eventual clearance, owners of its 'unfit' houses were effectively barred from making them 'fit'. The inspectors' lists of defects were normally a closely guarded secret, to be revealed if necessary only at public enquiries. Even should they be obtained, owners were told that they could not improve their houses on either or both of two grounds: that planning permission would be witheld, or

that, in the terms of the law, the houses could not be made fit 'at reasonable expense'. It was no use to protest that they would go to 'unreasonable expense', for then they would be acting outside the law.

There is no doubt that community action played a large part in the policy reversal that brought mass slum clearance to an end in the mid-1970s (DoE, 1975), although how important this was in comparison with wider policy and economic factors is impossible to say. Ultimately some 1.3 million dwellings were excised from the urban environment. This was equivalent to about a fifth of the older housing stock in 1945, and represented about 8.5 per cent of the whole housing stock of 1971. Well over a million people were removed before 1939 and the postwar clearances brought this total to between four and five million, not counting unknown numbers who spontaneously removed themselves.

The demise of traditional working-class neighbourhoods was, of course, hastened by many other things, including the closure of docks and heavy industries, many of them reprieved only for the war, and countless small neighbourhood enterprises that fell victim to national economic trends. But slum clearance played a significant part in their ending. Long before clearance actually began, the prospect of clearance discouraged investment. Building societies, for instance, covertly 'redlined' areas within which they would not advance loans. Between designation and clearance, and again between clearance and redevelopment, many years could pass, during which large areas lay derelict and menacing to their last remaining residents. If the sites were again used for housing (and many were taken for new roads, commercial and institutional buildings, rather than housing) it was more by chance than design that any of the original inhabitants returned; and any such returns could not make good the disrupted links with past communities and cultures.

IMPROVEMENT OF THE OLDER HOUSES

The idea that an unfit house might be improved was present in the earliest housing policy-making, but the more drastic 'solution' of demolition dominated practice – as, indeed, most writing on housing – for many decades. It was the case, however, that the bulk of older houses were dealt with by improvement rather than clearance. From 1960 onwards, improvement grants given outnumbered houses demolished or closed, in some years by as much as four to one. The earliest such grants were given to owners of farm workers' cottages in the 1920s. The first general grant was given in the 1949 Housing Act, but as it relied on voluntary action and had stringent conditions attached, it was little used. Throughout the 1950s clearance ran ahead of grants awarded until a 'Better Housing Campaign' made a concerted attempt to tackle the landlord-owned stock. Where voluntary action had failed, houses not in clearance programmes were to be improved by compulsory action and there was a new grant for converting houses into flats. The response of landlords remained disappointing and many authorities were reluctant to use the machinery.

The first effective action for improvement was the standard grant of 1959 for houses with at least fifteen years of useful life, used to install the five basic amenities: bathroom with bath or shower, wash hand basin, hot and cold water supply, WC, and food store. With an even more basic 'three point' standard and relaxation of various conditions, this measure is credited with bringing about the first postwar modernization of the older houses – but by owner occupiers rather than landlords. Even though the latter were allowed small rent rises after improvement, they were deterred, among other things, by the condition that houses receiving grant should be in good repair, for which no assistance was available. To address this problem, the Housing Act 1964 made standard grants exclusive to tenanted property, with compulsion in designated 'areas'. Tenants' agreement was a condition of grant and, without this, grant could be given only on change of tenant (and councils could rehouse tenants for this purpose). Outside the 'areas', tenants could themselves initiate improvement. Again, despite a vigorous publicity campaign, the overall impact was regarded as disappointing.

Some neighbourhoods were blighted for years, between designation and final clearance: Brunswick Avenue. Hull, 1976.

The first national housing survey of 1968 showed nearly twice as many unfit houses as had previously been estimated and this, reinforced by the messages of community action, encouraged a shift in official attitudes towards older neighbourhoods. They began to be looked on as potentially useful 'twilight areas' rather than slums, and one small neighbourhood, Deeplish in Rochdale, was chosen as a demonstration improvement project. Nearly three quarters of its 1600 houses were owner occupied and no more than half had basic amenities. As small, two-up and two-down dwellings, they might well, in another context, have been selected for slum clearance.

A new kind of improvement grant followed, in 1969, and was available to councils and housing associations, as well as landlords and home owners. It was now attached to a future dwelling life of at least thirty years and a higher twelve-point standard which included an internal WC 'if practicable' and gas or electric lighting 'if reasonably available' (Cullingworth, 1966, p. 210). The grant itself was discretionary and linked to a new kind of 'area', the General Improvement Area, where owners were to be persuaded rather than coerced into making use of it. For the first time there was also grant money for environmental improvements, typically taking the form of road closures, parking bays and tree planting. As it turned out, the majority of such areas were declared by councils on their own older suburban estates, while the majority of grants were awarded outside improvement areas, divided more or less equally between councils and owner occupiers, with landlords taking only a minor share.

Even more than the standard grant, the discretionary improvement grant amounted to a state subsidy to owner occupiers, rather than landlords or tenants. Although the costs of improvement were never covered in full, grants were not related to owners' means, and the enhanced value of the house benefited them personally. Up to 1974, they could be obtained

for second homes and more expensive houses, with few or no restrictions on resale: the possibility of abuse was evidently thought 'of less significance than the fact that a house had thereby been improved' (Cullingworth, 1979, p. 81).

The Housing Act 1974 attempted once more to address the needs of districts with high levels of private landlords, multiple occupation and other economic and social problems. In its new Housing Action Areas, local authorities were given powers for 'any action which is required to remove the underlying causes of housing stress . . . to arrest and reverse deterioration, and effect real improvements in the living conditions of those living in the area' (*Ibid*, 1979, p. 88). Strategies were to include limited clearance and the purchase of houses by councils, as well as an active role for housing associations and co-ops. House improvement grants, at up to 90 per cent of costs, were higher than before, and grants were now given for repairs. Houses in multiple occupation were no longer excluded from grant by conditions that were inappropriate for them, and environmental grants, though lower than in General Improvement Areas, could cover individual as well as collective improvements. Another completely unsolicited public subsidy was through 'enveloping', where a row of houses had its roofs and external works renewed, to encourage owners to carry out further work (Larkham, 1991). Some authorities also used 'packages' of interior improvements, with only a very small contribution being required from owners (Gibson and Langstaff, 1982).

By this time, earlier distinctions between housing, environmental and social improvement were becoming blurred. To prevent the rippling out of 'blight', Housing Action Areas could be abutted by Priority Neighbourhoods, where special powers applied. The underlying concept was a hierarchy of areas, each eventually qualifying for the status (and grant aid) of the one above it. Even so, the progress made with

Black Road, Macclesfield, before and after GIA designation and improvement, 1976. A rare example where local residents averted slum clearance and converted very small, 'unfit' houses and their surroundings.

this machinery was, generally speaking, disappointing. Eventually there were only about a third as many Housing Action Areas as General Improvement Areas, and the socio-economic decline of many inner neighbourhoods had clearly not been stemmed.

Slum clearance, meanwhile, had given way to the policy of 'gradual renewal', which envisaged 'a continuous process of minor rebuilding and renovation which sustains and reinforces the vitality of a neighbourhood in ways responsive to social and physical needs as they develop and change' (DoE, 1975, para. 23). Using this, authorities were to take a more flexible attitude to house improvement: 'It must be accepted – and willingly – that some houses of low quality meet a real need for cheap accommodation, a need which might not otherwise be satisfied' – for instance the elderly should if they wished 'remain largely undisturbed for the time being' (Ibid, 1975, para. 23). This was a marked change which set policy for the next twenty years, if not to the end of the century. As the triumph of improvement over clearance, it was 'tantamount to an abandonment of a century of housing philosophy'; as a shift of focus to social and community rather than technical concerns, it was moving to 'uncertain territory within which time-honoured signposts (such as plumbing deficiencies) are inadequate and perhaps even misleading' (Cullingworth, 1979, p. 96).

THE PRE-1914 HOUSE IN ITS NEIGHBOURHOOD

By 1991, houses built before 1914 still made up 27 per cent of the English housing stock, including 14 per cent built before 1890 and 6 per cent before 1871. The vagaries of policy, with other social change, meant that during its lifetime a house could have passed through different ownerships and tenures, involving landlords, councils and owner occupiers; and it could have had a number of different functions, including shops, rooms and flats, serving a variety of social classes. Depending on its location, it could, in the course of time, have been set in a populous neighbourhood street, a high-speed traffic corridor, or the carefully contrived cul de sac of a special policy 'area'. With its surroundings it might, at different times, have been put in a slum clearance programme, 'blighted', reprieved, modernized with or without grants, and eventually given some sort of an indefinite future.

One of the things the terraced house had survived was an idea current in the 1940s that any dwelling had a finite 'life', which was best made explicit by licensing every building. Then 'whole districts would ripen for rebuilding at given times . . . orderly redevelopment could proceed according to a time plan' (Bournville Village Trust, 1941, p. 105). The idea was implicit in slum clearance programmes that proposed progressively to eradicate houses

that were not so much unfit as obsolescent, and it was evident in the fifteen or thirty year 'lives' attached to different grades of improvement grant. Intended as minima, these were often in practice treated by health officials as maxima, and this was yet another cause of conflict between them and local communities anxious to hang on to their homes.

The construction of older houses lent itself well, in fact, to the installation of modern technologies, although doubts were sometimes expressed about the quality and durability of the improvement work which passed grant conditions. The bringing up to date of older houses was not, as we have seen, dependent on the state. Unquantified but undoubtedly large amounts of self-financed modernization were done at their own expense not only by owner occupiers but also by tenants (Milner Holland, 1965; Holmans, 1987). The early driving force was the desire for electricity, bathrooms and heating systems. After these, it was doubtful that there would again be such strong motivation to improve, unless perhaps for insulation when domestic heating began to be taxed, in the 1990s.

From 1988 the grant system was changed. It was now, for the first time, related to people's means, on a similar, far from generous, scale to social security benefits. Costs could be covered in full for those on very low incomes but above this, recipients were expected to take out loans to cover the share of costs allocated to them. By now, official concern was mainly with the growing number of houses in serious disrepair. The 1991 English Housing Condition Survey estimated that 7.4 per cent of the housing stock was 'unfit', through disrepair and other reasons; but around 15 per cent of the pre-1919 dwellings, and as much as 20 per cent of the landlord-owned properties, fell into this category (DoE, 1993). With a far from strong improvement programme, and in the economic conditions now prevailing, it was difficult to believe that many of the older houses would do other than progressively deteriorate as they entered their second century of use.

Their future was of course inseparable from that of the districts they stood in. As we have seen, the combined effects of clearance and suburbanization had left inner urban areas to cater for people who were non-family and non-suburbans, many of them with low incomes and living in multiple occupation. Some such areas contained numbers of council-owned houses, a relic of the 'municipalization' of landlord-owned houses that had been strongly encouraged by Labour governments in the 1960s and 1970s. Described as 'miscellaneous properties', they were commonly let to large families and others whom councils felt unable to place on ordinary estates. Some districts were more or less dominated by student populations. They were likely also to have large numbers of houses used as hostels and residential Homes, as well as purpose-built Homes and housing association flats, which could not have been placed in outer suburbs without invoking the protests of affluent home owners. At an opposite extreme, and most particularly in fashionable parts of London, the nineteenth-century terrace and genuine (that is, real stable yard) mews provided some of the most expensive and sought-after homes of the twentieth century.

The extremes of the housing shortage in London also tempted back many second-generation suburbans to be within closer range of their jobs. The trend was exploited, in the early postwar years, by the inventive property agent, Roy Brooks, who persuaded his middle-class clients to see the social as well as capital potential of returning dilapidated or subdivided houses to genteel family use. Like tourists, these colonizers were apt to destroy the very things they professed to admire: in this case the convenient and colourful working-class neighbourhoods they had just 'discovered'. They became adept at exploiting the improvement grant system, and also the new planning device of the Conservation Area, operative from 1967. In the classic case of Barnsbury in north London, which local property agents saw as 'a chicken ripe for plucking thanks mainly to Islington Borough Council's environmental improvement plans for the area' (Ferris, 1972, p. 95), middle-class gentrifiers saw their property being enhanced by becoming part of a Conservation Area, while hard-pressed working-class tenants escaped – at the time thankfully – into high-rise council flats.

More generally, the re-evaluation of older environments and its resulting conservation policies brought about not only the retention of older houses but infillings of new housing developments, typically of the mews court variety. This was most notable in historic cities like York, which had explicit policies to re-introduce residential use, particularly by the childless or elderly, to their centres (Larkham, 1991). Thus between the possible social extremes there were middle grounds where the pre-1914 terraced housing still functioned. Sometimes its ordinary family use continued from earlier times, and sometimes such use was renewed by immigrant populations. The emergence of a 'generic' postwar family house, applicable as we have seen to any location, made such continuing use more feasible. The main practical problem that arose was that terraced layouts did not lend themselves to the family car. It is not surprising, therefore, that as car ownership and traffic levels rose, on-street parking, residents' parking schemes and the exclusion of through traffic became salient planning issues of the older areas.

What would be the future of these various types of neighbourhood it was impossible to say – or whether, indeed, they were neighbourhoods in the traditional sense of that word, rather than accidental and temporary conjunctions of people and uses. The cohesive working-class neighbourhoods discovered and described by urban historians and sociologists around the middle of the century were now

'Scott, Dean, Neil and the Dog, sitting outside Scott's house which they couldn't do if they lived in the houses behind them.' A Portrait of Sheffield. Peter Mitchell, 1978.

clearly of the past – their longevity and stability had perhaps in any case been exaggerated (Meacham, 1977; Frankenberg, 1966). There was certainly no agreed pattern for what a 'normal' inner neighbourhood of the late twentieth century should be. Certain things would clearly influence its future development, perhaps its very physical survival. One of these was its place in the urban structure, always threatened by the demands of space for highways, retailing and expanding commercial centres. Another was future investment in the housing stock, for which the prognosis was doubtful. Yet another was the degree of official intervention. The attempts at neighbourhood revitalization in the housing policies of the 1960s and 1970s had been artificial and disjointed, fixed on buildings rather than economic or social structures. It was, however, an open question whether local authorities (or any other official bodies) could ever be 'sufficiently sophisticated to match a package demanding detailed and sensitive survey work, resident participation, and corporate planning at the local level' (McKie, 1975, p. 392). The policies undoubtedly contributed to the range of influences on such areas, but they could not in the end engineer a future that was deeply embedded in the nation's social and economic structure.

5

AT HOME IN 'HOMES': INSTITUTIONAL LIVING

PEOPLE WITHOUT HOMES

Both the design and policy of twentieth-century housing, including the pre-1914 stock, were devised in the interests of the nuclear family. The obvious justification was that this category included most of the population: it was, quite literally, the nursery of society. Given this bias, difficulties inevitably arose from those who, one way or another, did not fit the family stereotype. They included broadly two groupings: those who because of a particular infirmity were unable to look after themselves; and those who, in the view of society, should have done so but did not. The last included unmarried mothers and families who through unemployment, sickness or other accident had lost, or never had, a home. Even orphans were perversely bracketed with such deviants, for clearly they should have been part of 'normal' families.

Victorian society treated all such people harshly, for they breached the prevailing codes of *laissez faire* and self help. The New Poor Law of 1834, which governed all social welfare down to 1948, was founded on the principle of 'less eligibility': that life in the workhouse should be less attractive than the lowest level of life outside, to deter scroungers and wastrels. It sought to replace the earlier system of local, often small, general workhouses by a large

'parish union' workhouse where people could be sorted by age and sex into their respective categories, according to their deserts. The best part of a century later, however, the mixed general workhouse was still widely in force. All ages and moral conditions were thrown together, so giving the respectable poor 'a horror of it' (Royal Commission, 1909, p. 731). Infants and children were looked after by aged or feeble-minded pauper women, and never left the walls. The ablebodied were subjected to the 'labour test': usually picking oakum (unpicking rope) by hand or breaking several hundredweight of stone. Would-be inmates could be moved on to their 'parish of settlement' (a relic of Elizabethan Poor Law) and upwards of twelve thousand a year were still being thus deported across the country in 1909. The giving of outdoor relief, a dole to enable the needy to keep going in their own homes, was at the discretion of the Poor Law Guardians, who found acute problems in deciding whether those who had relatives or who used any ingenious stratagems to feed themselves, should be entitled to receive anything, or whether such relief only encouraged profligacy and immorality (*Ibid*, 1909). It is not surprising, therefore, that well into the twentieth century, the fear of going into 'the House', or falling 'on the parish' outweighed their fear of going to prison (Roberts, 1971, p. 64).

If it were a case of numbers alone, the history of institutional care for those without homes would not loom very large. No more than a tiny fraction of the national population were ever in such care at any time. In 1901, for instance, the workhouse population was well below one per cent, and after that date those in its successor institutions never reached as much as half a per cent (Parker and Mirrlees, 1988*b*). In 1981, around one and a half per cent of the population of Great Britain lived in residential Homes, children's Homes, hospitals and hostels (Pearce, 1983). At the start of the century around 25,000 old people, or 2.8 per cent of their age group, lived in the general mixed workhouse. By the start of the Second World War the proportion of old people in residential homes had fallen to 0.7 per cent (Parker and Mirrlees, 1988*b*); but after this, numbers rose both absolutely and relatively, to reach 126,000 or 1.7 per cent of the age group by 1980. The other groups in residential care were the non-elderly with physical disability, who decreased from 25,000 in 1950 to 11,000 in 1968; children, of whom there were some 40,000 in 1980 – roughly four-fifths of the number at the start of the century; and people with mental illness or disability numbering some 130,000 at this time. In addition there were homeless people who were found accommodation by councils. Less than 5,000 were counted in 1950 but they increased steadily from the 1960s, to reach a total of over 160,000 regarded as being in a priority category by 1991 (*Ibid*, 1988*b*; Social Trends, 1993).

We are talking, therefore, of a small fraction of the population; some hundreds of thousands of people, whose accommodation did not fall within the normal housing system. But there are reasons besides numbers for treating institutional housing as part of the history of the home. One is the human reason: the workhouse, and after it the residential Home, loomed large in the prospects of the elderly: it must have been a rare old person who did not think with

dread of 'becoming a burden' and consequently being 'put into a Home' or 'going into care'. The harsher aspects of such 'care' softened as the century advances, but the fear itself did not go away. Indeed, it was encouraged by the changing housing system. Up to the 1950s, the majority of old people still headed households of their own or were paying guests in their children's homes (Nuffield Foundation, 1947; Young and Willmott, 1957). This pattern was brought to an end by the suburbanization of young families, slum clearance, and the contraction of private rented housing, at the same time as numbers of the old and very old were increasing.

A second reason for including residential Homes and hostels is their visible presence in the environment, where they were in institutional buildings, or made use of ordinary houses in a distinctive way. Lastly, their history conveys strong messages about society's perception of people without homes and how they should be treated, including their right – or otherwise – to have homes of their own. Their development illustrates perhaps better than anything else could do the intangibles embedded in the very concept of 'home': 'there is hardly a better testing ground for examining the essential nature of "home" and the power of the modern domestic ideal' (Higgins, 1989, p. 159).

By 1914, although the general mixed workhouse was still common, the Poor Law had developed a range of welfare provisions, including general public hospitals, specialized mental hospitals, maternity and children's Homes. Inmates and users were beginning to be treated as valid citizens – for instance, all got the vote in 1918. The Poor Law Board was absorbed into the new Ministry of Health in 1919, but paupers and those needing temporary relief were still catered for in the workhouse system under Boards of Guardians. These were replaced by the Public Assistance Committees of local authorities in 1929. The mass unemployment of the 1930s, however, swamped this system and therefore the National Unemployment Assistance Board was created in 1934. The Poor Law itself continued in force until the National Assistance Act of 1948, under which the Public Assistance Committees were taken over by the National Assistance Board.

The limited old age pension introduced in 1908 was the beginning of independence for those too old to work, but the means test introduced in 1934, which was hated if possible even more than the workhouse, had the effect of driving old people from family homes to avoid prejudicing their sons' entitlement to dole. On his road to Wigan, George Orwell witnessed them eking out their days in private lodging houses which, mean as they were,

were preferred to Public Assistance Committee institutions that were workhouses by another name (Orwell, 1937). In the blitz and general turmoil of war that followed, further numbers of old people were dislodged, with little alternative, now, but to go into institutional care.

The Welfare State heralded by the Beveridge Report of 1942 was the culmination of a long policy progress since 1908. Just before the Report, in 1941, the abolition of the household means test had been a particularly momentous step, because it shifted responsibility for the individual from the family to the state. Under the universal insurance scheme outlined by Beveridge, all would live in freedom from fear of want, accident, sickness and old age, and all

'Public enterprise provides for the housing needs of old people'; with their universal pensions, the elderly could afford these new flats at Lansbury. After this, the hotel-like residential Home was their next step. (*Source*: LCC, *c.* 1962)

would have access to benefits in their own right, independently of the families they belonged to. There could no longer be any question about the aged and the needy being able to maintain their own homes and pay their own way. Under the Act of 1948, the workhouse was to be replaced by the purpose-built residential Home, which the health minister, Aneurin Bevan, likened to a residential hotel, whose residents would pay economic charges without any taint of welfare.

The situation of those with physical and mental needs waited on changes in the National Health Service, which was now responsible for them. In earlier times mental illness and mental disability were often confused and sufferers from both were cared for, when possible, by their families or in private asylums. The workhouse took in the residue of the 'feeble-minded' and people with disorders of many kinds. From 1845, large public asylums had been set up to counter the worst abuses of private care, and the Mental Deficiency Act of 1913 had established residential 'colonies' as well as training and supervision by local authorities for those living at home. To 1930, treatment for mental illness was dependent on 'certification' and so strongly linked to pauperism. Asylums were renamed hospitals in this year and the mentally ill, but not 'defectives', could enter as voluntary patients. It was not until the Mental Health Act of 1959 that the stigmatization of mental illness and disability began to be lifted.

People with physical disabilities would in the past have been found in the workhouse, if their families were unable to support them. The National Assistance Act 1948 gave local authorities powers to build specialist Homes for them, but they continued for many years to be bracketed with the elderly: as late as 1972 some 8,000 younger disabled people were still estimated to be living in old people's Homes and in the 1980s less than half of all local authorities had set up specialist Homes (Leat, 1988). In

the main, provision was through the voluntary sector, where a significant event was the foundation of the first Cheshire Home in 1948, which insisted on the principle that it was a real and permanent home for its residents, rather than a medical institution.

Children in need of care, historically, had been orphans or fatherless children whose mothers could not support them, and for centuries they had been taken in by charitable institutions, as well as workhouses. In these they were reared in special wards, schooled and sent out to work as early as possible, the girls to domestic service and the boys to apprenticeships or unskilled labour. Many were exported at an early age to the Dominions, a practice that lasted into the second half of the twentieth century. After 1900 there was a steep fall in the child population of workhouses, from 23,500 in that year to 6,000 in 1920, and only 2,000 by 1938. This was partly due to the 'cottage homes' and special colonies – virtually self-contained villages with their own schools and other facilities – which became numerous between 1910 and 1920; but the fall in numbers owed more to the growing preference for 'boarding out', which was used with nearly a fifth of children in care by 1938.

At the end of the war, when only a small proportion of children were still in old workhouses, the Curtis Report gave further encouragement to boarding out and by 1959 it applied to nearly half all children in care. Under the Children's Act 1948 local authorities had power to create Homes for children lacking ordinary family life, and the Home of twelve or more children superseded the large colonies. The other major shift was brought about by the effective end of real orphancy. Children were no longer without parents but needed care in periods of family crisis, and their right to return to their natural families was regarded as paramount. At the same time the age of those needing care was moving upwards, so that provision came increasingly to be dominated by adolescents (Berridge, 1985).

THE POSTWAR HOMELESS

In 1948, homelessness tended to concern families rather than single people, and it prompted the response of squatting, as we shall see in Chapter 6, below. It was dealt with under Part III of the National Assistance Act and for their so-called 'Part III' accommodation local authorities used former workhouse wards, sometimes supplemented by old tenement buildings. But on the whole, family homelessness was seen at this time as 'a diminishing and residual problem' (Burke, 1981, p. 64), and it was another ten years before there was a large rise in numbers (Parker and Mirrlees, 1988b).

The phenomenon of single homelessness was recognized somewhat later than this. There had always been vagrants, tramps or dossers: the wandering poor without their own 'parish of settlement'. In earlier times they had been whipped on, but in a more humane postwar climate they were regarded as 'picturesque and very often lovers of the countryside', or simply 'the misfits and drifters of society' (Hansard, 1947, col. 1607; NAB, 1966, para. 1). They were still in the main older men taking to the road after the end of a marriage or a family breakdown. Few were under thirty, and still fewer under twenty. Up to this time, unless they were catered for by private charities, of which the Salvation and Church Armies were the largest, they had been dealt with in the casual wards of workhouses, where the regime was penal: in return for supper and a meagre breakfast the usual labour task had to be performed before they were released, too late in the day to find other work (Roberts, 1971).

Under the National Assistance Act, responsibility for such men passed to the National Assistance Board whose duty it was to provide temporary lodging and to influence them to lead a settled life. A reduced number of existing casual wards, which had been falling into disuse since the Depression, were converted into reception centres, where the aged and those with jobs were to be kept away from 'habitual wanderers' (NAB, 1966, p. 264). Their former lock-up cells were converted to dormitories with curtains and other domestic touches, and the LCC organized an experiment where parties of old men were sent out from centres to visit and report back (favourably, it was hoped) on the new old people's Homes. 'Gentlemen of the road' never, of course, died out completely. The National Assistance Board found 920 men and 45 women sleeping rough in its nationwide survey of 1965 – the main railway terminals and Waterloo station, in particular, were their favourite sleeping places.

For the ordinary single person not living as a member or lodger of a family, the usual form of housing had traditionally been the rented room or common lodging house which, if registered, was defined as 'for poor persons'. Unlike men with families, single men who were unemployed did not get any rent allowance, and this reduced them to extremes of poverty (Orwell, 1937). Wartime conditions must have encouraged both the practice and acceptance of single people living independently. The Dudley Report recommended that the wartime relaxation of rules forbidding lodgers in council property should be continued after the war. It also acknowledged a particular need among women for self-contained flats, for which the special single-person subsidy could be used (p. 44, above). In the interests of creating balanced communities these, with flats for higher income single people, should be included on the new council estates to be built after the war.

In the event, few councils built any single accommodation. One deterrent was the cost, as we have seen, and to justify lower standards it was argued that single people did not want such things as gardens or balconies, or even full cooking facilities, since they spent most of their time outside the home. Where furnished accommodation was provided, the usual practice was to provide one of everything, including the easy chair, leaving none to offer a guest (DoE, 1971). One-bedroom flats did become part of many high-rise estates, but on the whole purpose-built single housing was so unusual that an experimental scheme of 1973 in Leicester, which provided both furnished and unfurnished, single and shared flatlets for young and middle-aged people, was repeatedly held up as an example (DoE, 1974; 1978). In general, single-person provision was left to the revival of housing associations after 1974, when small blocks of flats, 'cluster flats' (groups of bed-sits with common kitchens and dining areas), and houses converted into hostels became common in inner areas of most cities.

One particular population of single people consisted of students in the expanding higher education system. Traditionally, students had lived in colleges or halls of residence in imitation of the Oxbridge colleges. In the redbrick universities of the later nineteenth century it was assumed that students would come from local families and continue to live

A home thought appropriate for a single elderly or working person. (*Source*: MHLG, 1966*a*)

with their parents or, failing that, go into lodgings. The 1949 Housing Manual optimistically bracketed students with other single people, implying that local authorities would provide for them; but in the event provision was through special educational funding for halls of residence, which continued for awhile to be built in the old collegiate tradition. After the Robbins Report of 1963 refectory catering had to be justified by special arguments, and the growing preference was for self-catering study-bedrooms, single rather than double, arranged round staircases with shared bathrooms and kitchens. These new halls of residence contained no refectories, libraries or collegiate rooms, so in practical terms they could be located anywhere. After 1970 their costs were no longer fully covered by the government and private funding had to be sought. This led either to a lowering of standards of space and fittings, or alternatively to the adoption of higher standards to enable halls to be rented out for conference use when students were not in residence.

Rising student numbers led to a severe shortage of accommodation and it became the pattern for such halls to be reserved for first-year students only, after which they were expected to find rooms in the regular housing stock. This came to notice during the 1960s, when there was a spontaneous movement out of lodgings into furnished houses in multiple occupation, which were either rented direct from private landlords or through colleges as intermediaries (Raper, 1974). Either way, it resulted in a virtual student takeover of many districts surrounding large educational institutions, with consequent pressure on rents and neighbourhood services, but also strong impact on their social and cultural life. Colleges and universities sometimes rented blocks of accommodation, typically hard-to-let flats, from councils. Students' housing costs were for a few years supported by housing benefit, but this was later withheld during long vacations, and then removed altogether. By the 1990s student populations were becoming increasingly impoverished by the shift from student grants to loans, with consequent effects on their housing expenditure and standards.

FROM WORKHOUSE TO RESIDENTIAL HOME

The Poor Law of 1834 was not drafted with the intention of punishing aged paupers or those in genuine need, but its determination to deter the able-bodied who might be abusing the system, with the continued use of inhumane standards of earlier times, locked such people into a system that was 'dominated by destitution, madness and criminality' (Parker, 1988, p. 8). It was over thirty years before the New Poor Law thought it proper to provide aged paupers with backs to their benches; and it was not until the 'indulgences' of the 1890s that old men were allowed some baccy, old women a screw of tea, and pauper children a few toys. By the time of the 1909 Royal Commission on the Poor Laws three classes of accommodation for the aged were in use, a hierarchy that conveniently allowed demotion to be used as punishment for unruly behaviour. The highest class had the luxury of floor coverings, armchairs, jam and currant cake for tea, and possibly even private sleeping accommodation for husbands and wives. Inmates could go out or be visited with little restriction. The intermediate class went without jam and were allowed only a half day's leave of absence per week. The lowest class, reserved for the undeserving and dissolute, was restricted to one half day's leave per fortnight. Workhouse wards in massive two or three storey buildings had up to a hundred beds placed a foot or two apart, with bare floors and high windows. There was no privacy, even in bathrooms and WCs. Inmates were unable to have personal possessions or clothing; workhouse garb was worn (and only recently it had sometimes been marked with a prominent

'P'). Both at this time and later, voluntary, charitable Homes were often smaller, but this did not necessarily exempt them from similarly repressive regimes.

In 1947 Aneurin Bevan announced 'the workhouse is to go. Although many people have tried to humanize it, it was in many respects a very evil institution' (Hansard, 1947, col. 1608). But over a hundred of the buildings themselves remained, with sixty-three smaller, specialized Homes. They were now apportioned, either separately or jointly, to the local authorities and the new National Health Service which was now responsible for the sick and disabled. This marked a distinction between those with discernible illnesses, who could be looked after in hospitals, and those who were simply 'in need of care and attention', principally large numbers of aged people who then lived out their lives in geriatric wards little different, in practical respects, to those of the old workhouse system.

In 1960 the old buildings still housed nearly a third of all old people in residential care, and in *The Last Refuge* Peter Townsend laid bare conditions inside thirty-nine of them. The majority were over a hundred years old, without lifts and sometimes without central heating. In some, valiant attempts at improvement had been made: bare walls plastered, dormitories divided into cubicles, more sanitation installed; but only about 5 or 6 per cent of the residents had benefited. Most inmates slept on iron framed beds with thin blankets, sharing wardrobes and dressing tables, and many lived, slept and ate in the same ward. Only 2 per cent occupied single rooms. Meals were served to a hundred, two hundred or even more at a sitting. Furnishings were such that only a minority of institutions offered inmates the exclusive use of a chair, and none offered them sole use of either armchair, mirror, chest of drawers or wash hand basin. There was a dearth of such things as cushions, hot water bottles, occasional tables, waste-paper baskets, table cloths, glasses – in short, all the usual impedimentia of domestic living.

Men and women, including husbands and wives, were segregated. There were no quiet corners for conversations and in any case staff discouraged inmates from talking to or helping one another. With constant arrivals and departures, the switching of beds and dormitories could be used as a disciplinary device. It is scarcely surprising that 'most of the residents therefore led an extremely self-contained existence. They would wait stoically for their meals, conversed very little, thumbed their handbags or tobacco pouches and tried to give as little trouble as possible' (Townsend, 1962, p. 104).

In the same study Townsend visited fifty-three out of a total of 1,100 new Homes established since the 1948 Act. Only five of these were purpose-built. The rest were mostly converted mansions in spacious grounds, dating back to the previous century if not before. Though on the whole fairly comfortable, these mansion Homes were often deficient in lifts and sanitary accommodation. Their large, high rooms were difficult to divide and make cosy, and their grandiosity was at odds with the needs of frail old people.

Three-fifths of the newly established Homes were now 'mixed', for men and women; but in many respects workhouse rules persisted. Not all residents were allowed to wear their own clothing and, despite Ministry of Health advice to the contrary, the bringing of furniture was usually forbidden. Three reasons for this were advanced by one welfare officer: 'There is no room for it. It spoils the look of the Home. And often it's useless' (*Ibid*, 1962, p. 248).

For a long time it seemed obvious that reduced size was the best way of counteracting the workhouse legacy, but it was difficult to settle on an ideal size, not least because achievement of a homely environment and economies of scale were in conflict. An early ideal of thirty to thirty-five beds was displaced by one of up to sixty beds, which allowed more

single rooms; but in the end the concept of 'family groups' of around eight to ten residents seemed to offer a compromise which was adopted not only in newly built but also existing Homes. By the 1970s it was common to have forty or fifty residents arranged in such groups and sharing dining space and sanitary arrangements. A similar trend took place in Homes for the physically disabled.

The different types of local authority Home allowed a repetition of the social hierarchies seen before, with demotion to an inferior institution used as a threat. The inmates of former workhouses, though not necessarily any less well off financially, were of a lower social stratum than those in new Homes, and they still included unmarried mothers and people who were blind, deaf, dumb or with mental disabilities. Private and voluntary Homes, many with less than thirty beds, on the whole catered for a higher social stratum. The small voluntary Home, in particular, was used by retired spinsters, including former domestic servants. Women residents in general were of a higher social class than men, and women began significantly to outnumber men after 1950, whereas previously they had been numerically inferior. In postwar society it was increasingly the case that wives cared for husbands until they were widowed, when they themselves were infirm and in need of care. This difference became so characteristic of later residential care that it could be described as 'care by women, for women' (Higgins, 1989, p. 165).

FROM RESIDENTIAL CARE TO 'CARE IN THE COMMUNITY'

Townsend's *Last Refuge* was as influential in its way as the Nuffield Report of 1947 which had helped shift policy for the aged from large institutions to residential Homes. During the 1970s there was a marked improvement of physical standards in new Homes, including an increase in private rooms. Improved physical standards, however, might serve 'primarily to assist the work routines of staff rather than to enhance the lives of residents' (Willcocks *et al.*, 1987, p. 88). Thus they could make it easier for staff to bath residents, but still confront the latter with doors and windows they were unable to open or heating that they could not adjust. When private rooms were provided, they could almost never be locked from inside. Kitchens – the most attractive and convivial part of most ordinary homes – were usually in out-of-bounds staff space, leaving residents with nowhere to make an informal cup of tea.

Similarly there were limitations to the marked improvement of management practices. Entrants to Homes were no longer automatically subjected to a compulsory bath and confiscation of clothing on admission, and there was more sensitivity about the practice of keeping a 'Death room' to which people were removed in their final days (Townsend, 1962, p. 147); but the fundamental insecurity and unnaturalness of this way of living remained. Without legal security of tenure, ill and dying residents continued to be sent to another part of the institution, or away altogether. Few entered institutional care of their own free choice and it was not uncommon for old people to be tricked or coerced into taking up residence by being led to believe that it was a temporary or an only option. Coming 'into care' involved leaving perhaps lifelong associations, a home environment that could be personally controlled 'to conceal incapacities and limitations from others' (Willcocks *et al.*, 1987, p. 7); and most hurtful of all, it might involve the disposal of treasured pets. It was in many respects an admission of failure – both of oneself to remain independent, and of one's family to provide support (Higgins, 1989). Contrary to the spirit of the 1948 Act, there was not even, for most, the satisfaction of paying their own way; for all who were publicly supported had their charges paid for them and received weekly 'pocket money', usually distributed in public in the common lounge.

With this loss of identity and status, connections with the outside world were continued with difficulty. Half the residents in a survey of local authority Homes in the 1980s never went out (Willcocks *et al.*, 1987). Many had to receive visits from relatives and friends in common lounges or hallways. They lived in close proximity with strangers, often sharing bedrooms, when, with the possible exception of men who had once been in the army, they had no previous experience of collective living. 'For a person who has had a very private life the constant exposure to others is extremely taxing for both mind and body. It is difficult for the resident to make sense of the group process of which he or she becomes an integral part from the moment of stepping through the door' (Davis, 1982, p. 49). The presence of not one but two populations in Homes – staff as well as residents – created complex interpersonal politics where inmates had to learn not to challenge staff, not only for fear of reprisals, but because they depended on them for physical help and mediation with fellow inmates.

The best known sign of the tensions of institutional living was the arrangement of residents' armchairs which invariably seemed to line the walls of common lounges. This was noticed by a member of staff in Townsend's survey, who mistakenly attributed it to the stubbornness of old people (Townsend, 1962, p. 98). A later and more sensitive observer divined that the arrangement allowed residents 'to avoid prolonged social interaction and to withdraw to relative anonymity', while at the same time allowing the creation of personal territory by 'chairs adorned with blankets and cushions, defended by the owner's zimmer frame' (Willcocks *et al.*, 1987, pp. 91–92). Social retreat was further facilitated by the TV, switched on all day but not so much watched as allowing residents to withdraw into their own thoughts without giving offence to others. In a parallel way, it was noticed that children's Homes used the TV as a device to regulate group behaviour (Berridge, 1985).

A number of things contributed to changing policies for care in the later part of the century. They included changes in treatment of people with mental disabilities, whose release from long stay mental hospitals was under discussion from 1971, and the withdrawal from 1978 of government commitment to state provided residential care for the aged. After the Griffiths Report of 1988, local authorities become responsible for setting up care 'packages' for each person, to be paid for with a 'dowry' attached to each person, which could be used in private as well as public care Homes. For people with physical disabilities, in addition to providing special residential Homes under an Act of 1970, local authorities could give grants for adaptations to enable them to live as ordinary householders. Standards for mobility and wheelchair housing had been set in the mid-1970s, the former allowing access by wheelchair users, the latter so designed that all fittings and appliances could be used by anyone with severe disabilities. Through these years there was a growing acceptance that those with disabilities of any kind, physical or mental, had a right to live as others lived, in their own homes. Following the National Health Service and Community Care Act 1990, the policy of 'care in the community' was formally inaugurated in 1993.

At the same time a wave of reform was overtaking residential care, which was in effect the community care to which many inmates of hospitals were released. New principles and standards were laid down in the *Home Life Code of Practice* of 1984. They were based on respect for personal rights and emotional needs; the freedom to follow normal activities, and indulge in 'responsible risk taking'; freedom to have access to one's own room at any time, and to lock up both room and possessions; and the right to wash, dress and use the toilet in

private. It should be possible to receive visitors, letters and phone calls in privacy; to go out, take holidays, pursue interests and help in domestic tasks around the Home. Terminal care, when necessary, should if possible be given within the Home, and in the resident's own room rather than a special unit; for 'it gives a great sense of security to residents to know that they will not be sent away to die' (Home Life, 1984, para. 2, 7, 5).

The Wagner Report of 1988 generalized such principles to all categories of residential care, and *Homes are for Living in* (Department of Health, 1989) provided a model for evaluation of the quality of care given and life experienced by residents. The Wagner Report recommended, among other things, that old people should hold their own pension books and pay their own charges from housing benefit, and that sharing a bedroom should never be made a condition of residence. The principles and recommendations were, of course, ideals, and there was no mechanism for their immediate implementation, particularly since the greatest expansion of residential care was in the private sector, where even very high charges were no guarantee of private rooms or any other of the recommended standards. The ultimate safeguard of standards in the private Homes was intermittent inspection by local authorities. In the case of unregistered Homes with under four residents no inspection was required, and here some very low standards of care and accommodation prevailed.

For the aged, the principle of 'care in the community' came to be interpreted as the right to go on living in their own homes, as most of them preferred to do, and being supported by domiciliary services. These had grown up somewhat disjointedly since the first impetus given during the Second World War, when they were mainly used for maternity cases. The new National Health Service enabled councils to develop home help services, but on the whole they preferred to grant aid voluntary agencies and limit their own provision to the physically handicapped, so that they did not in effect fully use their powers until 1971. After this time there was a sharp rise in the numbers of old people and others receiving home help, which reached nearly three quarters of a million by 1980 (Parker and Mirrlees, 1988*b*). As well as help in the home, domiciliary care could replace certain household tasks, notably through laundry services and meals on wheels, which doubled in number between 1970 and 1980. It could also include attendance at day centres where meals, medical attention and leisure activities were available.

Living alone could be hazardous for frail people and this was partly remedied by linking their homes to the alarm systems of sheltered housing schemes, with mobile wardens who could respond to calls. The worries of elderly householders could be addressed by the 'staying put' scheme piloted by Anchor Housing Association in 1978 and the 'Care and Repair' scheme which was given state support in 1986. These helped elderly householders within designated areas to cost and arrange household repairs and improvements. They reached only a very small minority, however, and among other things they were not concerned with what was a very large problem for many, the garden. As a study of old people in three areas found, 'It is a source of great distress to some elderly people when their gardens are untended. Anyone . . . can see that gardens have often been their pride and joy for many years, and when they can no longer care for them, an important part of their lives is badly affected' (Allen *et al.*, 1992, p. 87).

This was only one illustration of the shortcomings of domiciliary help in general. Operating as this normally did, in conditions of shortage, it was seldom able to offer the amounts or types of help that were really wanted. Helpers and times were changed without notice and the person receiving home help had very little say in the help that was given. For instance, home helpers were customarily forbidden to do certain things which might be important to aged or ill people. They included tasks deemed inappropriate or unnecessary such as cleaning windows and unused rooms, and tasks which clients were supposed to be able to do themselves, such as dusting.

As a result of changing hospital practices, the policy of 'care in the community' resulted in many people being prematurely discharged from hospital wards without adequate homes or support to go to. In particular, the ill-judged discharge of psychiatric patients and people from long-stay mental institutions resulted in some ending up on the streets or in prison, and sometimes even committing murders. There were those for whom the closing down of institutions in which they had passed most of their lives was a dubious benefit. In such a context, the concept of 'care in the community' was rhetoric masking inadequate resources. This made the concept of 'community', in 'community care', as questionable as the concept of 'residential Home'.

FROM COMMON LODGING HOUSE TO HOSTEL

It had been the intention of the National Assistance Board to carry out five-yearly censuses of its reception centres for the homeless. Only two such censuses took place, in 1965 and 1972, and between them many commercial establishments closed down, owing largely to slum clearance and rising standards – for instance, the requirements of the Fire Act 1971 which prompted owners either to go out of business or to upgrade their property for use by a higher social class. By 1972, owners were becoming forgetful of the regulations covering common lodging houses and increasingly provision was covered by the term hostel. For the time being the majority of users were still men, white and never married. For half or more of hostel residents this was not a temporary but a permanent way of life (Wingfield Digby, 1976).

By this time, however, a transformation in the scale and nature of homelessness was under way, largely as a result of the diminution of older and privately rented housing. The first significant increase in family homelessness since the war began to be apparent in the late 1960s. It was the subject of Jeremy Sandford's never forgotten semi-documentary TV film, *Cathy Come Home*, first shown in 1966 and repeated three times in the next two years. Cathy and her young family slid down the housing ladder from over-expensive luxury flat to sharing with in-laws and death-trap caravan, finally reaching Part III hostels where her husband was banned and the family broke up. Her last refuge was a station bench where her children were wrenched from her to be taken into care, while she herself was told that she was of no concern to anyone any more.

In 1966 local authorities were instructed to convert their Part III hostels to not more than nine self-contained living units, and soon they were also being encouraged to patch up 'short-life' older housing. The foundation of Shelter and the militancy of this and other pressure groups (Child Poverty Action Group, Campaign for the Homeless and Rootless, Catholic Housing Aid Society) helped to bring about the Housing (Homeless Persons) Act 1977, which for the first time brought together the policy and administration of housing and homelessness. The Act made local authorities responsible for finding permanent homes for specific priority categories of homeless people, provided they had not made themselves intentionally homeless and (a relic of the 'parish of settlement') that they had a local connection. By the 1980s, when their stock was eroded through privatization, councils found it increasingly difficult to accommodate homeless families in their own property and some resorted to using commercial hotels – the notorious 'bed-and-breakfast' solution which cost more than buying a family house with a mortgage. It is not surprising, therefore, that in 1994 the Conservative government circulated a discussion paper which proposed to end councils' responsibility for finding homeless families anything more than temporary accommodation: in effect, a return to the situation prior to the 1977 Act.

By now a rapid rise of single, mainly young, homeless people had occurred, and by 1976 as many as 10,000 were estimated to be squatting

Multiple letterboxes and name plates on the door are often the only external sign of a hostel. Leeds, 1995.

(Burke, 1981). They were not one of the priority categories of the 1977 Act, unless they were pregnant or otherwise vulnerable, and their chances of finding a home were further reduced by changes in their right to various social security payments, including rent in advance which was required by almost all private landlords. By the end of the 1980s people under twenty-five received less than the full adult rate of income support, and those under eighteen, unless they were on a Youth Training Scheme, were denied any support at all – the assumption being that they should be living at home with their parents.

Even with the will, unless they had any hard-to-let property standing empty, councils could do little to help the single homeless who applied to them. Their only legal obligation was to provide advice – which a number did by handing out copies of the local paper or tourist guide. Apart from the Salvation and Church Armies, which were still the largest providers, with thirty per cent of all hostel beds between them, the main providers were housing associations, who were encouraged to develop hostels for vulnerable groups, with funding from the Department of Social Security and the Home Office as well as the usual housing sources. Overall, 23 per cent of their hostels were for ex-prisoners, 9 per cent for people with mental or physical illness, 18 per cent were women's refuges, and seven per cent exclusively for young people, in addition to the 30 per cent for general housing purposes (Berthoud and Casey, 1988). Those unable to gain accommodation of any kind lived on the streets and slept rough.

The numbers of single homeless are in the last resort unknowable, because authorities were not obliged to keep records of those that applied to them, and there were numbers more who did not apply. But on a crude estimate they amounted to over 100,000 in London alone (Greve and Currie, 1990) while no part of the country, rural areas included, was

without them. Rough sleepers were equally uncountable, but the 1991 Census actually recorded 2,397 men and 430 women in this situation.

Although hostels became the accepted form of housing for the homeless, the term itself covered many different arrangements, from large institutions to ordinary houses shared by a few individuals, with or without resident staff. The term also covered residential Homes for people with various handicaps, but not sheltered housing for the elderly, although the two might be closely similar. A hostel could also be a set of cluster flats or self-contained flatlets; and some hostels had satellites in the form of group homes for the use of their more independent inmates – typically adolescents leaving children's Homes, or people with mental disabilities leaving hospital, who needed practice in independent living.

The common factor in all such examples was provision for a selected group, with continuing control by others. Thus 'the establishment is run according to a set of principles initially conceived by someone other than the residents . . . What it means is that someone somewhere initially said, "We need a residential establishment for such-and-such – whether handicapped, old or young people" ' (Atherton, 1989, p. 7). Though not necessarily overt, authority is essential to the meaning of 'hostel'. In this respect, therefore, it is not the same as a 'house in multiple occupation', although their physical arrangements may be closely similar. On the other hand, in all respects but title, a bed-and-breakfast 'hotel' run to cater for the homeless and abounding in shared facilities and repressive rules is in fact a hostel in all but name.

Traditionally, hostel provision had been mainly for men. Towards the end of the century, while there was a limited number of mixed-use hostels, women-only places constituted little more than a tenth of the whole, although young women were now one of the fastest growing categories of the homeless. To those on the street it mattered greatly whether a hostel was 'direct access' (like the old night shelters) or whether it needed prior booking or referral from an agency. Emergency hostels were in the majority but there were also medium- and long-stay hostels, and there continued to be inmates who made permanent homes in these – either in one only or a number in succession (Thomas and Niner, 1989).

Inner city locations were almost invariable. In 1972 the great majority of hostel buildings predated the First World War. The balance was changed by hostels created after that date, but the majority were converted rather than new buildings, and sometimes left unimproved (Garside *et al.*, 1990). They ranged in size from a mere handful of beds to the several hundreds found in the larger Salvation and Church Army hostels, but the commonest sizes were not more than ten or between thirty and fifty beds. Much use was made of the 'domestic model' with twelve or fewer beds, 'an attempt to create a hostel building which is as close to a family house as possible and where residents can feel at home' – even though it also needed to contain staff accommodation (*Ibid*, 1990, p. 49).

In 1972 only a third of the hostels surveyed had any single rooms and the majority provided rooms for two to six people. By the later 1980s around half hostel residents had their own rooms. Sanitary facilities were normally shared by up to five people but catering facilities could be either individual or shared, the allocation being influenced by 'the common view that women can cook and men cannot' (Berthoud and Casey, 1988, p. 43). Cooking and housework were sometimes used as part of a programme for training inmates. In general, internal standards were highest in hostels for drug abusers and worst, including the worst overcrowding, in women's refuges. Residents were, however, surprisingly tolerant of low standards and shared facilities: for although many found living in temporary accommodation 'a depress-

ing and unsettling experience' they were 'often grateful for a roof over their heads' (Thomas and Niner, 1989, p. 150). It appeared to alter people's attitudes significantly if they themselves had chosen their accommodation rather than simply being placed there by others (*Ibid*, 1989).

The quality of conditions in hostels was very much determined by the needs and demands of the client groups. In particular, the disruptive resident could have a quite disproportionate effect on staff time and attitudes, and the reactions to hostel living of the other residents (Watson, 1987). A huge range of demands was made on the hostel, its staff and residents which, though not necessarily different in kind from demands made on a family home, were of a different degree of intensity. They included basic housekeeping skills (shopping, cleaning, cooking, care of clothes); health care, including treatment of various addictions; and a wide range of social skills such as obtaining information, form-filling, keeping appointments, dealing with the law and officials of many kinds, and the maintenance of personal relationships (Berthoud and Casey, 1988). The quality of these services was greatly affected by mounting pressure on hostel accommodation and changes in government funding of hostels after 1988, when grants to compensate for their high management costs and residents' board and lodging allowances were ended.

HOMES IN 'HOMES': CONTRADICTIONS OF INSTITUTIONAL LIVING

After 1948 institutional living was transformed in two particular respects: the domesticization of its environments and the giving of more privacy to inmates. The second, it could be argued, was the more successful because it was also the easier to achieve. It had a parallel in the twentieth-century prison where, although notorious degrees of overcrowding and lack of sanitation continued to be a disgrace into the

1990s, the prisoner's cell (particularly in women's prisons) was often allowed to become a personal room, with soft furnishings and private possessions (Fitzgerald and Sim, 1979).

The domesticization of residential Homes and hostels, on the other hand, seemed unaccountably disappointing, in spite of continuous efforts. Some of the constraints were physical, such as the special requirements of Homes catering for physical disability, which were 'space guzzlers' of necessity (Leat, 1988, p. 225), or the fire doors legally required in the interiors, even of very small establishments. But other measures seemed wilfully to highlight and stigmatize this particular way of living: the large name boards that advertize old people's Homes to the world at large; the official foundation plaques set in prominent positions; or the naming of Homes to commemorate local politicians, rather than letting them have ordinary names and street addresses. Lack of imagination and bulk buying contributed to an institutional atmosphere: for instance entrances halls covered with official notices and so furnished as to create 'something of the warmth and intimacy of an airport lounge' (Berridge, 1985, p. 77).

It might be argued that these were inevitable physical manifestations of a fundamentally unnatural and contradictory way of living. For one thing, residential Homes had to cater for not one but two populations, staff as well as residents. The collective environment was not under the control of the residents – which helps to explain why their insistence on privacy was so important. It did not necessarily follow, however, that it was directly subject to the control of members of staff. As we have seen, changes in design were based around their convenience, but there were many things in Homes and hostels, such as lounges, hobby and common rooms, visitor's rooms and gardens, which were provided for the benefit of residents but very under-used by them. It was the unfamiliarity and awkwardness of

living in groups, with the lack of any established codes and customs, that was responsible for this (Garside et al., 1990). Residents might be physically arranged in something called a family group, but it was not in any meaningful way a real family.

The artificiality of the situation also affected staff. It is true that, as Townsend saw in 1962, staff attitudes and procedures were slow to change, so that it took a very long time and natural wastage before the worst of the old workhouse management practices died out. The vulnerability of some residents to emotional and physical violence – particularly the frail elderly and the mentally confused – is something found at all times, and this should never be overlooked. The formulation of more enlightened policies, as in the Wagner Report, was not in itself a solution: in many respects it presented staff with new dilemmas. How were they, for instance, to encourage 'responsible risk taking' when they were professionally accountable for residents' safety? The crux is neatly illustrated by a new rule imposed on registered Homes in 1993: in their hot water tanks, water temperatures should be high enough to counteract Legionnaire's disease; but when it issued from the taps it should not be so hot that there would be a risk of residents scalding their hands.

The problem underlying these dilemmas was that institutional living involved collections of people who had not chosen to live together and who only came together because of need, and bureaucratic provision for that need. This governed all the interpersonal relationships within Homes. This was laid bare in the history of the original Cheshire Home, founded in 1948, which was based on the principle that inmates were ordinary residents rather than patients. By 1959 they were running most of the Home's affairs, but when a new warden and matron tried to impose new restrictions, among other things on bedtimes, resistance and a campaign for total autonomy ended in the realization that the real need was not independence from staff, but a sensitive and cooperative staff who shared residents' ideals (Miller and Gwynne, 1972).

The residents here were an unusually cohesive body, and the more normal situation was one where residents were atomized and powerless. For the aged, it was clear that residential care was a terminus, when all other options had been exhausted; but in the case of children reforms of the twentieth century led more and more to such care being used as a substitute, as temporary as possible, for 'real' family homes. Thus even when children sought to form child–parent relationships with members of staff, they were strongly discouraged from doing so. In preference, endless attempts were made to find foster parents or prospective adoptive parents, even at the risk of strings of failures and rejections. The implication was that a professional service, though providing for need, could not provide a genuine 'home'.

One way forward, as we have seen, was greater use of domiciliary care, to enable people to live at home. The other route went in a completely opposite direction, not towards more homely institutions but larger, better equipped and more fully professionalized ones. These could have a wider public role, for instance by providing day care and respite or temporary care for clients, and their facilities (social centres, hobby rooms, laundries) could be opened to people living outside. For many years, the refectories and sports facilities of larger YMCAs and YWCAs had been open to the public. Rather similarly, some housing associations designed the community rooms of their larger sheltered housing schemes so that they could be used by older people in the neighbourhood. This was also the trend in adolescent hostels, and in the new concept of the 'foyer' which was borrowed from France around 1990. As well as accommodation for homeless young people, the foyer contained a public restaurant run by residents, with other community facilities and training workshops for unemployed under-25-year-olds. New foyer buildings were being constructed in the 1990s, in London and other big cities, by the YMCA, YWCA and some of the older housing trusts, and a network of 250 was envisaged by the end of the century (Spring, 1991). If these and similar innovations became established, they might perhaps help to normalize institutional living. They could broaden public awareness of its potential benefits and help to close the ancient divide between the institutional 'Home', with its long, sad history of deficiency and repression, and conventional domestic life in ordinary homes.

6

SELF-HELP AND
ALTERNATIVE HOUSING

Conventional housing, as we have seen, allows little if any opportunity for individual intervention in its type or design, while those without homes would for the most part simply like the same sort of homes that others have. Falling outside the scope of these general rules is a mixed collection of exceptions, some deliberately motivated, others accidental or pragmatic responses to circumstance. Such deviations from the norm in housing may be crudely divided according to their motivation: technical and utilitarian, or social and ideological. An example of the former would be temporary shelter to meet a crisis need; and of the latter the adaptation of conventional housing to suit the needs of an alternative community. The two categories are not necessarily distinct: in particular, there is an area of overlap where a certain kind of dwelling, such as a solar or underground house, may be what ties a group together. This may also be the case with self-building; but another dimension altogether is provided by a distinct cultural tradition, such as that of the gypsies.

PREFABRICATED HOUSES

The use of prefabrication in housebuilding lies to some extent on the margins of these divisions. It was espoused by early twentieth-century Futurists and architects of the Modern Move-ment, who wished to see house production as fast and efficient as automobile production, as befitted modern industrial society. A later manifestation of this school of thought was Archigram, which proposed short life, expendable buildings and individual, plug-in and movable living 'pods' (Banham, 1976); but the real contribution of prefabrication was to mainstream building technology: for instance, in factory-made components that eliminated a good deal of on-site work by specialized trades. This was a cumulative contribution, starting in the 1920s but accelerating rapidly after 1945, one of its more oblique effects being in the DIY industry (Chapter 8, below).

A seemingly obvious use of prefabrication would be the provision of 'instant' dwellings to meet sudden emergencies; and innovative structures such as Buckmaster Fuller's geodesic domes have many potentialities for this (Fuller and Marks, 1973). But the opportunity was only occasionally exploited, for instance for the homeless and for students (Constable, 1975; Gililan, 1990). The most notable experiment in prefabricated housing was the postwar 'prefab' approved by Parliament in 1944, for a quarter of a million homes for victims of the blitz (Gaskell, 1987). The programme proved more difficult than expected and in all only 157,000 units were produced in redundant aircraft factories. Some

Owners of prefabs erected in Birmingham in 1946 have resisted demolition and used the 'Right to Buy', and they are about to become owners of listed buildings. (*Source*: Birmingham City Council)

dozen different varieties of house were used but the one first exhibited to the public (the Portal) was not in fact put into production, and only three different types were used in significant quantities. One of these, the AIROH aluminium house, took forty man hours to assemble on a prepared foundation and arrived fully plumbed and wired with connections to be made on site.

Never intended to be a permanent home, the prefab had many shortcomings in the view of the architectural profession. That it only had two bedrooms was condoned on the ground it was not intended to serve as a family home in the usual sense, for husbands were still mostly away at war; but its other defects were condensation, minimal circulation space and (in some types) internal layouts with rooms leading into one another. The prefab nevertheless became one of the most cherished of all twentieth-century dwellings, and probably the most popular of all types of council owned dwellings.

In essence it was simply a bungalow, usually detached and set in its own garden. Estates of prefabs were typically on small, bombed, inner city sites, or in outlying suburbs and urban fringes. Smaller groups were laid out in small closes, but estates of several hundreds were laid out like conventional council estates. The unusual luxuries of fully fitted kitchens and bathrooms, with running hot water, ample built-in cupboards and sometimes other fitted furniture (estimated to be worth £80) outweighed, for most occupants, the discomforts arising from thin walls and flat or shallow roofs. Tenants, therefore, clung fiercely to them, resisting demolition whenever this was proposed. As temporary dwellings they did not qualify for improvement grants; nevertheless some authorities modernized them, while their occupants were apt to lavish money on them. They lasted long enough to be bought under the 'right to buy' and in one case they became a tenant management co-operative (Gililan, 1990). Eventually prefabs were acknowledged to be particularly suited to the elderly, and in some places were managed as sheltered housing. The extension of their planned ten-year life to half a century or more was, therefore, an unintended conversion of a dwelling with precise and limited uses to a much more open-ended kind of 'self-help' housing.

NOMADIC HOUSING

Tents were well known as holiday accommodation but little used for more permanent housing, apart from the 'bender' – plastic sheeting or other material draped over a crude frame of bent branches – which was borrowed from gypsies of earlier times and used in the 1980s and 1990s by the women of Greenham Common and the homeless of London's Lincoln's Inn Fields. But the tipi, a conical tent of the North American Plains Indians which dated back to 1540, was a durable form of tented housing which was taken up in the 1960s and 1970s by 'hippies' and others, most notably by the Tipi People who colonized a Welsh valley site in pursuit of their non-industrial lifestyle. The tipi was a tilted cone of hide or canvas draped over a pyramidal arrangement of tall poles. Smoke from the interior hearth was guided out by smoke flaps and the undivided floor space had areas allotted to men, women and honoured guests (Faegre, 1979). The tipi's devotees maintained that living in it provided a unique, even mystical, experience.

Later twentieth-century people spent many of their waking hours in cars which, until the rising wave of car theft, they liked to personalize with special toys and fittings. It would be surprising if no one ever thought of inhabiting cars as permanent homes, and indeed the notices prohibiting overnight sleeping in lay-bys and car parks suggest that the authorities were alert to this possibility. A study of 1972 managed to locate over 700 people who did live in their cars (Wates and Wolmar, 1980).

The boat had always been used for permanent housing, and besides naval and merchant vessels there were enough lived-in canal boats for them to be regulated by a series of Acts in the nineteenth century. With tents, vans and sheds, boats were treated as houses under the Housing Act 1935. The houseboat population was boosted by the sale of government surplus stock at the end of the war, and converted Thames barges were taken so seriously as dwellings at this time that they were included in architectural books on housing (Yorke and Whiting, 1953). In one estimate as many as 15,000 people lived on boats (Shaw, 1985), although the 1991 Census found less than 5,000. For some, houseboat living was a necessary response to the housing shortage; but others chose it as a way of life, independent, unconventional and rich in the cameraderie of the moorings. Boats were bought and sold, but the rent of moorings could cost more than the boat itself. Indeed much of the cameraderie resulted from the insecurity, not only of the elements but of the moorings, for the number of these progressively diminished, while the only legal protection was provided by the law of contract.

The mobile caravan, like the tent or the boat, is well known as holiday accommodation, and it also resembles the boat in being used for utilitarian purposes by itinerant workers. An obvious use for the caravan would seem to be for the homeless, as proposed by the Department of Environment in 1974; but in general its potential in this direction was remarkably little explored (Shaw, 1985). The house on wheels

Both boats and caravans make cosy homes. (*Source*: Yorke and Whiting, 1953)

first emerged in the mid-nineteenth century and was not adopted by gypsies until the 1870s. Its first development was in fact by showmen (many of whom were gypsies) as transport for their menageries. It went on to serve various functions: touring and static holiday use, and eventually static permanent use for several distinct categories of people.

The heyday of the horse-drawn gypsy caravan or vardo was from 1875 to the early 1900s. Motor traction began between the wars, showmen again leading the way, but gypsies continued to use horses down to the 1970s. The vardo was not normally a self-made vehicle but built by specialist firms, rather than gypsies themselves. Its interior followed a conventional pattern: there was a two-tiered bed across the rear end, and a door with a porch at the front, where the driver sat. On the left or outer side was the stove, a seat and locker, which faced a seat and locker on the right hand side. Some vans had a bow top but a hard top would allow roof windows (borrowed from the Pullman railway coach) with plate racks or high-level cupboards. Furnishings were traditional, but not from a peasant tradition. As well as traces of Eastern origins, 'the Romany woman took her cue, not from cottages, but from the Victorian lady of the manor' (Ward-Jackson and Harvey, 1972): and this meant an abundance of mirrors, sequins, satins, lace, fringes, tassels and button upholstery. To the present day the traditional gypsy interior is a fairy cavern of reflecting and ornamented surfaces and exotic objects. On the outside, the elaborate painted and gold-embossed patterns of the horse-drawn caravan have been replaced by stream-lined, appliqued ornamentation of the mass-produced, bright gleaming trailer.

The compactness of this travelling home seems at odds with the large extended families and many children of traditional Romany culture. It was, however, intended to cater for a limited number of activities. For reasons of taboo, cooking, eating and sanitary functions, were originally performed in the open air, leaving the van interior free for social and leisure uses, including the display of ornate crockery and other valuables, and leisure use was in due course intensified by the installation of a TV set. Though this traditional arrangement was eventually displaced by the kitchen trailer or the site chalet with cooking accommodation, it was still opposite to the normal arrangement of the English home, which was expected to accommodate all functions. In strict Romany observance, gorgios or strangers were not allowed to pollute the interior of the home (and if they ate or drank from any vessels, these were afterwards broken). The home itself travelled to the workplace, rather than being spatially separated from it.

There is no reliable way of estimating the gypsy population but there appears to have been a growth between 1959 when there may have been 3,400 households (living in lorries, buses, shacks and tents as well as caravans) and the early 1980s, when another count gave around 8,000 (Wilson, 1959; DoE, 1982). By 1992 some 12,500 vans, representing 25–30,000 people, were counted (Home, 1994). Following a nomadic lifestyle clearly became more difficult as more and more land was developed and, most particularly, after the imposition of full development control in 1947. Gypsies were also affected by control of ordinary caravan sites, which would otherwise have increased alarmingly in the early postwar years. Under the Caravan Sites and Control of Development Act 1960 all such sites required a license in addition to planning permission and, though aimed primarily at controlling holiday caravanning, such licensing effectively barred these sites to gypsies, so further reducing their available stopping places.

Following the publication of *Gypsies and Other Travellers* by the Department of Environment, the Caravan Sites Act 1968 laid a duty on local authorities to provide adequate serviced, rented sites to meet travellers' needs. These could be basic or full facility sites, the latter having concrete pitches furnished with small brick chalets for washing and sanitation, resident wardens (who might themselves be travellers) and site services. From 1979 a hundred per cent grant was available for the capital costs of new sites. Nevertheless councils were notoriously reluctant to create them and the places available fell far short of the travelling population: by one estimate there were in the late 1980s 4,200 vans without legal stopping places (Gerlach *et al.*, n.d.). Whatever the exact numbers, the shortfall was largely to blame for a situation where 'the living conditions of many gypsies was scandalous' (Cullingworth, 1985, p. 97)

New Age travellers introduced a fresh dimen-sion to the problem of fitting nomadism into a settled society. They were not rooted in any ancient tradition as gypsies were, but rather self-selected 'drop-outs' from urbanized indus-trial society who came to prominence in the 1960s. Many were completely individualistic but many, perhaps the majority, had a strong sense of solidarity in their taste for illegal drugs and for national festivals of music, alternative therapies and cult observances, particularly those centred on Glastonbury and Stonehenge. They also turned up to support public protests against spoilations of the environment, as did the Donga Tribe in Winchester at the desecra-tion of Twyford Down by a motorway tunnel in

City of Leeds serviced travellers' site at Cottingley, 1995.

1993. For homes, New Age travellers use buses, vans, trailers – any kind of vehicle, in fact; but they use them differently from gypsy caravans, cultivating uncleanliness rather than cleanliness, and sharing none of the same pollution taboos, so that, for instance, cooking and eating were quite happily combined or strangers invited inside.

There is no way of discussing nomadic housing without touching on deeply engrained and polarized attitudes. As quintessential outsiders, the gypsies were always the objects of repressive laws and eventually of genocide by the Nazis under Hitler. In a pettier fashion, local prejudice which looked on them (as it happened inaccurately) as dirty and disorderly, led to innumerable incidents of harassment, wrecking and burning of caravans, and virtually automatic opposition to any proposed travellers' sites. Prejudice was further inflamed by conflating traditional with New Age travellers who in the capitalist-oriented 1980s were increasingly

seen as welfare-state scroungers. The civil rights stance was that all travellers should be treated as one, in spite of their differences and even conflicts of tradition and identity.

Prejudice aside, there were real contradictions in travelling lifestyles that were difficult for sedentary citizens to come to terms with. Thus New Age travellers liked to hibernate in winter (typically in otherwise hard-to-let council flats) and they were content to pay road tax and collect unemployment benefit; but come spring they wanted the freedom to roam, and their festivals and 'raves' made urgent physical demands on otherwise quiet rural districts. The needs of the more traditional travellers and gypsies, in addition to permanent, serviced sites, included permanent council housing for those who became too old for life on the road. At best, settled society tolerated nomadism when it could be accommodated on margins and fringes not wanted by anyone else; but whereas it found little

apparent difficulty in exempting a network of
Showman's Guild sites from normal licensing
requirements, it viewed other travellers as
deviants who, ideally, should be persuaded or
coerced into sedentary living (Swingler, 1969).

During the 1980s hardened attitudes of the
police, media and public generally led to the
increasing repression and criminalization of
nomadism. The Public Order Act 1986 made it
an offence to stay on land after police gave 24
hours notice to leave, and the Criminal Justice
and Public Order Act 1994 finally changed the
ancient law of trespass by making it illegal to
stop anywhere except on an official site. At the
same time the Act removed the duty of local
authorities to provide sites for travellers, who
in future would be expected to develop their
own sites; but it contained no special measures
to enable them to do this, although most
earlier attempts had met with planning refusals.
In 1994 police in several areas were reported to
be laying concerted plans to track individuals
and vehicles by aid of computers, and to take
draconian measures against all actual or potential convoys of travellers, whether on illegitimate
or legitimate business (Campbell, 1994).

RESIDENTIAL CARAVANS AND
MOBILE HOMES

The residential caravan began as a mobile or
touring holiday home, the 'land yacht' of the
1880s, and in 1907 the Caravan Club of Great
Britain was founded, its symbol a horseshoe.
Towing by motor cars only became practicable
after the Second World War, and from that
time the touring caravan rapidly multiplied,
the Caravan Club's 30,000 members of 1959
rising to 285,000 by 1992. Under the Public
Health Act 1936, stops were limited to 42
consecutive days; but in the early postwar
years touring or weekending in a caravan was
still represented as free from all taxes and
controls: it could be towed to any site where a
local farmer would 'oblige': and at this time

there was no need to suppose that caravanning
'entails living herded together in a shack
colony. Every self-respecting caravanner . . .
has a horror of such overcrowded sites' (Henry,
1950, p. 34). It was the effect of thousands able
to tow their own caravans and trying to avoid
precisely this horror that led, in fact, to the
Caravan Sites Act of 1960.

Technical improvements meant an increase in
size and sophistication of tourers, with awning
extensions, built-in sanitary facilities, heating
systems and better insulation (though still not
enough for permanent, year-round use).
Electricity was first taken from car batteries
and later from outlets at each stand. The
variant of the motor caravan or 'dormobile'
with a rising roof emerged, perhaps inspired by
converted coaches and buses. In spite of
growing site regulation, there developed a
special owners' cameraderie, with mutual visits
of admiration to each others' vans and
exchange of technical tips, which anticipated
the special, enclosed societies of the later 'park
homes'.

The holiday caravan, static either by chance
or on purpose, often ended its days as a home
for the homeless, with or without official
sanction. With shacks, old gypsy vans, buses
and canvas-covered carts, it formed colonies
on waste sites, urban and rural, where it was
'dumped like rubbish shot out of a bucket'
(Orwell, 1937, p. 54). Completely unserviced
and without sanitation, such colonies fell outside the scope of housing law until they had
been in continuous use for two years, when
they could be treated under the unfitness
legislation. The only other sanction was abatement of public nuisance under the 1936 Public
Health Act, which councils were unwilling to
invoke because they did not wish to become
responsible for rehousing the occupants. Thus
old caravans continued in informal use for the
homeless down to the 1990s (Seabrook, 1990).

The divergence of tourers from residential
caravans was noticed in the 1959 Wilson

'Some people have solved their
own housing problems in this
unsatisfactory way.' (*Source*:
City of Coventry, 1952)

Report, which criticized the continuing manufacture of caravans as though they were cars,
without any thought as to the sites and services
they would require. Nevertheless the Report
defended and justified the people who made
permanent homes in what it estimated to be
about a third of the 180,000 vans in use. 'Apart
from the fact that they live in caravans [they]
are for the most part indistinguishable in their
background and way of life from people who
live in houses' (Wilson, 1959, p. 7). This use
was evidently in process of change: around
two-thirds of the residents were young couples,
half of them with children, who were saving up
to become home owners and who were 'if
anything more endowed with self-respect, initiative and a keenness to get on and make a
decent life for themselves than many of similar
classes who are to be found in more conventional
types of accommodation' (*Ibid*, 1959, p. 14).
The remainder were retired couples or single
people, predominantly women, who formed 'a
particularly contented section of the caravan-
dwelling community' (*Ibid*, 1959, p. 15).
Among these it noticed an emergent bourgeois
lifestyle: the TV, a budgie in a cage, the
occasional refrigerator: that is, 'some of the

present-day material standards of middle-class
living' (*Ibid*, 1959, p. 21). In this context,
'keeping up with the Joneses' was not just a
matter of updating the contents of the home,
but 'buying a new model to replace the home
itself' (*Ibid*, 1959, p. 21).

Caravans continued to serve these populations but, of the two, the older, bourgeois one
became dominant, so that by 1990 only about a
third of an estimated 76,800 residential caravans
were used by families en route to conventional
houses (Niner and Hedges, 1992). The great
majority of residents were older people who
owned their caravans, typically financing the
purchase from the sale of a house. Freedom
from mortgage was one of the things most
valued, but there were extra costs attached to
this lifestyle. In addition to site rent, management charges and insurance (which was high
because of the risk of fire), any capital borrowed
was normally from finance companies over
short periods, and so more expensive than
conventional building society mortgages. But
although new and more luxurious models could
cost as much or more than a house, on average
the prices paid for second-hand models were
less than houses, and in 1990 they represented

only 38 per cent of average house prices. More particularly, such caravan homes were cheaper than any houses normally available in the preferred locations of coastal, rural and favourite retirement areas, especially in the Home Counties and the south of England.

Technical change had meanwhile transformed the residential caravan into the mobile home – one that, once delivered to site, would seldom in fact move again. The maximum width of units was dictated by the capacity of roads: up to 10 ft was possible, but 7.5 ft more normal. Standard lengths went in 2 ft intervals from 16 to 44, and eventually 60 ft. From the mid 1950s it became possible to bolt two units together, so that ultimately a 'duplex' of 20 by 60 ft with two or three bedrooms became possible. Now called 'park homes', such units came more and more to resemble the bungalow, which is what proud owners claimed them to be. The unsightly void between chassis and ground could be masked by a decorative apron, and add-on items which could be purchased included porches, pitched roofs, even fake chimney pots. Internally, standards were governed by BS codes, which specified ceiling heights, window to floor ratios, thermal insulation, and separation of functional areas. Solid fuel heating, pail closets and bottled gas for cooking and lighting were eventually replaced by full sewer connections and mains electricity, making possible central heating and all the amenities of conventional dwellings. Built-in furniture provided a last faint echo of a jaunty touring ancestry, notably the 'wrap-around' bench in the dining room. The one great defect of the mobile home, and the main technical reason for its rapid depreciation, was condensation.

Because of their peculiar ancestry, and unless they were rented (when they came under the Rent Acts), mobile homes fell outside housing law. The layout of sites, and particularly the important distance between units, were governed by site license conditions based on Model Standards periodically updated by the Department of Environment; but local authorities were often dilatory in enforcing these. Home owners were given more security of tenure against site owners under the Mobile Homes Act 1975, which required written agreements and extended legal tenure from the customary four weeks to five years. The legal situation was further regulated under a new Act of 1983, which gave home owners the right to assign their site leases or pass them on to successors. This made it easier for them to sell homes and slowed their rate of depreciation; but site owners were now entitled to take a 10 per cent commission on all sales.

In practice, mobile homes and their surroundings gave as much satisfaction to residents as any form of housing. Sites operated with little apparent conflict and the survey of 1990 found many residents who 'were positively lyrical about the merits of their home and life style' (Niner and Hedges, 1992, para. 662). The underlying reality, however, was a strange one, with deep conflicts of interest arising from the fundamental impermanence of the tenure and the home itself. The site owner's interests lay in protection of his asset, and therefore in its progressive updating. This required not only continuous rises in rent and charges but fairly frequent replacement of the homes themselves, and hence pressure on residents to replace old with new units. The interests of most residents were to preserve their security 'in a cheap and informal (if sometimes rather tatty) environment' (*Ibid*, 1992, para. 472). In 1990, most residents were still unclear about their legal entitlements and a majority of sites contravened the 1983 Act: for instance by requiring residents to replace substandard homes or to buy them only through the park owners.

This did not create discontent, however, because residents knew what they were opting for. Increasingly, parks were designated for the retired or the 'over-55s' and all undesirables were excluded: children, 'ethnics', even dogs and, of course, gypsies. The qualities of the home itself exactly met residents' aspirations, for park owners and manufacturers of units understood precisely the feelings they could appeal to: 'When you buy a park home you're not just buying a property. You're buying a new beginning. An opportunity to adopt a brand new life style' (Omar Park Homes, 1992). The key elements were fellowship, tranquillity, security, and freedom from worry. Social status was assured, wherever possible, by a converted mansion or stately home on the site. Healthy walks led not only to scenic viewpoints but, more ominously, to doctors' surgeries. Potential buyers were exhorted to realize the dream of a lifetime, enjoy the best of all worlds, and 'spoil themselves'. Those who bought into this dream were apparently content to trade personal autonomy for such controlled environments.

SELF-HELP HOUSING: SHACKS AND PLOTLANDS

There is no way of assessing how many garden sheds, allotment huts or holiday caravans – legally parked, but not legally inhabitable, in their owners' gardens – are used as residential accommodation. Britain has never had a policy for weekend chalets or leisure plots, as in many European countries, so that any such use must be surreptitious. The Census of 1901 enumerated 1,645 people living in barns and sheds, and this was a near 50 per cent reduction of the numbers ten years before. During the Depression in the coalfields, miners who had lost their tied houses with their jobs started to live in their allotment cabins. A generation later it seems to have been mainly the very old who clung to their right to live where and as they pleased, even when this breached public health codes. Thus the octogenarian Wrights of Ryedale went on living in their completely unserviced shed with three acres and 'the finest view in the land' (Bumby, 1976, p. 3); and

'The sad plight of Caddy Cates'. (*Source*: *Newmarket Journal*, April, 1976)

Caddy Cates, also an octogenarian, lived in a shed without windows and no room for a bed, by way of escaping an old people's Home (Lawson, 1976). Both households were protected by planning law which could not easily dislodge people from existing structures, but an attempt by a council tenant to build a traditional African mud hut at the end of her garden met with shorter shrift (Sinha, 1992).

Between the wars there grew up a market in small plots for weekend and holiday use, with or without structures, in coastal and holiday areas within easy reach of East Londoners and city dwellers generally. Many were equipped with an obsolete bus, caravan or railway carriage, the fashion for which had started before 1914. F.C. Stedman's Jaywick Sands, begun as a conventional housing estate in 1928, was converted to beach huts and chalets when it proved impossible to provide mains drainage. There ensued a quarter century of disputes between, variously, the development company, the local council and residents' association, concerning rates payable, the delivery of local services, and the legality or otherwise of sleeping in huts overnight. In 1953 the whole settlement was flooded and thirty-five lives were lost, so vindicating official caution. Fifty years after its foundation the settlement was protected by flood walls, drained and sewered, but was still in the process of being upgraded to full suburban standards (Hardy and Ward, 1984).

Another celebrated 'plotland' settlement, Peacehaven in Sussex, had a significant impact on planning policies. Begun by a developer in 1915, it was developed piecemeal to no overall plan, eventually achieving a water supply, electricity, shops, police, fire service, hotel and theatre. Among other problems it presented to the local authority was the cost of sewering and roads for 650 houses on more than the same number of acres, the 26 miles of pipes or cables needed, and the difficulty of preventing further development when plots with little use potential nevertheless had high compensation value. Jaywick Sands and Peacehaven were only two among many such settlements. Since many were small, their total numbers remain unknown; but when Basildon New Town absorbed Pitsea Laindon in 1949 it absorbed some 8,500 dwellings of which 5,000 were chalets or shacks; and an East Sussex survey of 1975 estimated 6,000 plotland dwellers in its area. The development control imposed under the 1947 Town and Country Planning Act made any further such spontaneous developments impossible, and the so-called 'leisure plots' marketed by sharp entrepreneurs in later years came, as their owners were to discover, without entitlement to erect any structures at all on them.

What has impressed later observers is the capacity of their makeshift dwellings to endure and evolve without any professional or official intervention, and indeed often with active official discouragement. The original core, even if only a bus or railway carriage, was often eventually incorporated into a much larger and more durable structure, usually of bungalow form, through the owner's own labour. The settlements themselves evolved through collective and individual self help from casual holiday or weekend enclaves to permanent communities which, it is held, commanded more loyalty than conventional neighbourhoods. At the same time they managed to preserve a spirit of informality and freedom. The plotlands have been presented as autonomous housing for the humble, starting as the cheapest holiday going for the small man and his family and developing into mature communities with a healthy disrespect for authority (*Ibid*, 1984).

In the context of normal English housing estates they are indeed a remarkable chapter; but it is perhaps debateable how far their eventual outcome was radically different from the norm. Many of the pioneers evidently depended on cars to take them out to their chalets (the early roads at Jaywick were even called after the chief makes of car) and they cannot, therefore, have been of the poorest. There are, it is true, many colourful first-hand accounts of the early days of pioneering and cooperation, but the eventual product was a low-cost although individualistic suburbia which was, as the planners complained, wasteful of land, blighting of natural landscapes, and in many respects in contradiction of a general public interest.

SELF-HELP HOUSING: SELF-BUILD

There has always been a minority of people who have built their own homes but, as a concept, self-build housing arose from two particular strands which came together in the 1970s. One was reaction against 'mass housing', a term usually applied to undesirable council estates but sometimes extended to cover the whole system of housing provision, in which users were merely passive consumers (Habraken, 1972). The other was the growing environmental movement which encouraged self sufficiency, to which a special type of house, or simply the act of building one's own house, was thought important.

The term self-build is imprecise, for it has been applied to both new and reconditioned buildings, as well as part-finished buildings supplied by contractors. It is applied to both individuals and groups, including private companies, housing associations and co-ops, and it may describe user control over commissioning, design and contracting, rather than actual construction. The Housing Act 1974 permitted the Housing Corporation and local authorities to sponsor and assist self-build groups, for example with land, loans and training; and self building was done in a variety of tenures, although its end result was usually home ownership. The dwellings produced might be indistinguishable from those produced through the normal channels, or they might be unconventional and innovative.

For the individual, self-building could offer a 'dream home' – a detached house, often a bungalow, standing in romantic isolation (Armor, 1978, 1991). More pragmatically, it reduced the cost of an ordinary family home, while the fact that an eye had to be given to its resale potential discouraged innovation. It seems likely that the application of self building to conventional family housing accounts for most of the 2000 new houses that it has been said to contribute annually (Broome, 1983). Much, possibly most, of it is done through specialist commercial firms who streamline the process from design to completion, requiring members of their schemes to submit to tight timetables, standardised plans and group discipline. Since all the costs apart from labour have to be financed, speed is essential. Thus in one survey of self-build groups only 24 per cent of the houses were adapted to individual requirements and only 4 per cent were actually designed by members (Purkiss, 1982). The largest concentration of organized groups was at Milton Keynes where from 1978 interested people were encouraged to form consortia of ten to twenty members and the rate of production was at times as high as five hundred a year, facilitated by fully serviced plots, approved consultants and loan arrangements.

Self-building became more socially innovative when it was aimed at low-income people for instance in homesteading schemes begun by the GLC and some other authorities in the 1970s, where people on council housing waiting lists rented or bought derelict properties for token amounts, on condition of making them habitable (Goodchild, 1981). Another strategy was the 'starter home' which the purchaser could finish at leisure, often by expanding into an unfinished roof space, or houses sold at any stage of completion, from serviced slab to full finish. More radical still were schemes for claimants, such as Zenzele in Bristol, where twelve black unemployed youths built a block of flatlets which they were able to buy as owner occupiers on completion. Strong sponsorship and access to funds were essential, not only to finance the project but to clear its way with Inland Revenue and the Department of Social Security whose rules would otherwise have made it impossible. The group then proselytized and inspired similar initiatives elsewhere (NFHA, 1988). A different approach was that of Great Eastern (with several other self-build groups) of former council flat tenants in London Docklands, who employed their own site manager and architect, using a basic terraced house plan which could be varied to suit individual requirements. Part of the group's design philosophy was to keep the river frontage open to the public (unlike private schemes in similar locations) but its members became owner occupiers on completion.

Self-building for special technical ends was seen in a small group of solar houses, Paxton Court in Sheffield, and in underground or 'earth-sheltered' housing, mostly done on an individual basis but attracting devotees of sustainability and energy efficiency (Carpenter, 1993). Lewisham Self-Build, on the other hand, was motivated by a combination of technical and social aims. Its modular, timber framework stood on stilts on a concrete pad, allowing a choice of one or two storeys and a

Lewisham Self Build, initiated by the Borough Council in 1978, utilized Walter Segal's light-weight prefabricated system, designed for anyone regardless of strength or experience. It is now used on schemes throughout the country. (*Source*: Town and Country Planning Association)

large amount of choice as to house shape and internal divisions. The first scheme was open to council tenants and waiting list applicants without any limitations of age, bodily strength or practical experience, the participants' work being converted into a share of the equity and taxed (Broome, 1986). The building system was later used by a number of other local authorities for homeless, unemployed people. Cheap and practical, it also expressed the social idealism of its architect inventor, Walter Segal: 'every house seems to exude Walter's great joy of life and achievement but is intrinsically the blueprint of the individual's own personality' (Walter Segal Self Build Trust, 1988, p. 2).

The idealism of self building was carried one further stage in the new towns. The first attempt, in 1979, was in fact abortive: 'Greentown' was to have been a 'third garden city' constructed within Milton Keynes as a self-sufficient urban community. The proposal fell foul of relations between Milton Keynes and the surrounding borough, as well as antagonisms between the Development Corporation and

the Town and Country Planning Association, and among its own members. From a proposed 500 acres it was whittled down to one small, self-build housing association, and eventually cancelled altogether, when the new town planners refused to allow homes and home-based industries on the same site (Wood, 1988).

The second and more successful attempt, under the guidance of Tony Gibson and the Neighbourhood Initiatives Foundation, was at Lightmoor in Telford New Town, where 'a new kind of neighbourhood' arose on a marginal site to a large extent exempt from planning and building regulations. The founder group of nine people together prepared the site infra-structure and then slowly built their own detached houses, some with associated work-shops or smallholdings. A later group of housing association tenants built a further five houses round a 'village green', using a timber-frame system similar to that of Lewisham. Lightmoor was treated as a social laboratory and intended to inspire similar initiatives. It was itself expected to expand, although early

Lightmoor New Community, Telford New Town. Self-built houses by owner occupiers and housing association tenants from 1984. (*Source*: Town and Country Planning Association)

indications were that the happy chance of obtaining cheap marginal land would not re-occur (Lawrence, 1987–).

SQUATTING

Like self-building and the plotlands, squatting embraced a number of dichotomies: it could be either an individual or a group effort; it could be pragmatically or ideologically motivated; and it could use new or rehabilitated buildings, in either conventional or unconventional ways. Its one invariable principle was that it was for housing the homeless: oneself or others. Beyond that, there might be secondary purposes, which could include taking a political stand or living an alternative lifestyle. These dichotomies largely account for the complex factional history of squatting movements, as well as official reactions to them. If anything, Labour administrations were the most hostile

to squatters, for challenging orderly programmes of housing provision and alloca-tion. Conservatives were more willing, at least from time to time, to do 'deals' with squatters, whose self help and initiative they might use to break through impasses in housing policy.

Contrary to popular assumptions, squatters seldom if ever invaded inhabited property, even when its owners were absent. They were concerned with empty, and so predominantly pre-1914 property, whether houses or institu-tional buildings. 'Skippering' – individual squatting by down-and-outs – had little general impact: for since it was furtive, those practising it did not try to restore services or make other changes, but simply moved on when squats became too fouled. Collective squatting campaigns, in contrast, sought both to draw attention to the scandal of homelessness and to exploit the legal status of squatting in order to get access to homes as rent-paying tenants. As Colin Ward pointed out, this was of necessity a post-1945 phenomenon, for it depended on buildings left empty for reasons of speculation, or in expectation of slum clearance (Ward, 1980).

A squatting campaign after the First World War left little lasting record (*Ibid*, 1980). That following the Second World War began with mass invasions of disused service camps in 1946. Eventually over a thousand camps were affected, involving some forty thousand people. Life in the camps was organized democratically with a weekly levy, communal kitchens, nurseries, and rotas for building work. Whitehall was not at first ill disposed towards the squatters and leant on local authorities in the areas concerned to take over the camps. Many did so and some of the camps that were squatted eventually evolved into permanent council estates.

The next stage of the campaign, which took place mainly in London, was more confronta-tional, involving takeover of a number of empty hotels, luxury flats and other buildings.

The Duchess of Bedford Mansions, a block of empty luxury flats in Kensington, were occupied by several hundred families, the fathers of many of them ex-servicemen. The Communist Party claimed to play the leading role, and although this was disputed by other participants, the police and press so far believed it that, in the event, five Communist borough councillors were brought to trial for conspiracy. The eventual outcome of the occupation was a negotiated settlement and peaceful evacuation. Some of the families concerned were resettled, first in residential Homes or Part III accommodation (p. 84, above), and later in normal council housing (Branson, 1989). Solidarity, self help and inspired improvization remained high in the memories of those who took part, evoking memories of wartime cameraderie. There was however no sign that the squatters' ambition was to achieve anything other than conventional family housing.

Twenty years later there were hopes of a new family squatting campaign imitating the successes of the 1940s (Bailey, 1973). It owed one of its origins to a protest of homeless families in a Part III hostel in Kent, where fourteen excluded husbands illegally moved in with their families. Two of the men were jailed, but the outcome was improved conditions, both there and in other hostels. The other origin lay in growing awareness of the scandal of empty houses. In the London borough of Redbridge a Conservative controlled council had boarded up a street of substantial houses, in anticipation of town centre re-development (the plan for which was eventually abandoned). Squatters broke into some of the houses and as far as possible made them fit for people to live as normal families (Ibid, 1973). Countering action by the council led to sieges, violent evictions by bailiffs, deliberate wrecking of interiors and services, and demolitions. In retaliation, some of the squatters carried out a campaign of personal harassment against individual councillors.

Support for the squatters came from the surprisingly wide alliance of ratepayers, political and religious groups, and eventually some of the houses were patched and handed over to short-life housing associations, with Ministry approval (Ibid, 1973; Platt, 1980).

Similar campaigns took place in many parts of London and a number of towns and cities, where office blocks and other empty buildings were occupied. The internal history of the movement shows a complicated array of organizations and alliances throughout the 1970s. Their achievements included two London-wide unions, a 'squatters' charter', the establishment of advisory services, a squatters' 'estate agency', handbooks, and an organized campaign against the proposal in 1974 to convert squatting from a civil to a legal offence. Squatters even invaded the 1979 Ideal Homes Exhibition where they briefly set up an 'Ideal Squat' (Wates and Wolmar, 1980).

The effects on housing policy were considerable. The publicity created helped to hasten the closure of Part III hostels, and the Conservative controlled GLC legitimized and licensed nearly 2,000 squatted properties, involving some 7,000 people. From 1977 the Department

The difference squatters could make. Postcard, Annie Ink, Leeds

of Environment urged councils to hand over short-life property to housing associations and some associations were set up specifically for this purpose, with access to a special grant from the Housing Corporation. Eleven par-value and two secondary housing co-operatives arose specifically from squatting, and another thirteen had a substantial squatting element. Altogether, considerable numbers of people were squatters: a conservative estimate was some 25,000 in London and 30,000 in total, but other estimates were much higher (Shaw, 1985).

The entirely new aspect of this later squatting movement was the involvement of single homeless people. This was apparent at Redbridge, where single would-be squatters were resented for spoiling family squatters' chances of re-housing (Bailey, 1973). The unmet housing needs of single people were the motive for a notorious squat of 144 Piccadilly in 1969. This large empty mansion was taken over by a hippy commune who at one stage invited in the Hell's Angels, whereupon the Skinheads came to fight them, with much ensuing violence and a police raid. This helped to colour public perceptions of all squatters as hippies, but for the most part young single squatters were more influenced by pacifist direct action and the painstaking local community action of campaigns against slum clearance. Many found inspiration in the 'free city' of Christiania in the heart of Copenhagen (Gimson, 1980), seeing themselves, therefore, as urban pioneers who followed different objectives from the family squatters. 'As well as raising questions about the *amount* of housing available, squatters increasingly challenged the *nature* of housing and the quality of community life' (Platt, 1980, p. 38). Their sense of community led them to develop street art, theatre, festivals, carnivals and communal street parties of a kind not seen since the demise of working-class neighbourhood culture some twenty or more years before. Their global as well as local conscious-

ness led them to become involved in wholefood shops, bookshops, recycling, community gardens, wind and solar power, and geodesic domes. In pursuit of its ideals one small West London squat (later converted to a housing co-op) declared itself the 'free and independent republic of Frestonia' (*Ibid*, 1980, p. 93).

The classic example of ideological squatting combined with practical achievement was Tolmers Square near Euston in London, a district with a background of local militancy dating back to the 1957 Rent Act and then fighting against both an unscrupulous private property company and a planning classification as commercial land, which ruled out housing uses. In addition it had a large demand for accommodation from students at local colleges – not least in two leading schools of architecture. To contribute to the planning stalemate, it had whole streets of condemned houses, council-owned but deliberately wrecked and boarded up, among many blighted shops and businesses (Wates, 1976).

All these strands came together in a creative alliance of students, squatters and established residents. Closed houses were opened up by squatters, who were regularly taken to court (where they usually won their case). This was an example of the conditions faced by those reopening a house:

the house was totally uninhabitable and full of rubbish and excrement . . . all the lavatories, soil pipes, cisterns and hand basins had been systematic-ally torn from their moorings and smashed. The floorboards in the back rooms all the way up the house had been torn up and thrown in the yard outside. The slates had been removed from the back slope of the roof so that rain poured right through the house from the roof to the cellar where it had collected in a stinking quagmire. Ferns and huge fungi fed by the downpour sprouted from the walls. The ceilings on the stairs and in many of the rooms had collapsed forming damp mounds of plaster and rubble. (*Ibid*, 1976, pp. 161–162).

It took three months to restore the fabric and services of this particular house, which was later listed as of architectural and historical interest by the Department of the Environment. Ultimately the Tolmers campaign dispatched the property company and achieved a primarily residential development of the area, much of it with council-owned houses of the same type and layout as those previously destroyed.

The campaigns of single squatters appeared to die away in the right-wing policies of the 1980s, but there still remained uncounted numbers of squatters particularly in inner London, and the main reason for squatting was, as ever, people's need of homes when no other affordable property was available. In 1994, the Criminal Justice and Public Order Act threatened squatters as much as travellers, and some local councils were already taking independent action to clear them out of their boroughs.

The longer-term achievements of single-person squatting were less obvious than those of the family squatting campaigns, although in some respects more pervasive. While some of the squatters must have joined the New Age travellers, they also contributed a generation of veterans to community and environmental politics, finding channels in various forms of advocacy planning such as Community Technical Aid Centres, the Tenant Participation Advisory Service, legal aid centres, and a host of local initiatives. More generally, they merged into the loose movement known as 'community architecture' which embraced both individual architects and consultancies, including those involved in the rehabilitation of hard-to-let council estates and multi-storey flats. Squatters also brought new populations and cultures to the areas they colonized, such as Hebden Bridge in West Yorkshire, where they attempted and partially succeeded in saving condemned houses, in some cases converting them to alternative domestic patterns to those of the conventional nuclear family (Ingham, 1980).

HOUSING CO-OPERATIVES AND ALTERNATIVE COMMUNITIES

Housing co-operatives shared the now familiar dichotomies of others kinds of self-help housing. They had, of necessity, to pertain to groups rather than individuals, but they could be pragmatic (as a route to normal housing) or ideological, to allow their members to practise a chosen lifestyle, whether in new or old houses. In operation, they were likely always to bear some traces of the ideological, if only because of the unfamiliarity of the tenure within the mainstream British housing system.

This in itself is something of a paradox, for the co-operative movement had begun in England and might have been expected to find an outlet in housing, as in retailing. But in so far as co-operative societies were interested in housing it appears to have been as conventional lenders or in the co-ownership societies that were strong around 1900, when they were welcomed by the Garden City and parts of the Labour movements (Birchall, 1988). Thus the Tenant Cooperators founded in 1887 eventually had fourteen societies providing over 6,500 conventional homes. Ousted by council housing, co-ownership declined between the wars but was revived briefly under the 1961 and 1964 Housing Acts, achieving some 40,000 dwellings before being drastically cut back by the reformed Housing Corporation after 1974. State subsidized co-ownership effectively disappeared after its members were given the 'right to buy' in 1980.

More significant in the last quarter of the century was the par-value co-op. This differed from co-ownership in that its members had no personal equity in the property but, as nominal shareholders, owned it collectively. Par-value co-ops were able to develop, improve and manage their own property. From 1957 local authorities could provide them with mortgages, but more importantly, from 1974 they could receive the same grants as housing associations through the Housing Corporation, which set up the promotional Co-operative Development Agency in 1976. A National Federation of Housing Co-operatives followed in 1981. Some of the co-ops now founded were initiated by housing associations and local authorities but the most vibrant were those initiated by their own members, particularly when these were local people taking flight from unloved council estates or landlord-owned property. For training and guidance in a complex and often daunting legal and financial process they could put themselves under a secondary housing co-operative, which was registered and funded for the purpose by the Housing Corporation but which did not build directly for itself. An alternative course was to use a housing association or independent firm of 'community' architects. Professional help in dealing with officials, red tape, contractors and unimaginably huge sums of public money was essential, although the self-confidence and expertise that were eventually gained could transform the lives of those involved (McDonald, 1986).

The largest concentration of par-value, new-build co-ops was on Merseyside, where strained local and central government relations of the early 1980s provided a special opening (Wates, 1982). Lesser numbers were found in London, Birmingham and north eastern England, and in total upwards of fifty bodies and 1,500

dwellings were involved. The briefly favourable position of the par-value societies from the later 1970s for the first time gave lay people an opportunity to become directly responsible for the design, construction, choice of materials and details, internal and external layouts of their own newly built homes, albeit under the then current rules and constraints of Parker Morris standards and Housing Corporation funding. Together with the sites allotted – typically in inner-city locations and of a size matching the co-ops themselves, which did not normally exceed forty members – such constraints led inevitably to the small 'mews'-type house in a courtyard cluster. Houses and bungalows took precedence, but low blocks of flats might be included. The housing co-op thus had the look of an oasis, especially in the more derelict parts of inner Liverpool, where the contrast with bleak council estates and byelaw streets was emphasized by imaginative paving and luxuriant planting of common areas, all lovingly tended by the members.

For ethnic or other minority groups the co-op became the vehicle of special kinds of dwelling and layout, to meet needs and provide a sense of security and identity. It could also be an expression of group philosophy and community ideals. Thus many groups purposely included dwellings for the elderly and

Eldonian Community Based Housing Association Ltd expressed its ideals through the image of the village. (*Source*: Eldonian Community)

wheelchair-bound. Funds permitting, some opted to include an old people's lounge or clubroom, and some were still more ambitious than this. Two of the most innovative were those of the Weller Streets and Eldonian Community, both in Liverpool and initiated by local residents, and both seeking to use their own experience to proselytize and train further groups. The Eldonians, in particular, set out to create a 'village' which would include not only members' homes but shops, new local industries, training opportunities, a community 'health villa' and projects for leisure and tourism (Owens, 1984; Cowan *et al.*, 1988). At this scale of activity they resembled the Coin Street Community Builders on the South Bank of the Thames who, with ownership of extensive and valuable metropolitan land, developed a series

of housing co-operatives through 'shell groups' of local people (who would not themselves be the occupants), together with a building and exhibition centre, an extensive street market with shops and restaurants, public riverside gardens and a museum and arts centre (Community Action, 1990; *Architects' Journal*, 1989).

At such a scale, the housing co-operative shared something of the scope of the larger alternative community. The difference was that it operated, when it could, with official funding and for the most part provided conventional housing for people who could be considered 'ordinary' members of the public. By definition, alternative communities set themselves apart from the normal world and among other things this meant that they were

Some of the Coin Street Community Builders of the South Bank, London. (*Source*: Town and Country Planning Assocation)

usually, though not invariably, rurally based. Typically they started from small beginnings with insecure finance, and consequent effects on the type of property they were able to occupy. A favourite choice was the large country house or redundant farm, which were adaptable for use as educational and craft centres. The main objective of urban groups was more likely to be simply to work out forms for living together, but they also took on crafts and various forms of social service. As well as large villas, the row of small houses that could be knocked through was suitable for their purposes (Michèle and Kevin, 1983).

The active period for the foundation of alternative communities was the 1970s. Most were very small and broke up after a short life in which sharing domestic space raised many problems of decision-making, privacy, child and house care (Rigby, 1974). The most durable examples were those with a strongly religious basis. Monastic orders, of course, had endured for hundreds of years, with a way of life actively followed throughout the twentieth century. A new initiative of this century was the Camphill community, begun according to the teachings of Rudolph Steiner as educational and curative centres for children with mental disabilities, and continued in the form of new 'villages' for adults with such disabilities. In the dozen or so Camphill villages throughout the country a new pattern was established where 'families' of houseparents, children, 'villagers' and volunteers lived in large purpose-built or adapted houses of a dozen or more workers and clients who shared meals, outings and cultural activities, as a family. The Camphill villages were also partly self-supporting, with workshops, gardens and farms. By the 1990s, some of their houses were being registered as residential Homes under 'care in the community' policies; but the care that was given was within the already established framework of an alternative way of life (Weihs and Tallo, 1988).

Whereas housing co-ops almost invariably produced conventional, self-contained homes, real co-operative housekeeping occupied only a small place in housing history. As an ideal it was cherished by socialist feminists who partly took their inspiration from some nineteenth-century experiments of the USA, in which domestic kitchens were replaced by centralized cleaning and meal delivery services (Hayden, 1981). In England, only fifteen co-operative housekeeping schemes of 1874–1925 have been traced, the majority for working spinsters and housed in dwellings that would now be classified as hostels (Pearson, 1988). The only family schemes were mostly very small and tentative garden city experiments: the sixteen houses of Homesgarth at Letchworth (1908–1912) had a professional domestic manager, and were for childless, middle-class households who wished to avoid the cost and trouble of domestic servants. A later scheme, Meadow Way Green, was principally for business and professional women who were jointly responsible for their collective catering. Guessens Court (1925) in Welwyn Garden City provided forty flats for households of all types, with a central restaurant block and maid service.

Around this time the radical ideas of Alice Melvin were attracting a following. The houses of her Brent Garden Village were fairly conventional but they had purposely small kitchens and an associated dining hall, nursery, laundry and common servants' quarters. Her most ambitious building plan was abortive but her conversion of large mansions into flats and of five existing houses in a Hampstead street expressed her ideas for centralizing and professionalizing housework (*Ibid*, 1988).

The idea of cooperative housekeeping circulated into the early 1920s, taking some of its inspiration from the national kitchens set up in the First World War, which many wished to see continued. The more radical feminists continued to assert that it would transform the lot of working-class women and that it was, in the words of Sylvia Pankhurst, something 'for which so many women long today' (Pankhurst, 1914, p. 90). But for all their painstaking fact-finding through the length and breadth of the land, the Women's Housing Sub-Committee of 1917 found no general desire for it, and they were forced to conclude that, however desirable it might be in theory, its time had not yet come. It appeared that most women 'wanted improved versions of the houses they already had' – if, indeed, they were lucky enough to have homes of their own at all (Pearson, 1988, p. 142). At most, as the Tudor Walters Report conceded, a laundry service, communal kitchen for occasional meals out, and play areas for children over and above private gardens, might be desirable; but no practical propositions for making them a reality were advanced.

Eventually all the co-operative housekeeping schemes that were built were converted into self-contained flats, hostels or hotels in the 1950s and 1960s. Cheap, municipally run British Restaurants were revived in the Second World War, some continuing under the Civic Restaurants Act of 1947 and not finally closing until the 1960s. The only lasting centralized housekeeping services to result from the war years were 'meals on wheels' and home helps (p. 89, above), which were quite unambiguously for individual householders in self-contained homes.

It was, therefore, mainly squatters, communards and alternative communities who experimented with new patterns. Some tried co-operative living only to revert to conventional privacy and self-containment, as did the free and independent Frestonians when they re-formed themselves as a housing co-op (Owens, 1987b). Exciting and innovative ideas put forward by others remained in the realm of fantasy, as did the Hebden Bridge proposal for a unified terrace incorporating children's houses, workshops, music room, organic garden and wind generator (Ingham, 1980). Though less ambitious, the unknown numbers of houses shared by young people who chose to share

expenses, catering and other chores were probably influenced by these examples. As for conventional housing, although the postwar women's liberation movement continued to rail against the self-contained home, it appears that it was driven by strong cultural imperatives, both for families and single people. Indeed, as a contributor to *The Freewoman* had pointed out in 1912, had there been any widespread desire for co-operative housekeeping, people could well have developed their own schemes within the homes they already had (Pearson, 1988, p. 122).

THE SIGNIFICANCE OF SELF-HELP HOUSING

While for obvious reasons the exact amount of self-help in housing is unknown, it is clear that, even discounting 'conventional' self build, upwards of a million people may have been involved throughout the century – more, that is, than all the subjects of institutional housing. But since so many different groups with different purposes were involved, this provides little guide to the real significance of these housing alternatives, for which a more discriminating approach is needed.

In the main, self-help in housing was an opportunistic response to housing need among the poor or marginalized, whose aim was usually to get access to a normal, self-contained home within the usual range of tenures. For the most part it was for the young and energetic, as well as the skilled, or those who were able to acquire skills quickly. But in desperate need, people of all kinds created homes out of anything that was at hand – including vehicles, sheds, boats – and then self help demonstrated not only people's ingenuity but their ability to be satisfied with self-chosen standards which could diverge very significantly from official standards or what was generally thought to be a proper home. It is, incidentally, interesting to observe how the 'bungalow' theme runs through many of the examples: the Wrights of Ryedale called their primitive shed 'The Bungalow'; the postwar prefab actually was a bungalow; and the tent, caravan or mobile home could be regarded as bungalow substitutes.

Technically innovatory self help was only socially innovatory when it expressed a different culture (as the gypsies) or new forms of social organization. Innovations with tenure were potentially more socially alternative, and in this respect co-operative tenure is interesting. It was often adopted for the duration of a self building scheme, only to be relinquished when the individual builders became owner occupiers, and it could also be treated as a slightly unusual form of renting. But the tenure had more radical potential than this, whether to create wider environments, or to bring about a new relationship to their homes among the members, through being collective rather than individual owners. In the early 1990s it was still too soon to see how far such potential might be realized, and little was yet known of the operation of housing co-ops following their pioneering phase, when the enthusiasm of the founder generation might have waned.

By far the largest number of social innovators were the squatter communards – not those who sought conventional ends, but the self-styled 'urban pioneers', who did report a different and 'unique' connection to their homes (Ingham, 1980, p. 173), although in the long run they could find themselves involved in a role not unlike that of landlord (Osborn, 1980). Older houses that were squatted lent themselves well to social experiments, especially when whole terraces could be adapted to a group. Thus twenty elegant terraced houses of the Villa Road housing co-op, saved in defiance of Lambeth Borough Council, made it possible for 160 people 'to remain together as a community . . . retaining many of the collective arrangements and physical adaptations . . . over the years' (Anning and Simpson, 1980,

p. 149). The dilapidated condition of such houses was regarded as an asset, allowing as it did a repudiation of conventional house-keeping and a stimulus to creativity.

Self-help in housing, therefore, has different functions: in one case it can be a means to an end and in another the end itself, and it is misleading to lump these together. The first case demonstrates the power of groups in getting homes for people whom the system does not serve; the second is part of a quest for alternative social forms. It was a distinction not normally made in the concept of 'freedom to build' which applied the observation of squatter, self-build settlements of developing countries to a British context – in particular drawing parallels with the English plotlanders and contrasting these to the problems of mass housing (Turner and Fichter, 1972; Turner, 1976; Ward, 1976). In such countries, officially imposed housing standards (often imported from the industrialized world) had a disabling effect on the lives of poor and struggling people; but when these people were given access to land they created homes appropriate to their means, gradually improving them over time. This conferred on them three 'freedoms': 'the freedom of community self-selection, the freedom to budget one's own resources and the freedom to shape one's own environment' (Ward, 1976, p. 80). From this a general principle was applied to developed and developing societies alike, that 'when dwellers control the major decisions and are free to make their own contributions in the design, construction, or management of their housing, both this process and the environment produced stimulate individual and social well-being. When people have no control over, nor responsibility for key decisions in the housing process, on the other hand, dwelling environments may instead become a barrier to personal fulfilment and a burden on the economy' (Fichter et al., 1972, p. 241).

The relevance to hard-to-let council

dwellings, and in particular the disasters of high-rise flats, was clear. It was less clear what dweller control might mean in practical terms. It could be argued that conventional home owners 'managed' their homes whereas the homes of tenants were managed by landlords, public or private; but whether this conduced to general social wellbeing was a subject of endless debate in housing politics and policy. When it came to personal fulfilment, it could be argued that a home (however built and tenured) was by definition a place that allowed autonomy over a personal environment. The English housing system was designed to make this accessible to a broad majority, who were therefore, not surprisingly, satisfied with their housing (Chapter 10, below). It was an open question how much suppressed desire there was for self building, self management or the working in groups which self help in housing entailed (Goodchild, 1981). Its history suggested that it was a resort of people on the margins of the main system, although – for both negative and positive reasons – these margins might grow wider in the future.

7

THE TECHNOLOGY
OF THE HOME

TECHNOLOGY AND THE DOMESTIC INTERIOR

The various technologies of the home are, perhaps particularly complex; for as well as going through the stages of invention, innovation and diffusion (Roy and Cross, 1975), they are dominated by housing tenure and physically tied to the housing stock. By 1914 the structure of the house was established in its recognizably twentieth-century form, and most of its services were in place. But it was for all practical purposes still in its pre-electric phase. The electric home dominated the rest of the century down to the 1980s, when it began to develop into the electronic home.

The points that continued to make a house 'unfit for human habitation' throughout the twentieth century are a good guide to the structural points that could not always be taken for granted in earlier times: stability, freedom from damp, natural lighting, ventilation, water supply, drainage and sanitary conveniences. After the byelaws it could be expected that a house would be a durable structure, made of hard materials, with a damp proof course, cavity walls, raised and ventilated floors, and internal division into a number of specialized rooms with windows. As we have seen in Chapter 4, the codes governing the structure

had emerged over a long period, but the byelaws marked 'the beginning of a completely new attitude to building legislation: that it should benefit everyone, including the poorer parts of the population' (Muthesius, 1982, p. 34). Eventually the byelaws developed into the current building regulations, which govern not only whole buildings but extensions and minor alterations, while since 1947 town and country planning law has required that most external changes and additions, including garages and new windows, should have planning permission besides. Only small garden structures are normally exempt.

Innovations in building technology, notably new materials and prefabricated techniques, were accelerated by the World Wars, particularly the second. Ultimately there was 'an almost complete reconstruction' of the fabric, which did not, however, prevent the house still 'ingeniously retaining its traditional image' (Pawley, 1971, p. 85). In optimal conditions these changes produced a warmer, lighter, more comfortable and usually more energy-saving home. At worst, the performance of prefabricated construction and new materials was fatally overestimated, giving rise to cold and damp conditions, most notably in high flats.

Ventilation of the home was by way of being

an obsession with the Victorians. The stench in the homes of the poor was associated with disease, so prompting public health and housing policies. But even in better-off homes there were plenty of things to cause stuffiness and smell: soot and coal dust, oil and gas lamps, untrapped waste pipes, not to mention heavily polluted external environments. Official concern centred on the volume of air thought necessary to maintain bodily health, and calculations were based on standards used in prisons and workhouses. Openable windows became mandatory for domestic premises from the 1850s and ventilators were incorporated in many parts of the house, for example in plaster ceiling roses above gas chandeliers. The open fire, however, was the main ventilating device, drawing in cold air from the floor and giving out hot air to escape at window level.

Ceiling heights of Victorian houses were normally 9 ft for ground floor and 8 ft 6 in for first floor rooms. By 1944, byelaws required a minimum height of only 8 ft and the Dudley Report debated, but decided against, reducing this by six inches. Eight years later, however, a new set of model byelaws permitted room heights of 7 ft 6 in which became standard practice. While there were many things to eliminate smells in the twentieth-century home – more frequently washed bodies and the end of greasy cooking, for example – the blocking up or elimination of open fires, and superior insulation in double glazing and cavity wall filling, brought the problems of ventilation back in a latterday form: that is, how to enable the escape of warm, moist air. This became an increasingly serious problem because of carbon monoxide and other pollutants emitted by gas fires, and the toxins given out by various synthetic building, decorating and furnishing materials.

Vermin was another problem apparently solved but later to return. At one time all classes had lived on intimate terms with cockroaches, black beetles, bedbugs, rats, mice and other pests, but direct knowledge of these gradually lapsed, except for slum houses, where

very serious disturbance of sleep is caused by the irritation of lice, scabies and skin diseases, and of that other scourge, the bed-bug. This last is, unhappily, very common in old property, where it lives and breeds in cracks and crevices of both structure and furniture, coming out to feed on human blood at night. It has a peculiar musty smell by which its presence can often be detected on entry into a room or building. Many respectable people keep the bed-bug at bay by the unremitting use of soap, water and scrubbing-brush, or literally flee before it'. (*Our Towns*, 1944, p. 27)

Slum clearance was the main mechanism for solving the problem, particularly since people were encouraged to move in the 'bug van', which took their household goods to be gassed with hydrogen cyanide overnight before delivering them to a new, vermin-free home the next day. In doomed areas there were reports of columns of refugee bugs retreating from emptied buildings.

The general rise in living standards also had an effect. In 1956, the Central Housing Advisory Committee noted that 'the incidence of bed bugs in slum houses is nowadays far less than was experienced before the war' (MHLG, 1956, para. 55) and disinfestation was felt to be discriminatory and embarrassing. A diplomatic way round the problem would be treatment for woodworm, for no stigma attached to this, though all would agree that it should not be carried into new homes. Making this the reason for disinfestation would, therefore, 'make the process more acceptable' (*Ibid*, 1956, para. 59).

Between the wars, all that most suburban houses knew of vermin were mice, bluebottles and flies, and long, sticky ribbons of yellow flypaper were a normal piece of household equipment. The 1951 Festival mounted a giant-sized and memorable exhibit on the disgusting habits of the house fly, and there followed a period when people's zealous use of DDT sprays led to its virtual disappearance. The Parker Morris Report, in 1961, found domestic vermin not worthy of mention. Very soon after this, however, rats and other species, including ants and pigeons, began to be troublesome in high-density environments, particularly flats, where regular cleansing was not carried out and where moist, warm conditions provided ideal breeding grounds.

The treatment of household refuse had grown haphazardly in times when no particular distinction was made between human and other waste. In byelaw houses the kitchen fire or range served as a waste destructor, while the contents of ashpit privies could be removed through small doors in backyard walls and carted away. Unburned refuse (of which possibly there was not a large amount) was collected in dustbins, but these lacked any obvious place of their own. In terraced layouts, unless they could be collected from a back alley, they had to be brought through the house for emptying, for to give them a place at the front of the house would have breached one of its most basic 'codes', the separate status of front and back. A semi-detached layout offered the obvious solution, of storing dustbins at the side. Council housing of the 1940s was the first to incorporate bin stores in the overall house design, placing them in rear outbuildings. In later council housing a bin cupboard containing gas and electric meters was often brought to the front, next to or near the front door; but this did not find favour in housing designed for owner occupation.

By the 1960s both qualitative and quantitative changes in domestic refuse were under way. Its volume had been growing steadily for some time, but its weight had fallen by about ten per cent in the early 1960s, and this was attributed to a decrease in ash and rise in paper packaging (a trend seen earlier in the USA). 'Good class' suburban areas were already following the American example (MHLG, 1967a). Waste paper generation continued to increase, owing

much to frozen and take-away meals and disposable nappies. Meanwhile the galvanized metal dustbin was replaced by a quieter plastic version, usually inscribed with caveats against depositing hot ashes, until at last these became redundant. The sorting of rubbish into separate bins for recycling was as yet only found in selected residential areas in the 1990s, but by this time it was common for householders to drive certain categories of waste, including items that local authorities refused to collect, to central depots or small bottle and wastepaper banks. With increasing difficulty, the ordinary householder could keep the growing problem of litter under control, but it easily became uncontrollable in high-rise flats and old housing with high levels of multiple occupation, where no effective provision was made for the amount of waste generated.

Noise similarly went through social and technical transformations. The intolerance of 'respectable' Victorian householders towards the racket in the streets had been a significant influence in suburban development (Daunton, 1983). There is little or no record, then, of noise nuisance from neighbours, apart from the taken-for-granted din in slum neighbourhoods; but doubtless parlour pianos and houses packed with children caused many a disturbance. The twentieth century had its own forms of noise torture, from loudspeakers and amplified sound, domestic and garden machinery, not to mention motorbikes and cars being repaired in driveways and traffic on the street.

Notwithstanding regulations for sound insulation of floors and party walls, noise in the home was a problem that could drive people to breakdown. According to a survey of 1948, the most intrusive noise was the neighbours' radio (Chapman, 1948), even though in the early days of broadcasting programmes were interrupted by requests to turn volumes down, particularly in summer when windows were open. In 1948, a fifth of people in bricks-and-mortar houses claimed to lose sleep through noise of many kinds, but many more in flats and steel-framed houses (over a third and over a half respectively). Twenty years later, a third of people living at high density were robbed of sleep through noise, and attitudes to the home were in general strongly conditioned by it: overhearing neighbours' snoring and 'pillow talk' being found particularly objectionable (MHLG, 1970c, p. 28).

One of the main benefits of a detached house was being relieved of this misery. Byelaw houses were better insulated for sound than newer suburban houses, even taking into account that they might contain less plumbing and noisy domestic machinery (Chapman, 1948). Most semis suffered the misfortune of having adjacent lounges, and already in the 1930s a house where 'the next door wireless cannot be heard' was a selling point (Jackson, 1973, p. 181). The Parker Morris-type open-plan house with open-tread stairs and thin internal partitions was still more at the mercy of noise transmission, but the worst case of all was flats, which had neighbours above and below as well as laterally, in addition to noisy plumbing, lift machinery, and stairwells acting as echo chambers. Gallery access flats had always been noted for their noise disturbance, but deck access flats were even worse, because their public walkways ran immediately above the ceilings of rooms, often bedrooms.

Previously dealt with under a Noise Abatement Act of 1960, noise was brought under the Control of Pollution Act in 1974, and domestic noise complaints increased by more than tenfold over the next ten years. The responsibility for deciding what noises constituted a statutory nuisance rested with local authorities, whose environmental health officers, however, usually had inadequate resources to deal with all the complaints made.

FUEL AND POWER

The main energy source of the Victorian house was coal, which had totally displaced the earlier fuels of wood and peat except in remoter rural areas. The impact of coal on the house was immense: it required means of delivery, storage, hearths and flues, as well as creating soot and ash. Gas began to enter the middle-class home around 1850, but its main period of diffusion was in the 1890s, when penny slot meters and the covering of installation costs by suppliers or their incorporation into running charges brought it within reach of most households.

Electricity was available from the 1880s, but it was mainly limited to lights and telephones in the homes of the very wealthy. At this time it cost about three times as much as gas, with which it faced half a century of competition, owing its eventual success to its superiority for lighting. At the turn of the century there was a chaotic mixture of supply companies (which included local authorities), of direct and alternating currents, and of voltages and fittings, so that appliances were not easily interchangeable. Housing tenure was also a factor, for a nation mainly of private tenants held back from the cost of wiring which brought them no capital return. The main channel for diffusion, therefore, was new suburban housing of the interwar period, private and public. Through this, electricity became symbolically associated with modernity in a way that it was not possible for gas, as a much 'older' fuel, to be.

After the First World War the number of households wired up rose from one in seventeen to one in three around 1930, and two in three by 1939. At this time only about a fifth of households lacked gas, although there were many rural homes which did not have either (PEP, 1945). Over the same period the electrical industry centralized and energetically promoted itself. A rather ineffective Act of 1919 was superceded by the 1926 Electrical Supply Act, under which the Central Generating Board and National Grid were set up. The value of electricity for health, hygiene and labour saving, was promoted by the Electrical Development Association of manufacturers, and more particularly by the Electrical Association for Women, founded in 1924 (and surviving until 1986). This participated in national and international conferences on power; its members sat on local electricity committees, and it mediated between industry, designers and users by producing publications and films, and by planning and sometimes constructing model kitchens for show houses and flats. These included an all-electric flat furnished by Heals at a 1930 'Bachelor Girls' exhibition, and another at an exhibition of the work of women architects in 1936 (Worden, 1989).

Meanwhile, under the 1926 Act, certain Labour councils had been cabling streets in working-class districts and assisting wiring with credit schemes. This enabled working-class consumers to buy electricity, like gas, through penny slot meters, and sometimes to hire electric cookers. Other devices, like 'cut-outs' which allowed only one appliance to be used at a time, helped to reduce the cost of installations. After nationalization, under the 1947 Electricity Act, wiring speeded up so rapidly that by 1951 nearly 90 per cent of homes were connected. Domestic electricity was soon virtually universal, even in rural areas. Installations were improved by the ring main, a circuit running from the main switch and carrying standardized, individually fused 30 amp sockets, rather than a collection of 2, 5 and 15 amp sockets separately wired back to a distribution board. Under this earlier system, one overloaded socket could fuse several sockets and all the lights, so that it was an unwise householder who did not keep a torch and card of fuse wire handy for this not infrequent event. The 30 amp socket could take any size of appliance without risk.

Both gas and electricity required meters. If these were slot meters they needed to be accessible, but nevertheless they usually contrived to be in awkward positions, high above front doors, in cellars, or at the backs of under-stair cupboards. New materials and styling after 1945 made then slightly less unsightly but they remained indoors, on the assumption that a housewife, though not now a servant, would always be available to let the meter reader in. It was not until the postwar period that houses began to be designed with meters that could be read from outside. For the majority still without these, a new policy of issuing estimated bills only partially remedied the difficulty that arose when homes no longer had fulltime housewives.

By 1939, newer houses were characterized by a mixture of fuels and energy and limited use of electricity. The home was still, therefore, very much 'a machine heated by coal, coke and gas, and powered by women' (Hannah, 1979, p. 208). The war years could do little to improve on this situation: on the contrary, coal rationing and frequent power and gas cuts, when people had to live and cook by candles, probably made them glad to have as many different heat sources as possible, and this to some extent explains the development of domestic heating and lighting after the war.

THE COAL-FIRED HOUSE

The Victorian open hearth and range were, at best, inefficient appliances, belatedly and imperfectly adapted from wood to coal. Even those that may once have worked well became increasingly unsatisfactory as they aged, and as those who understood how to use them passed on. The use of coal, in general, required a number of skills of no mean order: estimating future needs, budgeting for these, assessing the quality of different types of coal, laying, lighting and tending the fire in different weather conditions, regular cleaning – much of it in the form of vigorous blackleading – and getting to know all the various shutters, dampers and idiosyncracies of any particular appliance. Having the chimney swept (for if this was neglected it might catch fire) was a major domestic event which was estimated to take over nine hours of the housewife's labour (Mass Observation, 1943). When the only cooking appliance was a coal range – and this was still the case in council houses being built in some districts to at least 1960 – the day could not properly begin until the hearth was cleaned out, laid and lit.

The technicalities of coal, however, were almost secondary to its symbolic significance in the English home. This particularly struck Herman Muthesius in his exhaustive study of the early 1900s. Closed, space-heating stoves had long been used on the Continent, but he concluded that in England they existed only in catalogues. He was contemptuous of the so-called reforms of the English open hearth, which, as an inherently 'senseless device', he rated as only fourteen per cent efficient. On the other hand, he recognized it as a 'domestic altar' where 'all ideas of domestic comfort, of family happiness, of inward-looking personal life, of spiritual wellbeing' were centred. The fact that its devotees roasted on one side while freezing in a stiff current of cold air on the other, was unimportant to the English, to whom 'the idea of a room without a fire-place is quite simply unthinkable' (Muthesius, 1979, p. 181).

Fifty years on, others were still coming to the same conclusion. Mass Observation found the idea of houses without chimneys strange, and rooms without fireplaces lacking in focus, however warm, for 'there is evidently a feeling that unless something can be seen burning it is not a *proper* fire' (*Ibid*, 1943, p. 136). More prosaically, the Society of Women Housing Managers remarked that 'it can be sat around and provides something to poke' (EAW, 1946, p. 51).

In the mid 1950s the open hearth still bound the family together (Chapman, 1955). The mantelpiece was important to this, used as it was for the display of treasured possessions, including family photographs and trophies, with the best mirror or framed picture suspended above. When the open fire disappeared another site had to be found for these treasures. Out, too, went the fire tongs and toasting fork, and with them toast, potatoes baked in the hot ashes, chestnuts roasted on shovels, and days ending with 'pictures' watched in the dying embers.

Before its eventual disappearance, the use of coal went through various technical improvements. There was a particular incentive in flats where, between the wars, coke-burning grates, gas ignition pokers, and open hearths back-to-back with baking ovens began to be introduced. In the same period the Aga cooker was imported and, with other less efficient cooking ranges, this was to have a minority but loyal constituency to the present day. The open fire was made slightly more efficient by draught controls and ash drawers. But housewives often failed to appreciate labour-saving and efficient grates. They were reported to throw away covers designed to keep fires in overnight and to place firebricks in grates in misguided attempts at economy. They resisted coke, which they believed had 'most of the goodness taken out of it' and so should be cheaper rather than dearer than coal (WACSF, 1951, p. 15).

These gaps in consumer awareness and its own poor marketing were belatedly addressed by the Coal Utilisation Council, when it set up showrooms to compete with those long since established for gas and electricity. It claimed to have discovered that consumers still preferred coal for cooking 'because of the better flavour of the food' (Coal Utilisation Council, n.d.). The more likely truth, however, was that consumers cared more about the appearance of the open hearth than its efficiency, although they were concerned to save labour. The new fashion for cast, tiled surrounds, which started in the suburban semi and spread to millions of homes after 1945, made laborious and dirty blackleading obsolete. For several decades they were used as the cheapest and fastest way to modernize old rooms. Their thick, oatmeal coloured mouldings were influenced by motifs used in the interior design of cinemas, and their symbolism could evidently be counted on to arouse deep emotions, as Bell Fireplaces realized when they announced: 'The world's best fuel saver will be available again after victory! The design shown is of Muresque Stone and Rustic Faience . . . The natural markings suggest the foliage of trees, landscape and cloud studies' the faience being a 'Product of Nature [with] warm restful colours [and] an uneven surface similar to wooden logs'

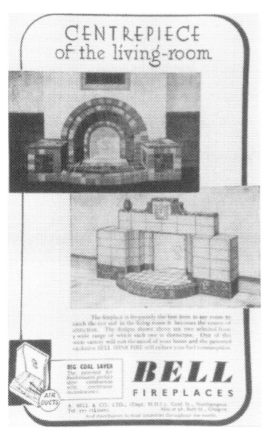

The state of the art tiled surround of the interwar and early post-war fireplace. (*Source*: Yerbury, n.d. *c*. 1947

(Pleydell-Bouverie, n.d., p. 164). The illustration of this product shows no sign of technical innovation, so confirming the view that expensive new fireplaces were not necessarily more efficient (Chapman, 1955).

The open fire was still taken for granted in the Parker Morris Report, but it now had a back boiler providing hot water and perhaps serving two or three downstairs radiators and a heated bathroom towel rail. It no longer had any cooking function. The biggest impetus for change came from clean air policies, at first attempted rather ineffectively by various local authorities but later given momentum by the increasing occurrence of smogs: lethal winter mixtures of smoke and carbon monoxide, which produced many fatalities. The first Clean Air Act of 1956, replacing the weaker provisions of the 1936 Public Health Act, applied to smoke emissions from new dwellings and allowed councils to contribute towards adapting old fireplaces. The much stronger Clean Air Act of 1968 permitted designated smoke control zones where it was illegal to use anything but smokeless fuel.

This made the survival of most open grates impossible, and their commonest replacement was the gas fire. The new law, however, also gave rise to the first general wave of closed stoves in England. PEP in the 1940s had regarded these as desirable yet 'continental' and controversial. They now became more common, being made both to insert in existing hearths and to be freestanding. They had fixed glass windows or openable doors, for it was still felt important to see the fire. Their spread was ultimately shortlived, as it was overtaken by a general desire for more heat in the home. This had been noticed as early as 1950 (WACSF, 1951) but was not given official recognition until the Parker Morris Report, which acknowledged that cold winter rooms inhibited the proper use of the house, and family life in general. Its proposed minimum of 65°F for all rooms including bedrooms was ultimately met by central heating. The open fire then survived only as an occasional luxury, or more commonly in symbolic form in gas or electric imitations.

GAS AND ELECTRICITY IN COOKING AND SPACE HEATING

One of the things that prolonged the use of the coal range for cooking was that it was a landlord's fixture, as well as the main heating appliance. It was therefore prudent to use it, especially in winter. In 1939 PEP estimated that over half of all households used it for cooking in winter, and over a third in summer; but in the north of England, where homemade bread was important, the proportions rose to over a third in winter and not far short of a third in summer (PEP, 1945).

The range had begun to be supplemented by a gas cooker or gas ring in Victorian times. House plans, and also the class associations of cooking by gas, determined their location in the scullery, where they laid the foundations of the twentieth-century kitchen (Ravetz, 1968). One of the things that had held back diffusion of gas cookers was the importance of the Sunday roast in family menus. True roasting was done in front of an open fire, where joints were turned and basted, and this was simulated with some difficulty in early gas cookers, which had a meat hook and could bring a current of cold air to play inside the oven. Such models seem to have been dropped by the early 1900s, after which the legendary Sunday roast became, in fact, baked rather than roasted. The gas cooker underwent various improvements, including detachable parts and enamelled splashbacks; but its most important, labour-saving feature was the regulo, or thermostatic heat control, introduced in 1915. This was at first regarded with some suspicion, for it displaced the older skills of judging oven heat; but once accepted, it led the way to automated cooking.

Gas cookers spread fastest between 1891 and 1911 when numbers increased more than thirty-fold, largely because they could be rented from gas supply companies. Numbers increased at a slower rate into the 1920s, when the prevalence of renting kept old models in circulation and was judged to be a brake on further technical improvement.

Gas fires of both radiation and convection types, many with simulated coal or coke effects, dated back to the 1830s, and portable gas fires were on sale from the 1890s. The diffusion of gas space heating was through middle-class housing: in particular, the interwar semi was often fitted with gas fires in the two main bedrooms and at least one of its day rooms (and it was common for gas pokers to be fitted to open coal grates). Mass Observation reported that fifteen per cent of its sample heated the living room by gas. Encouraged by smoke control, but then challenged by central heating, gas fires remained a source of radiant

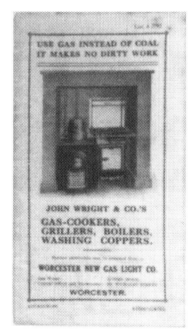

A 1923 advertisement promoting the use of gas instead of coal.

heat even in centrally heated homes. They were given a fresh boost around 1980, when increasingly realistic 'living flame' models were introduced. Many of these were inefficient as space heaters but what they offered, without dirt or labour, was the ancient symbolism of the coal – or still older log – hearth.

The development of electricity for cooking and space heating came the best part of a century after gas, but with a faster momentum. Cookers converted from or closely modelled on gas had just gone into production by 1914 but their distinctive development took place in the period between the wars. In 1912 the firm of Belling created the classic twentieth-century electric fire, where nickel-chrome wire was wound round fireclay elements – replacing the sausage-shaped 'glow lamps', or bulbs enclosing carbon filaments. Imitation coal effect fires where a lamp or fan simulated glowing or flickering embers were in use by the 1920s. Like their gas counterparts these were made to slide into empty grates or be freestanding, with small piles of 'coal' heaped above or below the radiants.

There was a rapid rise in sales of cookers and heaters from 1930, partly boosted by those local authorities who rented cookers to their tenants. This expansion of the market included electric kettles, toasters and many other small appliances invented long before but now updated; and it was encouraged by vigorous sales campaigns, including the building of 'all-electric' demonstration houses in many parts of the country. These provoked 'all-gas' rivals which, however, sometimes had electric wiring surreptitiously installed. Additional impetus was given by the all-electric postwar 'pre-fabs', whose electric fires, cookers, water heaters and refrigerators were widely admired.

At the time of Mass Observation only some 10 per cent of households were heating their living rooms by electricity, and the main period of diffusion was after 1950, when rising incomes allowed a steep rise in power consumption.

Much of this increase was directly attributable to the small, portable electric fire (typically the classic, one or two-bar fire with parabolic metal reflector) which was cheap to buy and could instantly be plugged in and used. The Parker Morris Report noted that its sales had doubled in the six years to 1960. Another device, originally of the 1930s, was now improved and revived. This was the overnight electric storage heater which, used in isolation, was a bulky and unfathomable device which gave out heat when it was least wanted and was cold when heat was most needed. With fan assistance, however, it could be used for whole-house central heating, and was adopted in many Parker Morris-type houses. In 1971 it provided over one fifth of all central heating installations, but by 1988 this had dropped back to less than a tenth (GHS, 1989). Nevertheless it maintained a place in the range of heating options, particularly in smaller and cheaper speculative houses and flats, where it was cheap to install, though not necessarily cheap to run.

At a time when virtue was found in variety, a further option was provided by paraffin, and the Parker Morris Report noted that three fifths of households had paraffin heaters. New types available at this time had mantles and bright reflectors to maximize output and give a cheerful glow, and they conveniently incorporated reservoirs of fuel. When properly managed they were almost odourless. Like the small electric fire, they had the convenience of being portable, and like coal, their fuel could be stored in advance, so giving protection against power cuts. The warmth they offered, however, was at the cost of much water vapour, and this was a particular problem in cold and damp high-rise flats.

CENTRAL HEATING

Central heating eventually brought the period of mixed heating systems to an end. It was not a recent invention, for in the previous century public buildings and grander houses had been heated from central furnaces, but in ordinary homes it was largely untried down to the 1950s (EAW, 1946; WACSF, 1951). District heating was also being canvassed at this time, having been tentatively tried before the war and incorporated into visions for New Towns and postwar town planning. In 1946 it was installed on a London estate, using excess heat from Battersea power station, and the following year the Ministry of Fuel and Power sent a mission to investigate American practices. District heating continued to be used on council and new town estates to the 1970s, but its high cost, inefficiency and faulty meters (where these were supplied) made it unpopular with tenants because they were charged for heat they had not consumed or could not regulate. It was even blamed for the outright failure of particular estates (Morton, 1994). Many of the same objections applied to central-ized electric heating systems of estates, which allowed no control over the times of switching on and off.

Such objections did not apply in houses with individual systems of central heating. Its spread had more to do with social class than climate, for it appeared first in London and southern England, where it was apparently introduced by those who had been abroad (EAW, 1946; Mass Observation, 1943). By 1960 only some 5 per cent of English homes, but half as many again in Greater London, had central heating, though a period of expansion was shortly to follow. This was accompanied by technical improvements, including better and lighter weight boilers and radiators, and the 'small bore' system where small diameter copper tubing used with an electric pump permitted faster, cheaper and less intrusive installations.

By the end of the 1960s, central heating had become one of the main official indicators of housing standards. All types of fuel were used, including oil, which had recently been as cheap as coal but was now beginning to be priced out of the market. Gas, formerly the most expensive in several regions, was now becoming the cheapest and most popular fuel. In small bore installations, however, it could not work without an electrically driven pump.

The point at which more than half the housing stock was centrally heated was reached in the late 1970s, and by 1991 the proportion had risen to over 80 per cent. Those who lacked it were distinguished by tenure, income and age: single, elderly and low-income house-holds were least likely to have it, and over half of the tenants of private landlords were without it. Arguably, such people had become more deprived since the disappearance of coal which, as something that could be bought in small quantities and used sparingly, had better suited the pockets of the poor. It was certainly the case with those in high flats, who, as we have seen, had no control over expensive electrical central heating systems (Chapter 3, above). Public concern over premature deaths from hyperthermia among the aged arose in the exceptionally cold winters of the early 1960s. It persisted through the century, in spite of the recommended minimum temperatures of Parker Morris and the later 'cold weather' payments for people on social security. In the 1990s there were still reckoned to be some two million English homes that failed to meet World Health Organisation minima (King, 1992). For all living on limited means, therefore, the imposition of Value Added Tax on fuel, first instituted in 1994, was truly alarming.

DAYLIGHTING

Daylight is so much a part of today's home as to be taken for granted; but in the last century it was very much the prerogative of the well-to-do: not so much because of the well-known window tax of 1823–51, which did not affect smaller houses, but because of buildings and layouts. Byelaw housing, although an infinite improvement on dark slum courts and alleys, was set out without reference to orientation and its rear quarters, in particular, were often overshadowed.

As indicators of social status, windows were second in importance only to the house itself. The dominant window of the nineteenth century was the sash type, used in classical architecture. The casement was considered oldfashioned and rustic until it was brought back into fashion in the Domestic Revival. It came back into favour in the twentieth century through garden city houses and their derivative council houses, as well as the interwar semi. Now it was the sash window which was regarded as inferior, because of its identification with byelaw housing and council housing designed in the classical idiom. The sash stayed in decline until the neo-Georgian revival in owner-occupied housing in the later part of the century.

As well as casements, the garden city school of design also adopted the bay window. A mark of social status in byelaw housing, this continued to be 'the acme of respectability' to at least 1939 (Mass Observation, 1943, p. 132). As we have seen (Chapter 2, above) the two-storey front bay distinguished the owner-occupied semi from the council house, which at best had one on the ground floor. At the rear of the house, bay windows were not so common. The ground floor room could be expected to have a 'french window', a glazed door or pair of doors connecting living room and back garden, which had begun to appear in terraced houses before 1914. This became a regular feature of the interwar semi and was only displaced by the postwar patio door, a sliding glass door that could be bought as a package and installed in houses of any age, in a way not possible with french windows.

How sensitive people were to the symbolism of windows is seen in the flourishing industry of replacement windows that sprang up in the later part of the century. Window replacement became necessary as houses aged (although it

CRITTALL
WINDOWS

FOR THE NEW HOUSES

By specifying STANDARD metal windows from British Standard 990 : 1945 you help to reduce the present unavoidable delay in delivery, and at the same time you ensure highest quality and lowest cost. Ask for leaflet 115 B.

THE CRITTALL MANUFACTURING CO. LTD.
BRAINTREE, ENGLAND

This advertisement which appeared in *Recent English Architecture 1925–1940*, published in 1947 epitomizes the symbolism attached to windows. (*Source*: Country Life, 1947)

tended to be needed sooner in postwar houses, with their unseasoned wood, than in houses built before 1914). The styles of replacement windows, however, followed fashion rather than what was appropriate for the period of the house. The most blatant anachronism was the 'Georgian' bow window, often glazed with imitation 'bullseyes', which in their original form had been defective and therefore cheaper panes of glass, but which were now distributed randomly to achieve a 'period' effect. Window replacements, as indeed windows in many new houses built for sale (but not council houses), were chosen with scant regard to the practicalities of external cleaning, and this became a serious problem for householders when window cleaners became expensive or unobtainable.

As was the case with other home technologies, people gradually forgot that the sash window was designed to perform technical functions. When properly fitted and used, it could be operated to control heat and ventilation. The top and bottom panels were adjustable to expel or admit air of different temperatures, or to admit a small supply of fresh air without causing a draught. The window was also designed so that the outside could be cleaned from the interior. In the course of time, sashes were broken and not replaced, and the mechanisms forgotten. Later, so-called Georgian windows were usually poor imitations, without sashes and sometimes with glued-on plastic strips instead of real glazing bars.

The casement windows of the interwar period had their own means of controlling temperature and air. They were usually accompanied by upper lights, some of which were made to open. These were often leaded and glazed with coloured glass, amber in particular being thought to deter flies (Pleydell-Bouverie, n.d.). Crittall metal casements became very fashionable during the 1930s and 1940s, making a fortune for their inventor, who built a model village with the proceeds. One of their main attractions at the time was that they could be made to 'wrap around' corners in modernistic houses, contributing to their reputation for sunshine and health. In use, however, metal windows were subject to rusting and cracked panes, so that they became unpopular and eventually went out of fashion.

In the Second World War all used rooms had to be blacked out at lighting-up time (and windows could also, if their owners chose, be criss-crossed with paper strips to prevent collapse from blast). Blacking out was usually done with special black cloth: 'black-out material' which was often made into clothes, because it was 'off the ration'. Endless ways of mounting and storing window black-outs were developed. In the postwar years, the huge numbers of pinholes where it had been tacked up mysteriously disappeared, presumably through innumerable applications of putty, polyfilla and paint.

The long and tiresome years of blackout may have helped to predispose people towards the postwar picture window. The stylistic origins of this were in the glass curtain walls of Bauhaus and Modern Movement houses, but it first appeared as a wide casement window with minimal glazing bars in the early postwar council house. The picture window became a selling point of speculative housing, providing an ideal opportunity for showing off all the

New windows update the image: a pair of 'modernistic' houses, Far Headingley, Leeds, 1995.

furnishings and appointments of the new home, and so replacing the bay window in this respect. In Parker Morris-type houses the window was taken down to floor level. Great store was set on keeping it highly polished, inside and out, and – to the despair of architectural purists – draping it fancifully with white nylon 'net', which had now replaced the lace curtains of Victorian respectability (Attfield, 1989). Sometimes householders dressed all their front windows uniformly, paying more regard to the appearance of the house from the street than its interior functions.

Eventually the disfunctional aspects of picture windows led to the fashion dying out. From the 1970s onwards, the role of windows in domestic energy use began to be taken more seriously, and window sizes became small again in 'mews' layouts with their 'village' style houses. The traditional means of heat conservation, external or internal folding shutters, had effectively died out with the byelaw house, for the fake shutters often fixed with replacement windows had no hinges and no functional use at all. At the same time, there was no English tradition of double glazing, as in most other northern countries. Curtains, therefore, were the main insulating device – and even the net curtain was useful in this respect, flimsy though it seemed.

Double glazing was not seriously thought about until the energy crisis of 1973, but from that time it became a thriving industry, allowing people to have sealed units installed or to buy secondary glazing panels to instal themselves. The cost of double glazing a whole house might be high enough to justify taking out a second mortgage, and it was doubtful how cost-effective it was, for it took many years to recover the outlay through reduced heating costs. Far larger contributions to energy saving could of course be made through design, where fewer, smaller and better placed windows could minimize heat loss and greatly reduce the amount of heating required.

ARTIFICIAL LIGHT

Perhaps nothing would have more surprised people of earlier centuries than the instant and unlimited artificial light of the twentieth-century home. To the middle of the last century, lighting after sunset depended on candlepower, albeit this was more technically sophisticated than is now remembered. Candles live on as emergency lighting – and a wise household keeps a box of white wax candles to hand for power cuts – and for ceremonial uses, as at Christmas and birthdays. Candlesticks, usually in pairs, continue to be an important part of the furnishings of the home, typically displayed on mantelpieces, when these are available. In Chapman's byelaw houses, candlesticks were the second or third most important ornament, but in his semis and detached houses they survived mainly in the form of electric candelabra, suspended from ceilings or on wall brackets, modelled to look like wax candles, even to their imitation 'drips' (Chapman, 1955). More recently, the ghost of the candle lingers on in decorative, coloured and scented candles which form a stock-in-trade of gift shops and have little value for lighting, and the more recent oil-filled imitation candle which burns with a naked, everlasting flame.

The candle was displaced by the oil lamp, which by the middle of the nineteenth century was rendered more efficient by the new paraffin oil and a series of technical changes. It gave a steady, gently hissing light, but the prevention of smell and pollution took much care in filling, trimming, and regular cleaning, so that not surprisingly it was readily abandoned when a better gas alternative was available. It was, however, a long time before this was so. Gas had been used in public places since around 1800, but it was another thirty years before it became a serious rival in the home. Although it was cheaper than most oil lamps, and much cheaper than tallow candles, its naked flames were smelly and sooty. It was therefore relegated to unimportant parts of the house until the introduction of the incandescent mantle in the 1890s. Gas lighting was further improved in the early 1900s by automatic switches using pilot lights, and by the inverted mantle, which was easier to replace and directed the light better. Like early electric light bulbs, early mantles could cost as much as a week's wages but the improved variety became much cheaper, while the unit cost of gas compared favourably with electricity, until this also fell in price shortly before 1914.

By 1920, some seven million households, half of them with slot meters, could have been lit by gas. The Tudor Walters Report, however, saw electric lighting as the way forward, even for council tenants, and it seems likely that from the beginning the overwhelming majority of council houses were fitted with electric light. Some insight into the novelty of this at the time is conveyed by the warning given to tenants on the Becontree estate not to wash the bulbs by dunking them in water (LCC, 1933, repeated in Dagenham Borough Council, 1956).

The gas industry did not, however, yield without a determined fight. It appealed to arguments that gas produced a mellower and healthier light than electricity, and that it was particularly suitable for the working classes because some heat came free with the light. It therefore sponsored 'all-gas' demonstration houses that were plausible rivals to houses wired for electricity, particularly after 1929 when pilot-less automatic switching was introduced. The fact remained that gas mantles were fragile and easily broken, while fittings were fixed and could not be portable, as small electric lamps could be. Yet gas, and even oil, lighting continued to have their advocates down to 1939 (PEP, 1945). It was many more years before gas lights were given up entirely in older homes, where the pipes and brackets remained, even after electric wiring was installed.

When first introduced, in the 1880s, electric light cost about three times as much as gas, partly because of the high cost of bulbs. This was partly remedied by the metal filament bulb, introduced in 1907, but it was not until the gas-filled, tungsten filament bulb just before the first World War that electric light had a decisive advantage over gas, at any rate in all new dwellings. The cost of installing a lighting circuit fell steadily from £11–£20 around 1919, to £7–£8 in the late 1920s, and £5–£6 ten years later. Bulbs also became cheaper and consumed less current, although savings here were offset by the progressive rise in wattage that was used.

The interwar semi set new trends in lighting, with two-way switching in halls and bedrooms (allowing the luxury of getting into bed before putting the light out), and increasing use of table and standard lamps, which Chapman saw as indicators of social status. The latter, for instance, were never found in his byelaw houses and seldom in council houses. Only a small minority of the former had any subsidiary living-room lighting, compared to 42 per cent of his semis and 76 per cent of his detached houses (Chapman, 1955). After 1945, there was growing dissatisfaction with the single ceiling light, most particularly in the scullery, where a woman working at the sink stood in her own light. Fluorescent lighting, already used in shops, was regarded by some as 'the home illuminant of the future' (EAW, 1946, p. 49), but PEP foresaw a rise in demand for multiple light sources.

Lampshades as well as lights expressed social status. Naked, unshaded bulbs were found in a minority of Chapman's byelaw houses but not at all in his council houses, semis or detached houses. Conical shades were mainly found in the byelaw houses, and two thirds of the council houses used the inverted ceramic bowl for their main ceiling light. This was also found in more than half the semis, but here it had to compete with electric candelabra.

Subsidiary lighting and changing fashions in

shades not only made for homes that were more pleasingly lit but gave more opportunity for individual household members to pursue their own activities. Inevitably, more lamps and increased wattage were associated with higher income. PEP remarked that 'families in the lower-income groups can seldom afford as much light as they would like, and certainly not as much as they should have on medical grounds' (PEP, 1945, p. xxxv). This changed to some extent in later years, when the current for lighting was a small part of total household consumption. If anything, lighting levels were higher in poorer homes, which relied on central ceiling lights; but the class associations of light fittings remained, in particular the association of the naked bulb with poverty.

WATER

Water was the last of the mains services to enter the home, which had functioned for centuries without a piped supply. It made its entry into the house at the scullery where, by definition, the wet work of the house was done, including laundry and bodily washing. Laundry was catered for by a 'copper', a metal cistern with a heat source in which clothes could be boiled clean. The scullery sink was made not to hold water but rather as a shallow slop tray without a plug, where buckets and bowls could stand. In later years, many such sinks, displaced from service, finished their lives as plant containers in gardens, where they are still sometimes seen.

By 1914, according to one historian, 'it was the rare house which did not have a piped water supply' (Daunton, 1983, p. 246); yet for many years to come this might be no more than a single cold water tap in the backyard. Subdivided houses did not normally have any increased plumbing installation, and here the burden of carrying water and slops up and down flights of stairs continued into the 1970s (Allaun, 1972). This was naturally a deterrent

to personal cleanliness, and as *Our Towns* remarked: 'the lack of proper washing of bodies and clothing is in part a housing problem resulting from the inadequate water supply and washing facilities in old property' (*Our Towns*, 1944, p. 93). Rural Women's Institute members found no other need more pressing than water supply at this time (EAW, 1946).

It seems, therefore, that too optimistic a view of water diffusion may be taken from looking at the better houses. In 1951 14 per cent of households still shared a water supply and a further 6 per cent were entirely without one. It was not for another ten years that a mains supply could be considered all but universal, and even then, homes might still be without a kitchen sink – as were 8 per cent of tenants of private landlords in Greater London (Gray and Russell, 1962). From this time on, however, fewer and fewer homes lacked an integrated system with both downstairs and upstairs plumbing, hot water supply, and water-borne sanitation.

English plumbing remained notoriously bad for some time. Inherited regulations and customs resulted in long lengths of unprotected, external waste pipes, and unlagged storage tanks in roof spaces. Winters regularly brought freeze-ups, followed by burst pipes. Eventually the problem was overcome by the lagging of pipes and tanks, replacement of metal by plastic fittings, and higher standards of house heating.

A steep rise in household water consumption accompanied these improvements, the main increase apparently happening, with little to document it, in the 1960s and 1970s. By 1990 personal daily consumption in Britain was 140 litres, some third of which was spent on flushing the WC. By this time the cost of water, which in early postwar years had usually been no more than a few pence weekly, was making serious inroads into ordinary incomes. The 1980s privatization of water companies was followed by steep rises in charges. At the same time, water rates were excluded from the 1990–92 'poll tax' and its successor, the council tax, leaving even poor households to pay full water charges. Further difficulties arose for council tenants when local authorities ceased to collect water rates with rents. Thus many households were faced with a charge they had not previously had to budget for, as well as one that was not covered by any Social Security benefit. In consequence there was an unprecedented rise of household disconnections, amounting to over 21,000 in 1992, which was related to a return of dysentery and hepatitis (Stearn, 1992; Hencke, 1993). A number of water companies were now introducing water metering, and new dwellings were in any case being fitted with meters. It was predicted that this would make it necessary for larger and poorer families to economize on water, and in this event unlimited access to running water would no longer characterize the late twentieth-century home.

BATHS AND HOT WATER

In 1900 Britain was regarded as leading the rest of Europe in the matter of bathrooms – a reputation based, of course, on the best houses containing an upstairs bathroom with full-length lounge bath, fitted basin, shower, and perhaps bidet. But even the humble byelaw terraced houses seen by Herman Muthesius normally had a bathroom with bath, basin and gas geysir for hot water (Muthesius, 1979). Several generations passed, however, before the bathroom became universal and Mass Observation still considered that 'whether a house has a bath or not is one of the major dividing lines' (Mass Observation, 1943, p. 116). For the majority of people, the bath was a zinc tub, used before a roaring kitchen fire, and hung on a nail in the backyard wall at other times.

In working-class houses the first fixed bath was normally in the scullery, where hot and cold water could be borrowed from sink or copper, but emptying might be by hand. A wooden board covered the bath when not in use and all other operations had to be suspended when it was. Some households found this so inconvenient that they took steps to have the bath removed (Mass Observation, 1943). The Tudor Walters Report thought an upstairs bathroom desirable, and a minority of its house plans show one. But to achieve economy in floor plan and plumbing, the bath would normally remain downstairs, either in a small room of its own or in the scullery, although the authors knew this to be unpopular. The arrangement of an 'old-fashioned type of bath standing like a chained animal in a bleak space off the scullery, without hot water', lasted well into the postwar era (Cleeve Barr, 1958, p. 56). It incidentally threw some light on the notorious 'coals in the bath' controversy – the allegation that baths were wasted on council tenants, who only used them for keeping coal; for, as the *Daily Mail* asked, 'Can one wonder that baths have been so used if the bathroom is near the back door, and there is no adequate supply of hot water?' (Pleydell-Bouverie, n.d., p. 60).

It was not until the 1923 Housing Act that a fixed bath became mandatory in subsidized dwellings, and the Housing Act of the following year stipulated that this must be in a bathroom. This requirement was later extended to subsidized houses built for sale, and from 1936 to all new dwellings, public or private. The bathroom did not necessarily contain a wash hand basin, a fitting that did not come into general use until after 1945 (Cleeve Barr, 1959). The Tudor Walters Report had agreed that housewives wanted a basin with hot and cold running water, and had even shown this in one of its plans, but in practice it was often dispensed with. In some of the more innovative interwar council flats, a basin was fitted over one end of the bath, whose taps and waste it shared.

There are still more baths than wash hand

The bathtub stored in a London backyard. This was a normal arrangement for many families until they moved in the course of slum clearance. (*Source*: Town and Country Planning Association)

basins in 1960 (Gray and Russell, 1962). In any case it was general practice, not confined only to the poor, to wash at the kitchen sink, especially among children and men coming in from work. 'People said it was a habit carried over from when they did not have a bathroom; the kitchen was warmer or more convenient [or] used when the bathroom was occupied and the basin in the bathroom was too small for a really good wash without splashing and making a mess' (Hole and Attenburrow, 1966, p. 31). The wish to keep the bathroom looking nice

KITCHEN FITTINGS OF A TYPICAL L.C.C. COTTAGE.

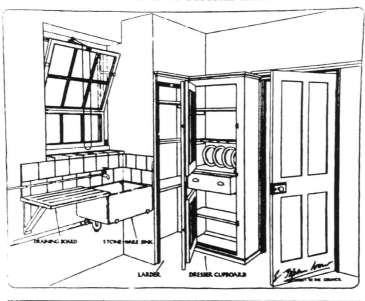

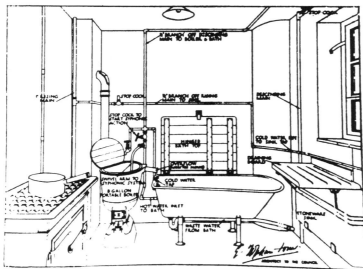

Kitchen, scullery and bath fittings of the 1920s on the LCC Becontree estate. (Young, 1934)

must often have taken precedence over convenience, for even in flats, where all rooms were on a level, the kitchen sink was still preferred.

It was the new, interwar semi which established the typical twentieth-century bathroom. The room itself was normally at the back of the house above the kitchen, adjacent to a separate WC compartment and often containing a heated towel rail and airing cupboard. The bath, with both hot and cold taps, was of enamelled cast iron, which after long use became stained and rusty. Before the period of relatively cheap plastic replacements, many people undertook the messy and chancy task of stripping and re-enamelling it. This type of bathroom was adopted without question in postwar council housing, although the Dudley Report had not quite abandoned the possibility of placing it on the ground floor. During the 1950s, the insertion of bathrooms into pre-1914 houses was done at the expense of another room, often a scullery or third bedroom. This wave of improvement did not benefit people in privately rented, and particularly subdivided, housing, the great majority of whom shared or had no access to a bath (Gray and Russell, 1962). It was only over the next decade that this proportion was reduced to less than ten per cent, and by the

early 1970s the subject had lost its interest for official statisticians, except when from time to time they examined differences of age, income, region, race or tenure.

The shower was now counted as an adequate substitute for the bath, although it had customarily been regarded as un-English – largely, one suspects, because of 'our chilly bathrooms' (WACSF, 1951, p. 25). Showers became increasingly common from this time, and were later of particular importance for certain ethnic minorities, for whom the custom of washing in standing water was abhorrent. Other bathroom developments were the use of plastic for baths, coloured bathroom suites, which increasingly included bidets, and the provision of window-less, interior bathrooms in flats and houses

The bathroom in transition. The bath has been panelled in, but the washbasin has a plastic curtain for a 'skirt', the WC has a high cistern and the hot water comes from a geyser. (*Source*: News of the World, *c.* 1950)

with a narrow-fronted, deep plan. Colours and varieties of style of bathroom fittings proliferated; for, as it was already pointed out in the 1960s, any bathroom more than twenty years old needed renewing and could become a showpiece as important for the value of the house as the lounge (*Household Beautiful*, 1961).

The bath and bathroom were not necessarily connected to hot water systems, which were slow to spread. Even after being moved upstairs, the bath might draw its hot water from the scullery. In council houses on the Dagenham estate, hot water was still raised by pump from the copper in 1959, an arrangement shown to a visiting American who 'flatly refused to believe that such a system existed in the Age of the H-bomb' (Dagenham Digest, 1959, p. 13). In 1939, about three quarters of poorer families lacked a hot water system, as well as some of the lower middle classes (PEP, 1945). The commonest method for heating water at this time was the back boiler, but more than a quarter of the PEP sample heated water in pans and kettles on open fires or gas cookers, a method still normal in the 1970s (Oakley, 1974*a*). This was an obstacle to bathing, for as PEP remarked, it was the difficulty of heating water, rather than the cost, that deterred people from taking baths more frequently (*Ibid*, 1945).

Over the middle decades of the century hot water systems were as diverse as space heating and cooking appliances. Independent coal-fired boilers were common in semis, especially those with a living kitchen or morning room in which they could be placed. The geysir or instantaneous water heater, invented in the previous century, was improved in the 1920s, and the Ascot variety spread rapidly in the 1930s, especially in new council flats. The electric immersion heater, invented in 1895, was used in only a small minority of homes in 1914; but once wiring permitted it became all but universal, because it was so cheap and easy

to install, and it greatly facilitated the insertion of bathrooms in older houses.

Households lacking hot water taps were still noted in the 1961 Census, when over a fifth were in this category. This figure halved in the next five years and continued to fall rapidly until, in 1974, *Social Trends* no longer thought it worthy of note. But until central heating removed all the stress of ensuring that there would be enough hot water for a bath, families had a regular bath night – usually Fridays – when they bathed in relays, often reusing or topping up one another's water. Whatever the heat source, the organization of this took some prior planning, and often hard physical labour, on the part of the housewife.

The history of bathrooms seems to contain a concealed history of popular attitudes towards bathing. At the Letchworth Cheap Cottages Exhibition of 1905 it was reported that working-class children, unlike their parents, were 'gradually becoming inured' to bathing (Gaskell, 1987, p. 74). But only five years later in Salford the proud tenant of a house with newly installed bath gave his neighbours a guided tour, pointing out the hot and cold taps, the purpose of plug, chain and overflow pipe: 'till then, some of them had never seen a bath, much less used one' (Roberts, 1971, p. 34). Countless anecdotes of families moving from the 1920s onwards confirm that they revelled in simply being able to turn a tap and soak. 'Mothers said their children were "bath daft". They'd be in there every night if you'd let them' (Hole and Attenburrow, 1966, p. 30). Thus over many decades, the humping of buckets of water and the emptying of the zinc tub became relegated to history. For children and parents, the pleasant ritual of 'bath time' with celluloid ducks took its place.

SANITATION

Sanitation did not depend on a water supply, for waste could be disposed of in middens and cesspits. In early times sanitary operations were performed outside the home, and the main domestic device was the chamber pot, normally sold in pairs or as part of a toilet set with basin, ewer and soap dish. The 'chamber' survived the second World War in boarding houses and institutions, and most notable of all in prisons, where the daily 'slopping out' of cells continued into the 1990s. *Our Towns* saw it in general family use in poor districts, and defended it as 'a highly functional piece of domestic equipment' provided it was regularly cleaned (*Our Towns*, 1944, p. 89). It was in its unclean state that it became offensive (Orwell, 1937). After the introduction of the internal WC, the use of the chamber pot survived only among small children, the aged and infirm. Many decorative examples ended their lives as antiques, fetching prices that doubtless would have amazed their original owners.

Our Towns was bold enough to discuss the sanitary habits of the urban poor which came to light in evacuation, when they were billeted on the hygienic and comfortable classes. In addition to males' urinating contests and use of public places as latrines, 'in true eighteenth-century style' (*Ibid*, 1943, p. 89), the report referred to the custom of wrapping solid waste in newspaper and burning it, which they credited as a rational response to bad housing conditions. The same strategy was used by convicts locked up in their cells for long hours, and it reappeared late in the century among residents of tower blocks whose water supply was cut off: only in these two cases the packages could not be burned and were simply thrown to the ground.

The first stage in the domestic privy was the earth closet: a sometimes unsavoury but peaceful shed 'down the garden path'. This survived in rural areas where, according to *Our Towns*, urban evacuees felt afraid to use it. A hygienic earth closet for inside use had been invented by Henry Moule in the mid nineteenth century, but it was adopted in hospitals rather than homes, and it was another century before the idea of covering waste matter with specially treated earth was revived, in the composting toilet.

A variety of appliances were found in back-yard privies, including simple pails that were covered and replaced when full, privies that drained into ashpits, and numerous forms of water closet, including some that were flushed with waste sink water. The modern type of 'wash down' closet with a water seal was not in general use until the last quarter of the nineteenth century. Placed in the usual privy compartment, it retained associations of un-savouriness and potential health risk. There was a clear difference, therefore, between houses with WCs in back yards and better class housing which had accommodated them in the interior for some time past.

By 1914, WCs were in the majority in 80 out of 95 of the largest English towns, and the rest had programmes of conversion in hand (Daunton, 1983). Different councils followed different policies and some northern and north eastern towns were notorious for clinging on to earlier systems. Oldham, in 1946, still had over 800 pail closets and nearly 24,000 waste water closets, forming over 60 per cent of its total (Nuffield Foundation, 1947). In 1962, in its St Mary's ward, only one house out of 132 had its own inside WC, and less than a fifth had their own outside closet; nearly half shared an outdoor closet in a common yard (MHLG, 1970*a*).

From 1919 all new council dwellings had their own private WC, but at the time of Tudor Walters, when common experience was of an outside privy, there was some doubt as to where it should be placed. In the words of the Report, it was 'easier to say where this convenience should not be placed than to find in a small cottage an entirely suitable position' (Tudor Walters, 1918, para. 126). In the end, the Report plumped for a covered lobby or small back projection off the scullery, rather than the upstairs (or half landing) position of better terraced houses, although this was the location 'generally desired by the artisan town dweller' (*Ibid*, 1918, para. 126). The unfamiliarity of early council tenants with their first flush toilets is reflected in their managers' warning to 'treat the flushing system carefully. Pulling the chain with a jerk damages it' (Dagenham Borough Council, 1956, p. xx).

Again, it was the interwar semi that set the definitive standard by invariably placing the WC on the bedroom floor, usually in its own compartment. The appliance itself might now have a low level cistern worked by a lever, but the old design, where water crashed from an overhead cistern down an awesome length of pipe, was still common. This could take long familiarity and much skill to 'pull the chain' effectively, to the frequent bafflement of foreigners.

After 1945, the public sector improved on this standard. Taking the upstairs toilet, now, for granted, the Dudley Report suggested that households with more than four people should have an additional downstairs WC with wash hand basin. After the Parker Morris Report this was, for a time, standard provision for any size of household. With such a 'cloakroom', it was felt permissible to locate the upstairs WC in the bathroom; but without it, the upstairs WC was expected to have its own compartment. Meanwhile the downstairs cloakroom became popular with owner occupiers, including those in pre-1914 houses where, with the aid of a ventilation fan, it could usually be inserted under the stairs.

There was no further technical innovation to rank with that of the water-sealed closet itself. Technical performance was improved by the siphonic pedestal, but many other changes were stylistic, involving 'close-coupled' seats and cisterns, and innumerable changes of shape and colour. In 1993, under a new European regulation, there was a reduction of 17 per cent in cistern capacity; but water recycling or the use of 'grey' (once used) water for flushing, though long talked of, was as far as ever from normal practice at this time.

The points at which households were able to gain the benefits of developments in sanitation depended on their housing history, with occasional small margins for personal choice. Among the elderly, old habits sometimes died hard, and it was known for them to prefer to use an outside toilet, considering it more 'decent', even when an inside one was available. People in general tended to dislike the placing of the WC in the bathroom (Mass Observation, 1943), or the location of downstairs WCs too close to front doors or kitchens, which they found embarrassing. Overall, the diffusion of the WC was slow and patchy: the decade of most progress was 1951–61, when the number of households sharing a closet was more than halved; but many people had no chance to experience up-to-date sanitation until well after the middle of the century. In 1971, over 10 per cent of all households still had to use an outside WC and it was not until the 1980s that those lacking any access to a flush toilet fell to negligible proportions. As ever, people unable to keep homes of their own were the slowest to gain from rising standards. Thus shared sanitation remained the rule in hostels and multiply occupied houses, while many old people living in Homes were, as we have seen, still waiting for seats, doors and privacy in the toilet in the 1960s (Townsend, 1962).

THE CHANGING TECHNOLOGY OF THE HOME: 'WHITE GOODS'

In the last quarter of the century, the electric home was well on the way to becoming the automated and eventually the electronic home. Its development was in the first place through the larger household appliances, the 'white goods'. After the cooker, the most important of these were the vacuum cleaner, refrigerator, and washing machine, all of which had pre-industrial origins and had been powered by hand or gas before 1914. Their main diffusion began in interwar semis, but their universal application was after the Second World War. Previous to this, their expansion was limited by a variety of factors. The electric vacuum cleaner, for instance, was limited by the electrical supply and restrictions of wiring, as well as the numbers of homes without carpets or for whom manual carpet sweepers were sufficient (PEP, 1945). These considerations changed after 1945, when the possession of an electric vacuum cleaner became so taken for granted

that it was not normally noted in official statistics. Similarly the refrigerator, limited to a minority of the middle classes before 1939, reached 90 per cent of households in the later 1970s, and the peak ownership of the electric washing machine, at somewhat less than 90 per cent, occurred ten years later (Social Trends, 1993).

A second wave of white goods included the deep freeze, the tumble drier and the dishwasher, which never reached so many households. In the 1980s, ownership of the deep freeze rose from 49 to 79 per cent, of the tumble drier from 23 to 45 per cent, and of the

The post-war prefab with its steel, back-to-back bathroom-kitchen core anticipated the range of fitted-in white goods to come. (*Source*: Avoncroft Museum of Buildings)

dishwasher from four to twelve per cent (GHS, 1989). There were in addition a multitude of smaller appliances, including the microwave oven whose rise to 47 per cent by the end of the 1980s was thought important enough to include in official statistics. These small kitchen appliances joined electric kettles, toasters and food mixers, all of which had long histories but were now going through a seemingly neverending process of technical and stylistic change.

The significance of this history of appliances for the home, housework and domestic life was not entirely straightforward. The large appliances obviously took up space, although they could also make less demands on space or change the location of activities, as in the case of washing and drying machines. They changed patterns of electricity, and sometimes gas, consumption. They transformed the nature of many household tasks, notably food preparation, which had far-reaching consequences for the pattern of meals. The wider implications for housework and housewives were, as we shall see in Chapter 10, below, a subject of debate; but it is indisputable that they eliminated most of the drudgery and dirt of cleaning, already much reduced by the substitution of coal by gas and electricity. One consequence was an altered status for the rear quarters of the house, which no longer needed to be associated with demeaning work. The incorporation of timing devices in cookers, automatic defrosting of refrigerators and 'programmes' of washing and drying machines were early steps towards 'interactivity' which would enable housework to be done with little human intervention.

TELECOMMUNICATIONS AND THE AUTOMATED HOME

The essential step in the creation of the automated home was the exploitation of the potential of the 'brown goods' (more often in fact black goods) of home entertainment: the radio and television set, and additionally the telephone. Broadcasting entered the home in 1922, through the battery radio, and around 90 per cent of households had a 'wireless' by 1939. After an initial stage of earphones, the loudspeaker set seems briefly to have been used as an occasion to invite friends and neighbours round, before it developed into a private family recreation. In the war years, it played a crucial role in drawing family members together and making them feel at one with the nation. The postwar development of small, cheap, transistor radios, headphones and cassettes helped to individualize the use of the radio. Families were no longer tied to one immobile set in the living room and headphones enabled teenagers, in particular, to remove themselves metaphorically if not literally from their family circles. A further stage followed after the heavy radiogram was replaced, first by a more flexible record player, and then by the music centre, where radio, compact disc player, recording and synthesizing facilities were combined.

Television broadcasting began in 1937 but it had reached only some thousands of London households when it was suspended for the duration of war. Once service was resumed, and especially for the 1953 coronation, rental or purchase of sets spread rapidly, to reach more than 90 per cent of homes within twenty years. Again, while it was a novelty, neighbours might be invited round to watch special events like royal weddings, but it soon developed into the main private domestic pastime, displacing the weekly or twice-weekly visits to the cinema during the 1950s, a generation before the video recorder brought cinema films into the home. The TV set became the focal point of the home's main living room, usefully filling the void of the absent hearth. At first, viewing was treated with formality, prompting dimmed lights, special chairs and tables, TV meals and TV crockery.

Colour TV, introduced in the late 1960s,

rapidly overtook black and white, and half the sets in use received colour by 1978. Reception was now greatly improved by higher definition and larger, flatter screens, giving a more realistic image. The ousted black and white sets were used in other parts of the house, and secondary sets were also bought for bedrooms, playrooms and kitchens, so that by the mid 1980s over half of all households had more than one set. Multiple ownership was stimulated by portable sets, and later the video recorder and computer games, which were sweeping the country by the early 1980s. Video ownership doubled within five years, applying to 60 per cent of homes by the end of the 1980s. These technical developments seemed indefinably to alter people's relationship with TV, perhaps by giving them more feeling of control. The infra-red remote control switch, which enabled 'grazing' (flicking from channel to channel without even rising from the chair) seemed to contribute to this. Video recorders could now be programmed to record a fortnight or more in advance, so that nothing need ever be missed and favourite items could be stored indefinitely. Subscription to satellite TV (which required a 'dish' to be attached to the outside of the house) brought a 24-hour menu of dozens of films, in addition to the four channels available to ordinary license holders. More and more, entertainment became one of the functions, perhaps the most important function, of the home.

In its earlier years of usage, the telephone seemed somewhat dissociated from the rest of the home, a mere substitute for the written word. Its very location was problematic, and it was most often relegated to the unheated hall: 'a draughty, awkward cranny in a passage where there's no space for a chair and every opportunity for everyone in the household to overhear one-sided conversations' (Drew, 1960, p. 59). The bulky telephone directories also posed a problem, which designers tried to cater for by the new telephone table, which combined shelf, stool and table top. Up to 1939, sub-scribers were confined mostly to a small minority of the middle classes, and telephones were found only in 12 per cent of homes by 1951. 'Being on the phone' was, however, beginning to be indispensable to those who ran businesses from home, and as an instrument for maintaining relationships within extended families scattered by rehousing. Indeed, it was now taking the place of 'chatting over the garden fence or at the back door' (Chapman, 1955, p. 70). By 1974 about half of all households were con-nected, and something approaching 90 per cent by 1989.

Domestic installations seemed to change very little until the 1980s, when plug-in sockets and telephone extensions became available at little or no extra running cost. Keypad and cordless receivers, receivers with 'memories', answering machines and fax machines (most of which could easily be installed by subscribers themselves) qualitatively enlarged the use of the telephone. Messages from answering ma-chines, for instance, could be picked up and answered from external numbers, and calls could be re-routed. In-house extensions allowed three-way conversations with outside callers; cordless phones allowed communication be-tween house and garden, or from vehicles outside the house. Receivers could show visual displays or amplify sound, with benefits for people with sight or hearing defects. In combina-tion with the TV and an adapter, subscriber programmes available from the 1970s offered consumer information and services, including 'teleshopping' from catalogues of goods.

The full potential of the telephone is held back, at the time of writing, by broadcasting restrictions and slow progress in cabling. This would be realized with the ISDN or Integrated Services Digital Network system in which copper wire would be replaced by glass fibres able to carry what for practical purposes were infinite amounts of two-way information (including visual images) at instantaneous speeds. Combining the use of telephone, TV and computer on one cable promised to offer the home user a choice of hundreds of films and videos, which could be called up, stored, halted or re-run at any time – viewers could split the screen, even print themselves onto it if they wished. All the libraries of the world could be accessed; newspapers could be 'personalized' to select only chosen themes and items. Health could be monitored and diagnoses given. Viewers could be kept informed of all welfare changes and entitlements. The ultimate experience of entertainment would be the 'virtual reality' of a computer-generated world, which would be entered by donning a sensory helmet, so offering total escape from the here-and-now.

Progress with cabling was left to follow market demand. The GLC had begun to cable London as part of its New Technology and Training iniatives prior to its abolition in 1986. After this, licenses were granted by a Cable Authority and cabling was actively under way, at any rate in larger cities, by the mid-1990s. The most critical part would be the linkage of individual homes to the trunk lines. Only around 600,000 were linked by 1994, but it was predicted that two thirds would be, by the end of the century.

Within the home, like other European countries, Britain was concentrating on making appliances and programmes inter-connectable, in 'Interactive Home Systems' projects of the 1980s. There was nothing to parallel the American legislation encouraging, among other things, the integrated 'smart house' project of 1984, where companies and service suppliers combined to produce a house where telecommunications and all appliances were run from a single cable, adding little to the initial construction costs. The 'smart' or fully interactive house would allow unlimited communication between people within and outside the home. Its white and brown goods, endowed with memories and programmes, and its self-reading meters, would be able to respond to any changes in external conditions – in weather, pollution levels, tarriffs, callers or intruders – to intercommunicate and adjust their own operations accordingly. The house would be able to service itself, monitoring and reordering supplies as these ran down, and carrying out its own programmes of maintenance and housework (Miles, 1988).

THE ENERGY-CONSCIOUS HOME AND THE SELF-SUFFICIENT HOME

The alternative direction for the home to take was that of self sufficiency or autonomy. This was gently mocked in the long-standing and popular TV 'sitcom', *The Good Life*, of the 1970s and 1980s, which showed a couple having picturesque adventures with food production and livestock in their conventional suburban home. The less dramatic realities of self sufficiency were to be found in practical attempts to free the home from fossil fuels and mains systems, in the interests of energy saving and technical sustainability. Such a home could also make active use of computers, but this was now for the purpose of entering into a closer rather than more detached relationship with the environment (Vale, 1975).

Compared to the commercial progress made towards the electronic home by the 1990s, the energy-conscious and self-sufficient home was still, for the public at large, a non-starter at this time. It had very limited government input, and only small and scattered commercial support. Other than individual, one-off houses, examples of development were few. They included the Homeworld demonstration houses at Milton Keynes Energy Park of 1986, and the Bournville Solar Village planned for around 300 houses in 1985. More generally, various local authorities were running controlled experiments with highly insulated and energy-saving houses at this time.

Early experiments had to be one-offs and the results looked not too unfamiliar. Milton Keynes low-energy house, 1981 Exhibition.

The aims of the domestic energy conscious-ness and self sufficiency must be viewed as operating along a continuum. At the simplest level, they aimed at economy of resources, using building design as well as insulation to achieve this. The next level was to replace non-renewable with renewable resources, the most obvious application being wood burning stoves rather than heating by gas or electricity derived from fossil fuels, or in the case of the latter, from nuclear power. Above this level, innov-ative technologies might be used, either to achieve household self-sufficiency, or in pursuit of wider social aims, including 'a stable, de-centralized society where each person is directly responsible for most of his survival' (*Ibid*, 1975, p. 16). In such a case, domestic gardens would be important for producing food.

By the last quarter of the century a variety of innovative techniques and appliances were available, some of them dating from the 1950s or earlier, and some commercially marketed. They were mixed in a variety of ways and no standardized system or package for a single

house had evolved. Most low energy houses used a combination of highly efficient wood-burning stoves, high insulation and some application of solar energy. At its simplest the latter involved a conservatory or glass wall with ventilators and shutters to control heat flow. More complex solar technologies were solar collectors mounted on roofs or walls, from which energy was collected and stored, and the Trombe wall which received sunlight and acted as a heat store inside the house. Other heating devices, making use of the laws of physics and chemistry, were heat pumps, described as refrigerators in reverse (and taxed as such when they first appeared in the 1950s), fuel cells, which converted the chemical energy of hydrogen and oxygen into electrical energy, and the solar cell, a small disc where sunlight produced direct current.

Some of these devices had been developed for space flight, but as far as normal domestic use was concerned, they had not passed from the stage of innovation into general diffusion. The cost and availability of suitable materials presented obstacles, as did the changes that would need to take place in dwellings to allow for heat stores, batteries and converters. Similar objections applied to domestic wind generators. Besides needing current converters and storage batteries, the tower with its generator needed to be set apart from the house and to be at least thirty feet taller than any structure within a hundred yards. Independently of any new technologies adopted, the most important energy-saving factors of all were the location and orientation of dwellings. To maximize natural resources, each individual site needed to be carefully chosen, while at the same time some of the devices chosen might require a lot of space. This was hardly compatible with the usual constraints of the land market and housing development.

At this stage of the various technologies, it was difficult to find a conservation justification for the high energy and capital costs some of their installations entailed, which might take many years to recover through reduced consumption. Another requirement, if they were ever put into general operation, was change in user behaviour, which would involve modifying habits and attitudes built up throughout the long evolution of the modern home. A Trombe wall, for example, required acceptance that a furniture-free and possibly windowless zone would be found in what was normally the best room, with the best outlook, of the house.

This was nowhere more clear than in energy-saving toilets designed to cut out the waste of centralized sewage systems and, in particular, the use of purified water for flushing. Some of the new types depended on electricity or chemicals to burn waste matter, but composting toilets relied on the heat of decomposition to convert it into a safe product. The Clivus Multrum, imported from Sweden in 1974, had a peat-lined collection chamber, which also received kitchen waste, and was activated each time the toilet seat was raised. After two years or more, the contents reached a storage bin

from which they were removed as dry, sweet, garden humus. The appliance was, in practice, used in institutions rather than ordinary homes; but if this or similar sanitary systems came into domestic use they would require a complete reform of attitudes to human waste as something 'dirty', to be expelled as soon as possible.

The purpose of an energy-conscious home, then, would be, not maximum independence from and mastery over the environment by means of high technology, but a closer personal and domestic relationship with the natural forces in the environment. Efficient use of solar heating systems, for instance, depended on observation and prediction of weather at the start and end of the day. Wood burning stoves and composting toilets required understanding of where resources came from and went to. Craft skills and, above all, respect for working with material things were required. The object was, not a home that managed itself without human intervention, but intelligent human intervention at the interface of home and environment.

DOMESTIC TECHNOLOGIES AT THE END OF THE CENTURY

The changing technologies of the home had always been driven by a number of competing industries and services. Greater efficiency was ever the overt goal, but rational use of energy and resources, and in particular their co-ordinated planning, was not a primary objective. Nor was social equity, although mains services and most machinery did ultimately reach all classes. For most, this placed the technical gains of the second half of the century beyond dispute: gains of warmth, comfort, hygiene, and the mechanization of domestic work. Those with less money to spend, including many of the largest families and the elderly, enjoyed the gains in smaller measure. In particular, their housing circumstances might debar them from the most economical use of services and efficient appliances.

At the time of writing, it is apparent that the working out of the two latest trends, of electronic and energy-conscious domestic technologies, would belong to the twenty-first rather than the twentieth century. By now, the great majority of English homes have the basic components of full automation, but as yet they are uncoordinated. The consumer response to the potentially momentous changes these could bring about has been understandably opportunistic. As with radio and TV at earlier dates, the main motivation for the acquisition of the latest and most sophisticated electronic goods has been home entertainment – in larger quantity, superior quality, more programmable, and above all serving the interests of children. Children's games, and to a lesser extent their education, were the main reason for a short boom in home computer growth in the early 1980s. This was not sustained, and many computer businesses went into liquidation after this time, but the computer game is nevertheless established as a virtually universal child minder and pacifier in the 1990s.

The second most important reason for home electronics was security, and the steep increase in burglaries in the later 1980s prompted an immense growth in intruder lights and alarms in middle-class housing (although in fact the incidence of break-ins was highest in tenanted housing, particularly council flats) (GHS, 1993). Electronic keys and personal recognition systems have an as yet unexploited potential to make the home 'more of a fortress . . . the doors and windows may acquire characteristics of hi-tech drawbridges and portcullises' (Miles, 1988, p. 111).

Three things are needed for people to take to the domestic use of electronics with enthusiasm: knowledge and money (which often in fact go together), and motivation. Learning an unfamiliar technology, its new terms made into a mystique by salesmen; the over-abundance of different machines and softwares, many of them not mutually compatible; rapid obsolescence and difficulties of getting machines serviced: all these things act as brakes on diffusion. People are concerned not only about the initial purchase price, but about what further expenses they might be drawn into. Lastly, a place in the home has to be found for the new machines, and this is not always easy. By 1989, only

The first family in Leeds to be connected to cable can look forward to a life of fibre-optic entertainment with more than 35 channels to watch. (*Source*: *Evening Post*, June 1994)

nineteen per cent of English households owned a home computer, and it was thought this often sat unused. Only a small minority of enthusiasts programmed their machines to do household accounts and other tasks. The main users of computers in the home were those who ran home-based businesses or consultancies, for whom 'teleconferencing', the ability to produce high-quality documents, and to receive or send fax and electronic mail became more and more essential. This 'telecottaging' or 'home commuting' was predicted to rise as the economy changed (Handy, 1984). 'Networking' from home would replace hierarchical organizations rooted in specific locations, making the home into the promised 'stop on the global, digital highway'.

In this way the new domestic technology would serve a new information élite – and members of such an élite might also be sufficiently knowledgeable to exploit energy conservation and self sufficiency. As always, when technology was applied to the home, automation was not driven by social equity, but left to follow market demand. Where it was potentially most useful, it would not necessarily be applied. Thus while it could enable people to overcome visual, aural or other physical handicaps, it was not specifically directed towards this. The history of the telephone already provided an example of the inequity of technological change. In 1977, nearly three-quarters of old people's and low-income households were still not on the phone (Toland, 1980). But by this time domestic phone usage of the majority meant that more services, including booking medical appointments and obtaining essential information of many kinds, were effectively only possible by phone. Public payphones became increasingly rare and vandal-

ized, and the emergency telegram service was ended altogether. If this could be the impact so early in time of a single appliance, it seemed even more likely that sophisticated 'Home Informatics' would fail to meet, and in fact exacerbate 'the very real needs of the impoverished elderly and homeless' (Miles, 1988, p. 363).

Thus while liberating its occupants for more 'interactivity' and personal choice, the main thrust of domestic technological development is socially exclusive. Its enormous potential for change is largely undirected, and in a sense a virtue is made of this. 'There are the applications [of digital systems] which haven't been invented yet simply because no one has yet got their brains around to thinking of the products to fill the gigantic capacity that may eventually be in your living room' (Keegan, 1994, p. 2). Among the applications that were sometimes suggested were robotic servants, therapists, comforters, even pets (Miles, 1988); but perhaps more importantly they were expected to include the delivery of medical and other vital services. The fully automated home offers the potential of almost unlimited personal autonomy and privacy: it is the ultimate development of the 'domestic encapsulation' begun two centuries ago, but its unprecedented levels of comfort can now be achieved without even the intervention of servants. Should the systems on which this encapsulation depends break down, however, the inmates would be pitched back into candle and bucket days for which nothing in their previous experience (unless, perhaps, holidays under canvas) has prepared them. As with all technologies, a more sophisticated system is vulnerable to breakdowns in the wider technical or social systems that support it.

8

ROOMS

THE EVOLUTION OF THE HOUSE INTERIOR: CULTURAL CODES

The starting point of the twentieth-century interior was the byelaw, terraced house, with its strong distinctions of front:back, and upstairs:downstairs, and its functional division into rooms. The interior was not designed to accommodate primary production (although home-based and backyard industries most probably lasted longer and on a larger scale than is normally allowed, until they were scoured out by slum clearance). Nor was it designed to accommodate religious observances – the only vestige of this once important function of the home was in the parlour, with its hearth, family photographs and family Bible. The internal divisions of the house, nevertheless, constituted codes of use that were broken only under some strong imperative. This might, for instance, be the infirmity of the aged who had to bring their beds downstairs – something they would resist as long as possible; or it might be the intrusion of other cultures with different and overriding domestic codes. Thus Muslim households needed separate accommodation for men and women; many cultures separated inmates and strangers; and many brought the sacred back into the home, needing shrines, special places for prayer, ritual washing and perhaps religious gatherings (NFHA, 1993).

To breach the codes of room use was a serious thing. When it was enforced by poverty and shared housing, the fact that rooms were forced out of their 'proper' use was a significant part of the problem. When a new type of dwelling contradicted the code, it operated under a special handicap. This explains the inherent difficulty of flats, which could not have 'fronts' and 'backs' in the usual way. Private house developers took care to conform to the codes, which they not only enhanced but exploited; but the designers of council housing were in a different position, both because their tenants were captive and because they were social reformers as well as designers. In the interests of maximum cost effectiveness, rationality, or enabling people to have better lives, therefore, they could feel entitled to produce unconventional, 'upside down' or 'back to front' dwellings, and above all the inherently risky family flat.

Users also played a vital role in the history of rooms. For the most part they confirmed and enhanced the expected use of rooms through furnishings (draperies and ornaments as well as items of furniture). They changed and updated them by painting, wallpapering and small 'DIY' modifications, or more occasionally through structural alterations.

It is far from clear what, other than site and technical factors, was responsible for the internal arrangement of the pre-1914 terraced house. When the German visitor, Herman Muthesius, scrutinized it in the early 1900s, he concluded that its plan was 'almost exclusively in the hands of the developer. This explains why the stereotype prevails and why the ground-plans show very little variety and, in general, little intelligence' (Muthesius, 1979, p. 148). It was precisely this stereotyped and unintelligent design that Arts and Crafts and garden city architects tried to address. Their most significant contribution was the abolition of the back extension, which made it possible for the narrow, paved and walled backyard to develop into the back garden (Chapter 9, below). It also had far reaching effects on the house interior, by bringing the scullery and also the third bedroom (if any) under the main roof and resulting, ideally, in a wider-fronted house plan.

This reformed internal arrangement seems to have sprung principally from architectural theory, most particularly Raymond Unwin's ideas about the ideal domestic arrangements for working people (Unwin, 1902). There was one special effort to consult public, or rather women's, opinion, when Christopher Addison, the Minister for Reconstruction, briefed a Women's Housing Sub-committee in 1917 to advise on official house plans 'with special reference to the convenience of the housewife' (Ministry of Reconstruction. 1918a, para. 1). The plans were those recently used by the Ministry of Munitions or put forward for future municipal housing by the Local Government Board, and the housewife in question was to be a working-class woman.

The members of the Sub-committee were professional, public service or upper-class women, who, elated by their success in getting votes for women, set about their task with great energy, canvassing the opinions of thousands of working-class women. However, their draft report gave so much offence at the Local Government Board, whose house plans they criticized, that it was nearly suppressed, and in the end was published in a modified form (Ministry of Reconstruction, 1918a,

1918b). The Board had strongly questioned the women's ability, let alone right, to read its plans, and ridiculed their suggestions as utopian, so that these had little or no immediate effect on council house design. They were, in fact, in fairly close agreement with what was about to become the standard suburban home: larger, wider fronted, with a kitchen-scullery and two other rooms on the ground floor, and fitted with electric light, hot and cold running water, and (although this only came much later) some form of central heating. The Sub-committee also elaborated on many practical details of fittings and finishes, such as a double draining board at the sink, and a well for the front door mat (Ravetz, 1989).

Although this initiative was largely abortive, the government continued to be committed to involving women in housing design and encouraged local authorities to co-opt women onto their housing committees. When the Dudley Committee was set up in 1942, it had a substantial amount of research into women's preferences to draw on and consulted many women's organizations, including the Society of Women Housing Managers. Over a third of the Committee's members were women, including the secretary, an eminent woman architect. The bias of its report, however, was similar to that of the Tudor Walters Committee, in that its concern was with what it saw as the housewife's convenience, rather than jointly designing with her (*Ibid*, 1989; Matrix, 1984).

After this time, the conditions in which professionals and others felt it necessary to dialogue with people about their homes no longer obtained. Private developers habitually claimed to respond to customer demands, but they did not publish any surveys, and seemed mainly to draw their conclusions from sales figures, which could of course reflect many other things besides people's satisfaction with house interiors. In contrast, public sector housing was copiously researched, not only by central government's Housing Development Directorate and Building Research Station, but by many of the larger local authority housing departments (although these did not normally publish their findings). Government studies were impeccably carried out, but they too ignored the non-design variables that might influence people's attitudes, and their aim was to record rather than canvass opinion. Thus while they examined people's behaviour and feelings with almost clinical correctness, there was no suggestion of drawing them into any stage of the design process. This changed only in a small number of instances in the 1980s, as we shall see below.

SPACE IN THE HOME

It is a truism that more money buys more space. But over a century or more from the 1870s, the space that middle-class money could buy diminished, perhaps by around 45 per cent (Hole and Attenburrow, 1966), while for many others, particularly those housed by local authorities, there was an overall gain of space. A new optimum was set for council housing after each World War: for a three-bedroom house, this was 800 ft^2 in 1919, and 900 ft^2 in 1945. In practice, these standards were often exceeded: 'parlour' houses of the 1920s and houses of the 1940s, for instance, had areas of over 1000 ft^2. But after each of these leaps forward, space standards fell back. At their lowest, under the 1923 Housing Act, they reached around 600 ft^2. In 1961, the Parker Morris Report recommended areas of 960 ft^2, a standard that was met in public housing until the early 1980s, when councils were obliged by government to build to the lower space standards of private developers.

Middle-class and working-class standards, therefore, converged. Houses with more and larger rooms were of course always provided for those with money to pay, but, taking like for like, council houses were 'considerably larger than most speculative semi-detacheds' (Burnett, 1986, p. 227). In addition to its overall dimensions, the house after 1914 gained internal space from the reduction and eventual elimination of flues, and from a better internal layout – although this, it might be argued, was at the cost of some of the more interesting nooks and crannies of older houses. The council house gained space by severe reductions in the hall and circulation space. Typically, interwar examples had a front door that opened onto a tiny lobby, from which the stairs rose. Access to the back of the house, containing scullery and WC, was through the main living room.

Plans of the 1940s restored the hall to more generous proportions and its conventional function of providing access not only to the upstairs but to all ground floor rooms (although sometimes a working kitchen was accessed only through a dining room). Great importance was now attached to the hall having sufficient space for a pram. This was a fairly recent acquisition of poor working-class families, and as a postwar status symbol large sums were now spent on it. Twenty years further on, in the various house plans based on the Parker Morris Report, the entrance hall again shrank to a mere lobby, but open-tread stairs now rose from one of the living areas of the house. Although this now had central heating and was luxurious in comparison with earlier times, in its ground floor plan it was not unlike the humble terraced houses of the previous century.

The hall, as we have seen in Chapter 4, was functionally and symbolically important to servanted houses and 'respectable' homes before 1914. The private semi followed this tradition by fitting in a hall, however small, and emphasizing its meaning of panelling, newel posts, delft racks and coloured window glass (Barrett and Phillips, 1987). It was particularly appreciated that such halls eliminated the long unlit passages of the older terraced house (Mass Observation, 1943). The hall continued to be an important part of the house as long as the economics of development permitted, but in smaller and cheaper houses it became a mere lobby, as in public sector housing.

After the bay window, the front door was the most important indicator of a household's status. Much store was set on keeping the brass door furniture, and even the paint of the door itself, well polished. Hence the acquisition of a front door was in itself a social step, and the managers of early council estates felt bound to remind their tenants of the responsibilities entailed: 'Have you ever thought seriously about your front door and what it symbolises? . . . Make it the envy of your neighbours' (Dagenham Borough Council, 1949, p. 12). Dagenham tenants did, indeed, take their front doors so seriously that they raised strong objections to the shared porches of their houses, presumably designed in the tradition of the east London 'half house' (p. 41, above; Mass Observation, 1943).

The importance of the front door did not, however, mean that it had to be in regular use. Like the whole front of the house, it was for public and formal use, but the back door was for service and informal use, for neighbours and familiar friends of the family, who might be allowed to see the back quarters of the house with impunity. Codes of use, however, varied in different social classes and regions. In some circumstances the front door was never, in practice, opened, while in others it was a matter of fine social calculation which door a caller should go to.

As the century advanced, front doors retained their importance, even as the house changed internally. Proud home owners, and most particularly those council tenants who had bought their houses, went to much trouble to change doors and door furniture. Mock Georgian doors with integral 'fanlights' and flanked by brass 'coach lamps', were a particularly popular choice. Letter boxes in any case

The front door as a symbol of status. Leeds, 1995.

often needed changing, for those originally fitted were often too small to cope with later twentieth-century newspapers and bulky mail. The front door was another respect in which flat dwellers were disadvantaged, for the postman did not always deliver mail to their own doors, and any alternative arrangements had drawbacks. A sinister confirmation of the front door's social importance is found in a common and dangerous form of racial harassment where faeces or lighted rags are pushed through the letterboxes of targeted ethnic minority households.

The other great spatial change in the house plan after 1914 was the elimination of basement and attic levels which had previously been common. Basements had been used for coal cellarage and frequently housed a copper and sink, if not an entire kitchen. After 1919, houses were virtually never constructed with more than a ground and first floor, until the advent of new dwelling types in the 1960s. In this, English tradition is unlike that, say, of the United States, where basements remained a valued part of the twentieth-century home, used among other things for laundry and informal 'dens'. There is no clear evidence that people wished to dispense with attics or basements and some of the evidence collected by the Women's Sub-committee suggests that they regarded them as useful (RECO I. 1918). It is an interesting question, therefore, why they were abandoned. The answer as regards basements must lie in the practicalities of suburban development, where lower densities made the necessary excavation uneconomic. But additionally, their association with servants' working quarters, or with cellar dwellings in the slums, may have helped to rule them out. If, after 1919, a third or attic storey was provided (and it appeared in one of the Tudor Walters house plans), it was as a fully finished room rather than an attic. Many owners of private suburban housing later colonized their roof space by means of a 'loft conversion', reached by means of a retracting ladder. This was made possible by the high, pitched roofs of interwar houses, and the 'V-lux' skylight window, which was fairly cheap and easy to instal, helped to encourage the custom, which enabled expanding families to stay in homes which they would otherwise have outgrown.

THE SCULLERY AND KITCHEN

How functions were allocated to ground floor rooms depended on their number. The 'through' terraced house had, by definition, a front and a back room, each with a window. If it had a third room, this was placed in a back extension which covered less than the full width of the house, to ensure that the rear room could still receive natural light. Normally such an extension housed the scullery, but sometimes it also contained a third living room, usually described as a breakfast or morning room, and if the house had a resident servant this could be used as her sitting room. Morning rooms were on the whole more characteristic of earlier and larger semi-detached houses, where their windows could be placed on the side wall of the house.

Where there were only two ground floor rooms, there were two possible arrangements of use: a kitchen-living room in the front and scullery at the back; or a front 'parlour' with a combined kitchen-living room-scullery at the rear. Where there were three rooms, the standard arrangement would be front parlour, rear kitchen-living room, and scullery in the back extension. Thus a minimum of four, and perhaps five, functions were to be accommodated in two or three rooms: wet work, cooking, daily living, meals, and the more formal function or functions assigned to the front parlour. This in itself was a confusing situation, but it was compounded by the shedding of servants in some families, the acquisition of more house room by others, and a general change in domestic standards. It is not surprising, therefore, that there was a fairly lengthy transitional period, involving among other things confusion about the names of rooms.

The scullery was, as its name implied, for wet work. Besides food preparation and washing up, it normally accommodated laundry work, which needed a copper and mangle, unless, as was sometimes the case, the house was in a group sharing a separate wash house. Monday was habitually wash day, and the long and complex operation of boiling, scrubbing, mangling and putting out the washing effectively immobilized the rear of the house, while drying, ironing and airing might dominate the kitchen-living room to the middle of the week.

The Tudor Walters Report briefly considered the case for providing individual houses with washrooms but found this unjustified in a small workingman's 'cottage'. Laundry work therefore remained in the scullery, and was later transferred with the scullery's other functions to the kitchen. This contrasted with housing traditions of other societies, where laundry and cooking did not share the same space. The Dudley Report favoured a utility room, but there appears to have been no strong public demand for this (CoSMITH, 1955), perhaps because at this period most middle-class and many working-class housewives sent their washing out to commercial laundries (Mass Observation, 1943). This remained an option in the early postwar years, ending as a 'bag wash' (which returned laundry in a damp condition), until the automatic washing machine displaced it altogether.

The first step towards automation was the single, or later 'twin' tub machine to which an electrically powered mangle or wringer was attached. The machine had to be wheeled up to the sink and connected to the taps with hoses, so immobilizing the sink. It remained popular with older people into the 1990s, when it might possibly cost more to buy than the fully automatic washing machine which succeeded it. This was fully plumbed in and did not need to be moved, thus enabling laundry to be done without interrupting any other kitchen task.

Food storage was another function of the rear of the house. Grand houses with servants had had arrays of pantries, cellars and larders, but the absence of anywhere to keep food was one reason why the urban poor had to buy their food daily in penny quantities. Byelaw houses were normally provided with a walk-in larder with a window or ventilated panel, an arrangement to which the Tudor Walters Report adhered. In later years many householders demolished their larder walls, to enlarge the scullery into a more modern 'kitchen'. Whether or not a dwelling had a ventilated larder

The single tub machine with electric dryer (*Source*: House Beautiful, June 1957)

became an important criterion of 'fitness', and as late as the 1980s the more pedantic environmental health departments refused to allow a refrigerator as a substitute. The larder had in fact started to be displaced by the refrigerator after 1945. In the 1960s, depending on region, between a third and a half of home owners and lower numbers of council tenants had this (Gray and Russell, 1962). Some local authorities in the early postwar years supplied or rented out refrigerators to their tenants, and in high-rise flats they were sometimes fitted as standard.

In the byelaw terraced house, the scullery was habitually a step below ground floor level, with a stone or tiled floor, and numerous doors, for access to kitchen, back yard, larder and perhaps coal shed. It might contain a covered bath, in addition to copper, sink and gas cooker. The sink was normally placed under the window next to the back door (see p. 210, below), allowing room for only one draining board. Made of wood, this rotted fast, and was often replaced in later years by a detachable enamelled board. The only other appliance that was squeezed in, if at all possible, was the combination kitchen cabinet, which came on the market around 1914. With storage shelves, flour bin, drawers and pull-out enamelled worktop for pastrymaking, this had to serve in lieu of any other work surfaces. The scullery of the Tudor Walters Report was not a great improvement on this, as regards working space and convenience. It was more likely to be on the same level as the rest of the ground floor, but it usually had to find room for a bath or, if there was a ground floor bathroom, it might have yet another door leading to this.

A strong contrast with the scullery was provided by the warm and cosy kitchen (Hoggart, 1957). This was the place of the coal cooking range or its successor, a space-heating grate with trivets and perhaps an oven above. Kitchen work was therefore divided into two functions, revolving around water and heat respectively and accommodated in different rooms (Forty, 1975). Food preparation might be done in either room, but that done in the kitchen took place on a solid deal table, containing one or two knife drawers and serving for meals and other family activities. Victorian and Edwardian examples were too bulky for post-1919 kitchens, and increasingly they came to rest in junk shops, where they were eventually bought by the 'gentrifiers' of older houses.

The Tudor Walters Report felt that it was witnessing an important transition in the use of sculleries and kitchens: 'the tendency is to require a scullery in which cooking, washing up and all other similar work is carried on. The kitchen becomes the living room in the ordinary sense, which may be kept for use as a sitting-room, as a meal room, and for the cleaner activities of the family' (Tudor Walters, 1918, para. 87). It wished to improve on this change by fostering better patterns of use, but it regarded as out of date the two-room ground floor plan where cooking and meals were combined in the rear room, so that the front one could be used as a parlour.

The transition had, in fact, been going on for a good generation, largely owing to the diffusion of gas cookers and their location in the scullery. So also had one of the compromise solutions the Report now proposed, that of adapting the living-room fire so that it could be used for cooking (Ravetz, 1968). It appears, therefore, that the authors of the Report were not fully abreast of current trends – they might perhaps have done well to listen more closely to the Women's Subcommittee – and their main obsession was with whether or not the house should contain a parlour. After rehearsing the many sound arguments for this and the emphatic preference that people had for it, it declared that 'we do not consider that the parlour should be secured by cutting down the desirable minimum sizes of the living-room, scullery, or other essential parts of the house, and, where it is not possible to provide it except in this way, we recommend that it be omitted' (Tudor Walters, 1918, para, 86).

This, however, then brought in its eyes a further hazard; for in a ground-floor plan with two rooms only, the pattern of use might be the very one it regarded as obsolete. Some tenants 'would even be willing to adopt the old type of houses with combined living room and scullery, in order that the second room might be retained as a parlour' (*Ibid*, 1918, para. 86, italics added). What it was anxious at all costs to avoid was cooking and eating in the same room. Any enlargement of the scullery, there-fore, would be 'somewhat dangerous', as it might encourage tenants to live and take their meals in it.

The Report had got itself into a position where nothing would be ideal, because of its own requirements for economy in design and construction, and its commitment to continue providing a coal cooking appliance. Lacking total conviction, the Report continued: 'Perhaps too much weight should not be given to the danger of improper use of the rooms, in view of the strongly-marked tendency of working-class families to live in the living room and to confine the cooking, &c, to the scullery' (*Ibid*, 1918, para. 89).

What most strikes the latter-day reader, perhaps, is the moral earnestness about the use of different rooms. In seeing the kitchen-scullery dichotomy as a moral dilemma, the Tudor Walters Committee seems to have missed the main point: that in whatever sort of house they found themselves, working-class people now wanted two day rooms, in addition to a multifunctional (cooking and wet work) kitchen. One of the day rooms would be for day-to-day activities and the other set aside for 'best'. A generation later, *Mass Observation* reflected, 'there used to be a big social dividing line between those who ate in the same place as they cooked, and those who had a separate room in which to eat' (Mass Observation, 1943, p. 99). It noted two then current contra-dictory tendencies, people who ate in the kitchen but wanted to expel the sink, copper and gas cooker (if any) to a scullery, and those who already had a scullery but wanted it enlarged so that they could eat in it. The study also noted a dislike of eating alongside the sink – something that may still hold good today.

Official concern with which room people used for meals lasted down to the final quarter of the century (GHS, 1976). Once wet work and cooking were finally brought together, concern was channeled into the question of kitchen size, for if there was inadequate room for a table people ate off any other surface available, such as the tops of washing machines (Gray and Russell, 1962). This then became an issue which no socially conscious architect could afford to ignore: how small must kitchens be to exclude any possibility of their being used for meals, or alternatively, what was the minimum size to permit this? At the level of public health, whether or not a room was used for meals determined whether or not it was classified as a 'habitable room', and this affected the assessment of overcrowding (*Ibid*, 1962, p. 67).

THE PARLOUR

The Victorian parlour occupied the premier position on the ground floor. Provided with the most elaborate hearth and mantelpiece, it was left unheated except on formal occasions and Sundays. It contained the main entertainment source of the home, the piano, as well as family treasures: ritual objects like religious and royal portraits, candlesticks, the best clock. It contained the best furniture, although this was often designed for show rather than regular use. Ornamental linoleum or a carpet square, if this could be afforded, long lace curtains, and a table with aspidistra or other plant in the bay window, completed the effect. For the functions of the parlour, the Tudor Walters Report is probably a reliable guide. They included socializing, use in sickness and con-valescence, homework, serious reading and writing, and interviews with formal callers. The parlour might also, perforce, serve as storage space for bike, pram, or sewing machine. In all, it represented 'a triumph over poverty and a challenge to the external environment which was too often one of dirt, squalor and social dis-harmony' (Burnett, 1986, p. 172).

Attachment to the parlour was deeply rooted in English culture. Any amalgamation with the back kitchen or living room was prevented by 'the power of prejudice'; for 'nothing in the world would persuade people to forgo a drawing room such as real "well-to-do" people have' (Muthesius, 1979, p. 146); but to Raymond Unwin the parlour was 'worse than folly', because of the space it took up in a small workingman's home, and his Cottage *Plans and Common Sense* proposed that it should be dispensed with (Unwin, 1902, p. 11). In Tudor Walters plans it yielded place to the living room, as 'the most important room in the cottage' (Tudor Walters, 1918, para. 104).

In the event a compromise was adopted and council houses were divided into 'parlour' and 'non-parlour' types, the former with higher rents, while flats of necessity fell into the non-parlour category. A fair proportion of houses built under the Addison Act had parlours, as well as subsidized houses built for sale. The critical moment for the parlour came with the Housing Act of 1923, which by reducing house areas seemed to its critics to rule out any possibility of a parlour. This, they argued, inferred that 'the working classes have no friends, and do not require any place in which to entertain their friends' (Hansard, 1923, col. 335). The Act's author, Neville Chamberlain, protested that his houses were large enough to provide a parlour that, at 10 ft 6 in by 9 ft 3 in was 'big enough to court in'; but his critics vowed that this was 'not room for a china dog' nor 'a mug of beer' (*Ibid*, 123, cols. 310, 352).

The larger houses made possible under the Housing Act of 1924 could in theory have had parlours, but in practice this was discouraged by the costs involved. In one district, twelve non-parlour houses might be built for the cost of nine parlour houses, so that, as Ernest Simon remarked in *How to Abolish the Slums*, it was 'pretty clear that a parlour must be regarded as the beginning of luxury' (Finnegan, 1984, p. 127). The parlour was therefore jettisoned. A generation on, Mass Observation observed that, in expressing their preferences

for which room to eat in, people were not in fact returning to the old scullery-kitchen issue but were, as before, asking for two ground floor rooms, in addition to the kitchen. 'Seen in this light, the question of which room to eat in is part of the old controversy about parlour and non-parlour type houses'; and people still had a strong aversion to 'eating in what they regarded as their "best" room' (Mass Observation, 1943, p. 102). By this criterion, pre-1914 houses with parlours were preferable to non-parlour council houses; but the aspiration for a second day room was not again going to be met, in the public sector.

THE CONTRIBUTIONS OF THE INTERWAR SEMI

The real step forward in the evolution of the ground floor was taken by the interwar semi, although it was more grounded in convention than the council house. Its basic plan had generous front and rear rooms, with a narrow 'kitchenette' matching the width of the entrance hall. The kitchenette had a back door to the side driveway or back garden, and sometimes a serving hatch into the rear room, to facilitate the use of this as a dining room. The kitchenette combined all the food preparation functions of scullery and kitchen, but it might or might not have a wash boiler and larder, and it had no room for a table and chairs.

Mass Observation picked up signs that some women were already critical of its meagre size, which they attributed to an ingrained middle-class prejudice against kitchens. On the whole, however, such houses seem to have been popular and the kitchenette in particular was valued as 'labour saving'. A fictional wife in *The House You Want* of 1923 declares: 'no separate scullery and kitchen for me . . . In preparing dinner I have to make endless journeys from one place to the other. That's why I want the kitchen and scullery combined'. She feels that it would be a mistake to make this new room too big, because that 'simply means you are walking about in one room almost as much as you did when there was the ordinary arrangement of separate kitchen and scullery, pantry and larder . . . You ought to have all these various places grouped together . . . then your kitchen-scullery becomes the proper "workshop of the house" it should be' (Phillips, 1923, pp. 37, 40). The 'wife' adds that 'as we have only one maid, she can't do everything, so we ought to eliminate all unnecessary work' (*Ibid*, 1923, p. 37). The vast majority of the new suburbans, of course, had no domestic help beyond a daily char, but their standards, whether inherited or self-imposed, led them by the same logic to the small, 'labour-saving' kitchen, a prototype of which, the Frankfurt kitchen of 1926, was in fact designed by a woman (Mang, 1978). Its narrow, corridor shape made it particularly suitable for modern flats, which it helped to make more widely acceptable.

Various women's organizations set up model kitchens in the 1930s: that of the Council of Scientific Management in the Home (CoSMITH) toured the country (Wheatcroft, 1960), and the Women's Gas Council created at Port Sunlight a kitchen where 'everything works itself' (*Fanfare*, 1939, p. 4). An important feature of such kitchens was their range of fitted cupboards and worktops which had been pioneered in the Bauhaus in the early 1920s and produced commercially in the USA by 1930. Most English women of the 1940s were still unaware of these and other benefits to come: deep sinks with double draining boards, and gas or electric refrigerators which would replace the larder (Pleydell Bouverie, n.d.). In later years the acquisition of these with other bulky equipment such as washing machines and dish washers was to make the fitted kitchenette impractical. With the alleged isolation that it imposed on housewives – since its small floor space precluded the sharing of chores – this brought on it the criticism of

feminists (Craik, 1989; Watson, 1987). However, this largely overlooked the domestic traditions and expectations of its early users, as well as its position in the ground plan of the suburban house. Small it might be, but the kitchenette was strategically placed to survey front door, hall, stairs and back garden, and so to monitor all the comings and goings of the household.

The main reason for the small size of the kitchenette was, of course, to release space for the two main ground-floor rooms, which were now increasingly defined by estate agents as 'reception rooms'. Their respective functions were resolving into a front sitting room and a rear dining room, often provided with french doors to the garden. The latter room had taken over the role of the Victorian kitchen and become the main living room. The use of the term sitting room for what had previously been a parlour is significant. Before 1914, it is claimed, the parlour started to be used as an everyday sitting room by the middle classes (Daunton, 1983). Clearly, this would have been dependent on the income and servants necessary to keep its coal fire burning. Between the wars, gas fires, for those who could afford them, brought the front room into more frequent use, although it was heated for many fewer hours than kitchen-living rooms (PEP, 1945).

The emergent sitting room reflected a social shift: 'the desire for such [an] extra room is not a mere fad on the part of women; it may have a deep social significance' (Pleydell-Bouverie, n.d., p. 54). This was now, however, not so much to do with social status as the needs of different members of the household, most particularly teenagers, who might be driven out of the house altogether in the evenings unless they could get away from the family circle in the living room (*Ibid*, n.d.). Larger terraced houses could have both a parlour and a sitting room, but in smaller ones there was a transitional phase when users opted to have

The new suburban ideal: the rear room of the house is used for everyday living with French windows into the garden, wireless set and easy chairs. (*Source*: McAllister and McAllister, 1945)

either one or the other. In Chapman's Liverpool sample there were still twice as many parlours as sitting rooms, each with distinct functions, and those of the parlour remained strongly traditional (Mogey, 1956). While it still served primarily as a storehouse for treasures, sometimes arranged as a set piece to be viewed from the street, the sitting room was used to live in during the second half of the day (Chapman, 1955). A full ten years later, 'the concept of the parlour [was] not yet outmoded' (Hole and Attenburrow, 1966, p. 20).

THE DOWNSTAIRS AFTER 1945

After 1945, the public rather than the private sector led the evolution of the ground floor. The Dudley Report produced three alternative ground floor plans, only one of which had the traditional living room, scullery and third room, which it termed 'sitting room' on the grounds that 'the expression "parlour" carries an implication which is old-fashioned and obsolete' (Dudley Report, 1944, para. 43). This traditional plan, in fact, was proposed only for rural areas, for a transitional period. The other two plans re-thought and catered for the three functions of cooking, eating and 'living'. In one, the kitchen was designed simply for work, and meals were taken in a dining recess in the living room. In the other, the kitchen had enough space for both dining and cooking, so that the living room was smaller. This second option would ideally have a separate utility room for laundry and other rough work. These plans were more than an

'Opening up' the kitchen to the rest of the house after 1945. (*Source*: Pilot Papers, 1947)

update of the non-parlour house. All the complications of the old scullery had gone, and kitchens were fitted with sequential working areas. Both bathroom and WC were now without question upstairs, and this, with built-in cupboards, bigger windows, elimination of dust-gathering details and reduced chimneys created a more open and flexible ground floor layout, no longer dominated by the technicalities of servicing the home.

What the Dudley Report was most concerned to address was the housewife's actual working day, which was dominated by endless relays of meals served to different family members, from seven in the morning to nine at night. This was a significantly different approach from the Tudor Walters Report, which tried to reform the traditional arrangement of interiors without analysing the housewife's work patterns. To a later generation of feminists, the Dudley approach appeared gender biased, particularly as one of its illustrations portrays the wife cooking and waiting on the man (although it must be said that in another picture he is seen in the utility room cleaning the family's shoes) (*Ibid*, 1944, pp. 36, 34). The Report, of course, reflected the prevailing view

that to be housewife and mother was a woman's crowning role. It was the view that continued to dominate public housing design down to the late 1960s; for though by the time of the Parker Morris Report it was expected that women would have jobs outside the home, the housewife's working day still ran, with only short breaks, from seven in the morning to ten at night – and even then she got up in the small hours to attend to the baby (MHLG, 1968*a*).

As we have seen in Chapter 2, the lead established by the public sector in the early postwar years was more or less maintained, and speculative housing followed its functional building techniques and design. Pure modernism, according to the principles of the Bauhaus and le Corbusier, continued to be applied to only a few specially commissioned houses, and the Span estates were virtually the only popular application (p. 33, above). But many features of modernism were widely adopted, including large windows, non-load bearing internal walls, open-tread stairs, and free-flowing internal space, as little broken up by solid walls, furniture or clutter as possible. Indeed, these may even have become more common in speculative than council houses, because of the savings they offered.

The single living room was now standard, often a 'through' room with windows at either end, but there was a shortlived fashion for two rooms which could be thrown together by means of dividing doors. The term 'lounge' was more and more used from this time, although evidently the house-proud home owner had begun to use it before the war (Rowntree, 1941). In the first postwar *Ideal Homes* book of house plans the 'lounge' is shown as a new room tacked onto the house, and so additional to the living and dining rooms; but in a minority of cases shown it takes the place of the living room (Ideal Homes, n.d.). It is in this sense that the term came into common usage in the postwar home, but it was regarded as a substitute for 'sitting room' by Liverpool's premier furniture store in the 1950s (Chapman, 1955).

In 1961, the Parker Morris Report took one last, backward look over the evolution of the downstairs before laying down new official guidelines (which were in fact a restatement of the 40-year old principles of the Modern Movement). 'We have heard it said on more than one occasion that the kitchen should be planned so that it is impossible to take meals in it, with a view to raising the social and living standards of the occupiers. We believe that this is an unsuitable motive on which to choose a plan; and even if it were not it would be necessary now, after ten or fifteen years of trying it out, to recognise that it is misconceived;' for 'in all parts of the country, and in whatever social and economic group [people] have at least some meals in the kitchen . . . whether or not there is room, that is what they will do' (Parker Morris, 1961, para. 33). There needed, therefore, to be a separate dining area in the kitchen, or, in larger houses, a separate dining room. The Report further commented that still, at the time of writing, even in modern houses, the kitchen 'retains some of the

character of the 19th-century scullery', lacking both efficiency and cheerfulness (*Ibid*, 1961, para. 79).

THE PARKER MORRIS HOUSE

It was the main concern of the Parker Morris Report to offer principles rather than ground plans. The chief of these was to make an 'adaptable' house, to accommodate both social change and the life cycle of any one family. The first priority, therefore, was to use the whole volume of the house, and in particular to liberate the bedroom floor from its previously limited uses. This could only be achieved if the whole house were heated. This would then allow open planning, which it admitted had been disliked by such council tenants as had experienced it because of noise, distraction and lack of privacy. 'These are weighty considerations, but as there has been little experience of it in local authority housing, it would be easy to attach too much weight to these views' (Parker Morris, 1961, para. 30). In private housing it was alleged to be liked for the sense of space it gave, but in order to work well it needed not only good heating but 'suitable arrangements' for private activities. In houses intended for four or more people, therefore, there should be at least one room which could be kept free from disturbance.

To try out these principles in practice the Ministry of Housing built a small estate of two and three storey houses in London and a study of their operation after one year led to a recommended house plan which became 'a seminal influence on the low-rise, medium-density council housing built in all parts of the country since the mid sixties' (Pepper, 1977, p. 273). The plan, drawn and analysed in great detail (MHLG, 1968a) shows a deep, narrow-fronted house from which circulation space has been virtually eliminated. A built-on garage takes up about a quarter of the ground floor area and projects beyond the front of the

The functional use of the interior carried to its logical conclusion. (*Source*: Parker Morris Report, 1961)

house. In consequence the house has, in effect, no facade, the front consisting of front door, garage door, and the blank wall of a refuse cupboard. The circulation arrangement consists of a small lobby, off which there is a downstairs cloakroom, and the open-tread stairs rise from a room-sized 'dining hall' in the interior. This gives access to the kitchen, a narrow room where husband and wife are depicted working side by side, while all meals are taken in the dining hall. The recommended 'private' room also opens off the dining hall, from which it is separated by a movable partition. During the course of one family's occupation of the house, this room is expected to serve in succession as a play recess (without the partition), child's bedroom, study, guest room and old person's room. The whole house appears mysteriously to operate without a heating system or at any rate not one that would take up any space or create any nuisance. This suggested an unrealistic situation where the use of space was unhindered by practical constraints.

The exercise also combined two somewhat contradictory approaches: tailoring a house to fit a family exactly, and maximum flexibility of room structure and layout. The latter continued to be the ideal of progressive architects, including followers of the Dutch architect, Habraken, whose 'Supports' proposal, which allowed

people to choose and later change their internal room divisions, was later tried out by the GLC (Ravetz and Low, 1980). Flexibility was also the aim of a demonstration estate where the Parker Morris ideas were put into practice. Its housing managers agreed to put up or take down internal partitions according to tenants' wishes (MHLG, 1969a); but although tenants exercised some personal choice at the outset, the present housing managers have no record of any subsequent changes to partitions being made.

What in practice was much more significant for flexibility of design was the way that allocation of council housing operated. Since demand invariably exceeded supply, applicants were assigned the number of bedrooms that exactly fitted their needs. Thus in a totally functional and rationally designed dwelling they could end up with less real spatial flexibility than in much older houses (Rapoport, 1968).

The influence of this new internal plan was considerable, not only in public housing but among housing associations and private developers, who by now were trying to increase densities and reduce selling prices in order to extend home ownership to a wider market. Dressed in a variety of facades, the plan lent itself to the newly fashionable mews layouts, and to situations where it was necessary to turn a blind wall to an environmental nuisance, such as a motorway. The deep, narrow fronted dwelling, which was helped by internal bath-rooms, could be fitted into deck access blocks of flats and maisonettes, and it was applied to three-storey houses, where the ground floor contained a garage (see p. 31, above).

Liberation from traditional circulation space allowed front doors to be placed on any level and living rooms, kitchens, bathrooms and bedrooms to be distributed between floors in any combination, without reference to their traditional positions. In very small dwellings interior planning was helped by a counter rather than a wall separating living room and kitchen, and by an open stairway rising from the living room. In speculative housing a positive virtue was made of this space-saving device, which in pre-1914 housing was considered a defect. Such housing also abandoned the built-on garage, which was replaced by car standing space only. Private developers took pains to keep this next to the house, but on public estates, in accordance with Radburn theory, cars were segregated in garage courts, often out of sight of their owners' houses.

The minimalization of domestic space in its most extreme form is found in the 'starter home' or 'studio flat' of the private sector, where all functions were condensed into an area about 15 ft². The living room housed a foldaway bed and dining table, and dressing was done in the tiny bathroom. Weekly mortgage charges included carpet, curtains, cooker, refrigerator and washer-drier, which the purchaser therefore bought on very expensive terms. This ultimate shrinkage of the home was made possible by new lifestyles in which cooking and laundry were reduced to their simplest terms and it was expected that much of the occupants' time would be spent outside the home.

THE UPSTAIRS

The association of the first floor or upstairs with sleeping seems to have been well established by the time of the byelaw house. Two or three bedrooms were normal: the third being over the scullery extension, if there was one, or in an attic. A third bedroom was thought essential by social reformers, to permit the separation of sons and daughters: a not unreasonable concern in the large Victorian family. The Tudor Walters Report, ever anxious to ensure higher standards for working-class tenants, was firmly in favour of three bedrooms, since 'there already exist in nearly all parts of the country such a large number of houses having two bedrooms only that it is undesirable to add to the number' (Tudor Walters, 1918, para. 94). If a fourth bedroom were needed, the most sensible room to use would be the parlour. 'Unfortunately, however, experience as regards England and Wales shows that the extra downstairs room is seldom used as a bedroom, even when overcrowding and inter-mixing of the sexes result in the two upstairs rooms' – although it was suggested that the return of the war wounded might change this (*Ibid*, 1918, para. 94). The oblique reference here was to Scottish tradition, where the box bed enabled parlours, and even kitchens, to double up as bedrooms. In Tudor Walters plans a fourth bedroom could only be fitted into the larger first floor of a parlour house, or into a third or attic storey. The Report stipulated that all bedrooms should be large enough to accommodate a 4 ft bed, which was the only type that many tenants owned. Two at least of the bedrooms should have a fireplace, which was thought necessary in event of illness.

Twenty-five years later, the Dudley Report demonstrated the bedroom standards that had meanwhile become established. It recommended minimum areas and heights of a 'best', second and third, single bedroom, the first needing to be big enough to accommodate a

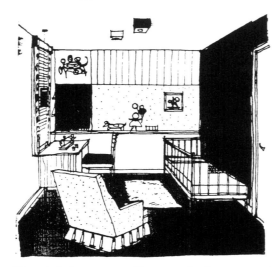

The baby's room. (*Source*: Stephenson and Stephenson, 1964)

baby's cot, and one of the two main bedrooms having a heating appliance. The bed positions, it advised, should always be drawn on plans: a reminder that in speculative housing the so-called third bedroom, situated above the front door, often turned out to be too small to take an adult-sized bed. At the same period, the *Daily Mail* confirmed that it was regarded as good practice for babies to sleep in parents' rooms (Pleydell Bouverie, n.d.). Twenty years later this was still normal, although by now Doctors Spock and Bowlby, the child-care experts, advised otherwise. The professional and managerial classes were the first to give under-fives their own rooms (Hole and Atten-burrow, 1966). The *Daily Mail* also insisted that all bedrooms, including the third, should have a heat source, although only older women now thought that this should be an open fire: 'opinion seems at present to be divided as to whether a bedroom, heated by an electric or gas fire or panel, can be healthily ventilated unless a flue is installed' (Pleydell-Bouverie, n.d., p. 58).

In postwar conditions, the moral concern

about bedrooms died away, to be replaced by a new concern that the adolescent of the family should have 'the privacy, the feeling of personal possession, and responsibility in his or her own room, which are so essential to the formation of character during these important years' (*Ibid*, n.d., p. 59). This was facilitated by new furniture in the form of shelf units lining the walls and perhaps a divan bed decked with cushions. The younger child's bedroom was also becoming more self-contained, with a desk for study. Since the previous furnishings of these rooms might not have been very grand it may have been comparatively easy for parents to consider re-equipping them. It was their own, the so-called 'master' bedroom, that was burdened with an expensive 'suite' of double bed, wardrobe, dressing table and perhaps other pieces, making it considerably less adaptable.

It was, of course, only people in newer houses, or not overcrowded in older houses, who enjoyed these higher bedroom standards. In poorer districts between the wars it was still exceptional for children and adolescents to

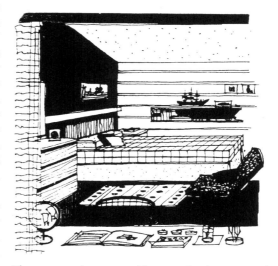

The teenager's room. (*Source*: Stephenson and Stephenson, 1964)

have their own rooms and many shared beds, sometimes with several others. Some slept on floors, covered with old coats; for while it may have been possible to keep up standards of clothing, the entire family stock of blankets might consist of a single pair, bought on marriage and 'worn to a shadow' (*Our Towns*, 1944, p. 64). Such deficiencies were overtaken by the welfare state and full employment, but people did not lightly give up the reassurance of sleeping with others, even when they had enough accommodation for private bedrooms (Hole and Attenburrow, 1966).

In Parker Morris-type houses the bedroom became more compact, particularly since the first floor area might be smaller than the ground floor, and from this time the custom of providing above-eye-level, strip windows in bedrooms became common. The Parker Morris Report recommended that all adolescent and adult children should have their own rooms, even when of the same sex. With the aid of adequate heating and bunk beds, children's rooms could also double as play rooms.

In practice, departures from conventional bedroom use were felt to need special justification (*Ibid*, 1966). As people continued to double up in their sleeping accommodation, a substantial minority of third bedrooms were unused. Gas fires in bedrooms, if present, were lit for getting up and going to bed only, rather than to make bedrooms into bed sitting rooms. When toys, sewing machines and such like were found in bedrooms, it was for storage rather than use.

'It is better to keep bedrooms as bedrooms', was a remark made by many housewives who disapproved of using these rooms in any other way . . . They were also very conscious of the extra wear and tear on their furniture which would result from children playing upstairs unsupervised by an adult. 'Too much running up and down wasted the stair carpet.' (*Ibid*, 1966, p. 29)

It was as if housewives were determined to make up for the overcrowded conditions they had put up with for so long. Friends and relatives already in new homes provided a model where, among other things, bedrooms were laid out for strictly limited uses, and for show (*Ibid*, 1966).

Eventually the trends anticipated by Parker Morris were confirmed and went even further. Children of the family were given decorative name plates to put on their doors and encouraged to personalize their rooms. These were made more self sufficient by the addition of radio and TV (according to market research of 1994, half of seven to ten-year-olds and two thirds of eleven to fourteen-year-olds watched TV in their own rooms); but it was the computer that finally entrenched them. Their independence became complete when it became accepted practice for even parents to knock on their doors before entering.

THE CHANGING INTERIOR: SPACE AND FUNCTION

The evolution of rooms after 1914 both reflected and influenced changes in domestic life, which were marked by a periodic redefinition and renaming of rooms. The trend that most stands out is an enormous improvement in working-class accommodation, and a consequent convergence of middle and working-class standards (Burnett, 1986). But there was also a downward drift of space standards, although this was partly compensated by domestic technology. Standards, however, cannot be evaluated in isolation from the actual use of the house. While there was an overall reduction in sharing and overcrowding throughout the century, there were individual patterns in the use of space. Space was apt to be tightest when people were family building – even owner occupiers could not then always buy as much space as they would have liked. Many would have liked to have a spare room (Mass Observation, 1943; Jennings, 1962). But during the Second World War any empty room was apt to be commandeered by the government or filled up by lodgers, so that this was an amenity that did not begin to be realizable until the postwar period. It was particularly useful for messy and creative activities, and in its absence these were often carried out in garages and garden sheds; but people on high-density estates and in flats did not have this option, and often abandoned their hobbies altogether (MHLG, 1970c). The lack of a spare room was also deterrent to overnight hospitality. The expedient generally resorted to was the bed settee, but the use of this could cause much dislocation in the household.

Towards the end of the century, while the homeless single were limited to a room, or even a bed, changing demographic patterns brought unprecedented amounts of space to some people, including parents whose families had left home, and well-paid young professionals. Indeed, it was not uncommon for young couples or partners to own two dwellings between them. A novel statistic used in 1991 *Social Trends* was, not 'persons per room' (the old measure of overcrowding), but 'rooms per person'. Well over half the national population by then had over two rooms per person, although the minority ethnic groups were excluded from this general improvement.

Another aspect of the changing interior was a subtle transition from status to function, in which the ancient dichotomies of front:back, formal:informal, public:private, leisure:work, and clean:dirty were at least partially dissolved.

The kitchen becomes open and visible. (*Source*: News of the World, *c*. 1950)

Before 1914, internal layout expressed the domestic standards of a socially stratified society, and these accounted for much of the concern of the Tudor Walters Committee. A quarter century later it was the running of the house rather than social propriety that was the main concern. While this prompted the feminist response that it expressed control of women by men, in the revised interior layout the kitchen became more integrated with and visible to the rest of the house. While housewives did not gain any personal space, they were less cut off in the kitchen and better able to monitor the other occupants of the house.

The 'affluent worker' in a new council house in the later 1950s recognized what it did for his status when he said 'We've moved to the front' (Zweig, 1961, p. 5). More exactly, his house no longer had a front in the old sense. A more open plan, whole house heating, the mechanization (and eventual automation) of much kitchen work, clean and stylish kitchen and bathroom surfaces, meant that there was no longer any part of the house too disgraceful to be seen. The whole house was available for living in with pleasure and, other taboos aside, it was accessible to anyone.

The weakening of status did not mean that non-functional aspects of the interior were no longer important. Rather, personal style and expression replaced the class codes dominant in the age of the scullery and parlour. After the Second World War, householders were increasingly encouraged to think 'what your home says about you' (Murdoch, 1986, p. 88). The domestic interior was expected to make a statement in the public arena.

A change in the nature of domestic privacy accompanied this trend. While the personal space of the children of the family increased, the parents were no more likely than before to have any defined personal space. This was of particular concern to feminists, who argued that husands could have garden sheds or garages to withdraw to, while wives had no comparable space (Watson, 1987). In practice, the strategy used by housewives was to take over the whole house when other family members were absent. Neighbours and women friends could then pay calls, and sewing or other work be spread out in any room – often on the kitchen or dining room table. Privacy was thus achieved by 'time zoning', a device always used by parents when they resumed control of the downstairs after their children went to bed. When all adults were at home – and with rising unemployment this was bound to be more frequent – the single family living room did pose problems, as architects had foreseen. If either husband or wife had confidential business to transact, the pattern was for the other to withdraw tactfully to a different part of the house or to the garden until the coast was clear.

THE CHANGING INTERIOR:
USERS' CONTRIBUTIONS

Design change, as we have seen was driven by professionals and developers who confidently prescribed for people little able to express their own preferences. After the Women's Housing Subcommittee, the 1940s was the only period when the public was actively involved in design debates, and even then opinion was channelled and edited by the BBC, the press, film and government inspired education and propaganda. Before this time, people felt so little able to practice choice in housing that they would 'take their homes for granted, and they just live there with little further thought' (Mass Observation, 1943, p. 53). After the coming of the Welfare State, general public interest in housing abated, on the assumption that the battle had been won. Women's organizations either abandoned their interest or focused it on very specific topics. The Council for Scientific Management in the Home, for instance, turned its attention to the performance of the postwar 'prefab' (CoSMITH, 1951).

Our understanding of people's reactions to postwar housing is very much limited by the bias of research towards council housing. It is clear, however, that the underlying conservatism on which private housebuilders traded was universal. The conventions of room naming and usage changed, but the great majority of people continued to behave according to the conventions of their time. There were strong inducements for such conservatism in both public and private housing. Would-be council tenants were visited by an official housing visitor who noted the type and quality of their furnishings in order to assess the standard of accommodation that they should be offered. In owner-occupied houses, the way rooms were decorated and set out strongly influenced estate agents' estimates of market value and how a house should be marketed. Unconventional room uses or furnishings would be prejudicial to these. The housing market was in any case so structured that people with unmet needs would be better advised to sell up and move on, than to make idiosyncratic changes. The logic of the situation, therefore, was that the only room offering a real flexibility of use was the spare room, if any. With impunity, this could be turned into an office, study, guest room, games or hobby room.

Understandably, some of the early reactions to postwar, functional design were negative. Some distress was felt when the function of rooms in new houses was unclear, or in houses without parlours (Kuper, 1953). Some tenants tried to recreate parlours by erecting their own partitions, which they felt bound to take down, however, when the rent man called (Mogey, 1956). There was soon a tempered acceptance of functionalism, although less tolerance of its later and more extreme applications. People expressed appreciation of the space and light that it gave, but disliked small kitchens and bathrooms, and the placing of a downstairs toilet too near to the kitchen or front door (MHLG, 1969b). Windows reaching down to

the floor were considered dangerous, draughty and lacking in privacy, and open-plan interiors were in general disliked for most of the same reasons (MHLG, 1969a; NCWGB, n.d.). A later twentieth-century craze for the 'farmhouse kitchen', with space enough for family and friends to sit round a table, in addition to a generous range of work units, indicated what the most popular priority would be.

From the 1970s on, however, the small, single living room plan seems to have been widely accepted. Not only were private developers and housing associations using it, but also members of housing co-operatives and the few scattered groups of council tenants who were involved in the design of their own houses. In the Merseyside co-ops the flexibility of a plan where internal walls could be placed in various positions, to accommodate individual preference, was appreciated and exploited to the full (Innes Wilkin et al., 1984).

Perhaps the strongest evidence for people's acceptance of the new interior layout was that they tried to reproduce it in older houses. A craze for modernizing broke out in the newly affluent, postwar working class. Picture rails were taken down; panelled doors 'flushed' with hardboard; door handles replaced by ball catches; baths, sinks, banisters and other mouldings boxed in (see p. 137, above) – so much so that it fell to later generations painfully to undo and reinstate many such details. With the replacement of an old fireplace by a modern grate and tiled surround, these were the simplest and cheapest way of updating older homes: keeping up with the times no longer had to depend on getting a new house.

In due course it became standard practice for their users to make structural changes in all older houses, including those built between the wars. Larder walls were knocked down to make sculleries into kitchens, and front and back rooms knocked together to create 'through' lounges. Built-on glass porches and conservatories further enhanced an impression of flowing,

The house extended and
overflowed. A Leeds suburb,
1995.

and therefore modern, space – although the ready-made conservatory which became so fashionable from the 1980s was tricked out in Victorian-style details.

Much of this internal change was done by people's own hands. The practice of 'Do-It-Yourself', which must have owed something to wartime campaigns of 'Make Do and Mend', did not gain its full momentum until the later 1950s, when it owed a huge debt to new synthetic materials. Probably the most important of these was formica, which could be used to cover a multitude of surfaces, but fablon, a roll-on adhesive plastic covering, was an acceptable substitute. In privately rented houses at this time, people were just beginning to paper their walls and whitewash outside WCs, but they left more radical improvements to their landlords. The real challenge was taken up when they moved out to the new council houses, which provided 'almost endless opportunities for work' (Willmott, 1963, p. 31).

As landlords, local authorities undertook the modernization of their stock, fitting new wiring, bathrooms, central heating and so on, but this was done only on long cycles, and often without consulting the occupants. Housing management practices were far from encouraging to tenants who wished to carry out their own improvements. People were discouraged

and frustrated by having to seek permission even for small changes – a mere rabbit hutch in the garden had to be built and located according to standard specifications – but the strongest deterrent was probably the formal requirement, on giving up a tenancy, to reinstate anything which had been changed or removed. Nevetheless, over the years huge quantities of work were carried out by tenants: in two northern estates of the 1960s, for example, over two-thirds of the tenants put in a new fireplace, and between a third and a half fitted new sink units and power points, boxed in their baths or 'flushed' doors (Kirby, 1971). It was possible, on particular estates, to watch fashions for specific improvements sweeping through sets of neighbours (Ravetz, 1974b).

Once theirs had become the dominant tenure, owner occupiers were generally assumed to be the most active home improvers. In the early postwar years, however, this was not always the case, and their homes could be shabbier than the better-kept council houses (Newson, 1968), perhaps because they had not yet adjusted to the fact that specialist help was expensive and hard to come by. Home owners eventually became tireless do-it-yourselfers, although their priorities tended to be cosmetic and superficial compared to the more structural and systematic improvements carried out by councils as landlords. This was particularly observed in houses bought by tenants under the 'right to buy', which were given the outward trappings of ownership, including the inevitable new front door, but not the more basic structural improvements (Forrest and Murie, 1990; see p. 40, above).

At first the effect that home improvers aspired to was 'contemporary' rather than consciously modern. The effects could be striking: the choice of a tenant in Dagenham, for example, was a 'grey, yellow and blue patterned [wallpaper] on three walls, contrasted with a red and white check on the fourth, the woodwork painted in grey, with red plastic handles and finger panels on the doors' (Willmott, 1963, p. 92). Fashions changed, but the work itself continued, greatly aided by technological improvements such as water-based emulsion paints and easily handled wallpaper adhesive or, eventually, ready-pasted wallpapers. Cumulatively, such work made a more than cosmetic contribution, for it contributed to a feeling of space which was further enhanced by investment in 'fitted' kitchens, bathrooms and bedrooms, by wall-to-wall carpets and central heating. All such things worked in combination to bring remote or unused corners of the house into use, and to make space for all the white goods that were now invading the home. Sometimes the re-modelling was carried out with a deliberate intention of re-assigning rooms. Thus the artist of the colour scheme described above also carried out other work to enable meals to be taken in his kitchen, which he then renamed 'kitchenette', so freeing both his front room and living room from meals (Ibid, 1963).

USERS' CONTRIBUTIONS: FURNISHINGS

The one contribution that householders could not avoid, even if they did not indulge in DIY and took little interest in their homes, was providing some sort of furnishings. It was here that most people felt they expressed their originality, although objectively speaking their choices remained strongly conventional (Hole and Attenburrow, 1966; Kirby, 1971; Holme, 1985). Furniture had always been important in confirming the functions of rooms. That of the Victorians and Edwardians had been craftsman built; heavy and durable, it was a major investment that was expected to last a lifetime. This was an expectation not easily discarded and it created problems for old people when they had at last to move into a small bungalow, flat or bedsitting room (MHLG, 1968c). This attitude towards furniture survived into the period between the wars, when the 'suite' of matching items seems to have risen to import-ance. 'To own a suite was . . . a symbol of the capacity of the breadwinner to provide for his family' (Oliver et al., 1982, p. 176); and in early postwar Liverpool, it was the bedroom rather than the lounge suite which took the lion's share of a young couple's resources (Chapman, 1955).

Furniture of any kind had always been scarce amongst the poor, who made do with what was scavenged or passed down. When they moved into new council homes, therefore, their lack of furnishings, and most particularly their inability to curtain their windows, advertized their poverty to the world. Consequently it was a valuable service when local housing authorities used the powers of the 1936 Housing Act to sell furniture to their tenants on hire purchase arrangements (Ministry of Health, 1938). This was not without active opposition from commercial interests and it was abused by those tenants who did a flit taking the furniture with them, but it was further encouraged by a Hire Purchase Act of 1938 and by the Housing Act of 1949, which renewed local authorities' powers in this respect.

It was essential to the aesthetic of both Arts and Crafts and Modern Movement houses to use specially designed and appropriate furnish-ings, without which their respective architec-tures could not achieve their intended effects.

The sitting room or lounge in pre-post-war transition: a furnished prefab. (*Source*: Avoncroft Museum of Buildings)

Furnishings of the Arts and Crafts school were sufficiently close to the traditional to be readily adopted – and indeed, they provided much of the inspiration of interwar suburban style. But those designed for the stark and unadorned rooms of purist modern houses were deliberately distant from the clutter and stylistic confusion of everyday homes. Thus the one-off houses built for wealthy clients in the 1930s and again in the early postwar years were designed as settings for particular objects such as chairs or lamps, which were regarded as works of art in their own right, and it was impossible to make such houses function as their designers intended unless the usual domestic paraphernalia were eliminated. This was at odds with the situation in most English homes, whether of owner

occupiers or council tenants, which had hetero-geneous and accidental accumulations of objects, including 'ornaments' valued for senti-mental reasons and draperies, coverings and paddings in profusion. But whereas the owner occupier could if he wished escape all the manifestations of modern design, the postwar council tenant, as we have seen, could less easily do so. The fact that many such tenants were at the same time enjoying their first opportunity to acquire furnishings and to explore and express their own taste resulted in the situation where progressive architects, who believed themselves to be conferring rationality, light and space on the working-class home, despaired at its occupants' determination to cover the purposely large windows with draperies and to create a familiar, cosy, cluttered interior (Attfield, 1989).

From the 1950s, shopping for furnishings became a joint interest of husbands and wives (Chapman, 1955), and many – new council tenants in particular – took on far larger hire purchase repayments than they could afford, for goods that were often poorly designed and overpriced (Manchester & Salford CSS, 1960). It appears that wives mainly took the lead in deciding what was needed and how to set it out within rooms; and most particularly housewives expressed themselves through soft furnishings, many of which they made themselves, egged on and instructed by the women's magazines. Oblivious to the scorn of 'progressive' architects, they had a clear idea of the contemporary but nevertheless domestic effect they wanted to achieve, so that the resulting homes were 'bulging with visual evidence of the home-maker's deep aesthetic involvement in the domestic environment' (Hunt, 1989, p. 75; Partington, 1989).

The first chance that many people had of seeing new, simple but well designed furniture was under the Utility scheme which ran from 1943 to 1953. This allowed those setting up home for the first time and anyone who had been bombed out to purchase a range of basic items that were designed to be economical of both materials and space. The purpose and the very name of the scheme, however, invited disparagement, and this was perhaps one reason why as soon as restrictions on furniture making were lifted postwar home-makers elected for elaborate but inferior pieces. Before the scheme had quite ended, the Festival of Britain in 1951 provided a further means of popularizing a modern idiom, both through the furnishings of the exhibition itself (notably its Charles Eames chairs of moulded plastic) and its specimen rooms in the Homes and Gardens Pavilion and the Lansbury 'living architecture' estate. In these displays, special emphasis was laid on space-saving items to enable rooms in small

Utility replaced by 'contemporary'. (*Source*: Stephenson and Stephenson, 1964)

houses to serve dual functions, an issue that had in fact begun to be taken up in the 1930s. Such items included studio couches doubling as divans, bunk beds, and extendable ranges of standardized shelf and cupboard 'units'. At first used for lining walls, these acquired a particular use as room dividers in the postwar home. Such things were a godsend to people with limited incomes and little house room:

a chest of drawers or a cupboard can be crowned with shelves which turns it into a dresser, a sideboard, or a tall bookcase. The shelves can be filled with different kinds of household possessions to give a varied aspect to the final picture. A vase in

The lounge achieves its late twentieth-century peak of luxury. The advertiser's image of the comforts of the modern home.

one small space is balanced by several brightly coloured books in another, while a cactus, a ship in a bottle, the radio, magazines, or books lined up another way, make up a satisfying and changing pattern on the other shelves. In later years another set of shelves can be added . . . or a small cupboard, specially made as part of the whole set, goes between the sets of shelves to give variety and extra use. And this is only the beginning. (Smithells, n.d., p. 85).

Should their readers be unable to afford even this instalment approach, magazines were full of useful tips on how to dismantle, convert and disguise large, junk furniture with the aid of fablon and plastic handles. It was thus that an appropriate repertoire was assembled for the postwar interior.

Throughout the second half of the century furnishings continued in the twin channels of functionalism and traditionalism, both separately and in combination. The diffusion of fitted furniture and extendable units, important to the subtly changing function of the home, was greatly facilitated by the spread of large 'DIY' stores which sold them, as well as other, freestanding items, in flat packs to be taken home in the car for self assembly. More formal pieces of furniture, meanwhile, were strongly influenced by the growing leisure uses of the home, notably TV viewing. Early signs of this appeared in the 1950s in the occasional tables

introduced into 'sitting rooms' for the serving of afternoon tea 'informally from trays' (Chapman, 1955, p. 64). It was, in fact, as not tea but coffee tables that they became a virtually indispensable part of the domestic furniture repertoire, undergoing many metamorphoses of shape including 'palettes', 'kidneys' and ovals, before finally settling down into a long rectangle that could be placed parallel to a deeply padded couch.

This last object had by now become the most important item of the updated, three-piece lounge suite (Kuper, 1953; Mogey, 1956; Manchester & Salford CSS, 1960), and it cost more if it was also a convertible bed-settee. Other items important to the increasingly opulent and leisured home were the cocktail cabinet, replacing the more sober and traditional glass-fronted china display cupboard, or its substitute, the built-in bar, which could be designed and installed by a creative handyman (Barrett and Phillips, 1993). With the special furniture of the new patio garden, the dining set and awninged swing couch (p. 194, below), these reinforce the atmosphere of the later twentieth-century home as a seat of relaxation, luxury and leisure.

Important though such trends were for re-defining the home, English home-makers never really embraced modern design. In this respect they lagged behind some parts of Europe, which had been much more influenced by modern architecture and by a series of international exhibitions through the inter-war years, from the 1923 Weimar Exhibition onwards. Nor was there any serious formal attempt to educate consumers (other than scattered instances of new council show houses and flats), unlike Sweden, whose Consumer Association provided an active link between designers and consumers and influenced consumer behaviour. Britain's government-sponsored Council of Industrial Design from 1944 was intended primarily as shop windows for manufacturers, while the Design Centre set up in the wake of the 1951 Festival was remote from the experience of the ordinary householder. The independent Consumers' Association, founded in 1957, was in business to test products and advise on value for money rather than quality in design. The main influence on style, therefore, was in women's, housekeeping and house and garden magazines whose thrust was in the main strongly conventional, particularly in view of the bias of most of the latter towards the stately home and all that this represented in stylistic terms. Another influence was television which, although its set designers aimed to represent rather than form taste, must have helped to disseminate new fashions.

The interruption of war had given the lead in furniture design to Sweden and the United States, whose new ideas were seen for the first time by most Britons at the 1951 Festival. This was the one exhibition (interestingly, a national rather than an international one) which gripped the imaginations of many and so helped bring the British consumer into the world of modern design.

The Festival's immediate influence on the home was mainly through small and often cheap items such as coffee tables, kitchen chairs, coat or newspaper racks. Its longer term and more diffused influence was on

movements in design, as in the popular G-Plan range, introduced in the 1950s, and Terence Conran's Habitat furniture, made and sold in a chain of stores from the mid-1960s. Eventually, using the increasingly popular means of mail order catalogues, the Habitat chain offered virtually every item, large or small, that would be needed in a household, at prices within the reach of people of modest means. Not all the items were visibly modern, for as time passed the stores stocked many plushily upholstered pieces and revivals, more and less genuine, of folk and 'cottage' traditions. But in general Habitat furniture used bold, basic colours, good, natural materials and simple, distinctive shapes, conveying an image that sat comfortably with both the Arts and Crafts and Modern Movement schools. Habitat also offered copies or derivatives of *avant garde* pieces in moulded plastic, aluminium or tubular steel, so bringing truly 'modern' design into the homes of the more adventurous; but in general such products were mainly found in suppliers of furniture for offices, public and institutional rather than domestic buildings.

After the 1960s, with the ending of detailed sociological-ethnographic studies and the government Design Bulletins, and with occasional exceptions (Noble, 1982), there is no easily accessed record of people's choices and priorities in furnishing the home. Distinct gender differences are suggested by the fact of the home being women's workplace and having different meanings in the lives of women and men (Foo, 1984; Madigan et al., 1990). This was borne out by a TV documentary series which showed that what to women was 'home' was simply 'a place to live' to men, who furnished it to look stark and technological, in contrast to the profusion of ornaments, textiles and clutter preferred by women. At the same time, both men and women in the series frequently agreed in their taste for nostalgia (BBC2, 1992).

Technically, non-traditional techniques and

materials – notably veneered chipboard and foam rubber – were happily accepted by home-makers but they were concealed under a wide range of exteriors. Modern and unconventional-looking pieces were more readily accepted for utilitarian or 'new' parts of the home – patios and conservatories being good examples – but elsewhere the popular choice of style was more often traditional. Thus, as with the house itself, there was no more than a limited acceptance of functionalism. This conservatism was no doubt encouraged by the survival of older houses, which most people felt would be inappropriate to furnish with modern pieces, as well as a national reverence for stately homes and 'heritage'. Such reverence was catered for by a craze for the rustic and picturesque that had always existed but which was particularly promoted by Laura Ashley designs, originating in 1953 and sold in a chain of stores from 1960 onwards.

The dominant objective of twentieth-century home furnishing, however, came increasingly to be, not choice of any particular style but free and individualistic expression of choice from many styles. There developed a wider and wider repertoire from which the individual was expected to choose. Thus, 'when you furnish with G-Plan, you have exactly what you wanted, tailor-made to your way of life, and each room becomes an expression of your personal tastes and fancies' (*House Beautiful*, 1959, p. 9). This was the more possible because the entire range of types, styles and qualities became available from many different types of store, including antique and junk shops. Whether very large or very small amounts were spent, the idea was that the home should express one's individuality – or, when making choices for others like babies and young children, or the more perfunctory selections for bedsits in hostels and institutional Homes, what one conceived to be the individualities of others. Ideally, the furnishings were expected to be changed and updated as individuals' personae and means changed (Hunt, 1989); but apart from the more affluent, usually youthful householders, the old customs of accumulating and keeping furniture over long periods, or – in the case of the poor – acquiring chance accumulations of the discards of others, were still the normal way of turning empty domestic interiors into functioning homes.

9

GARDENS AND EXTERNAL SPACE

The twentieth-century garden was primarily a nineteenth-century creation. By the turn of the century, two conventions dominated the garden's design and use. The first had evolved from the English vernacular tradition of rural cottage gardening. Although the cottager's plot, with its fusion of vegetables, fruit and flowers was a model of efficiency and aesthetics, it was largely displaced by a different style of gardening adapted to a suburban setting. This style was marked by formal design and constrained by the availability of land. The contrived landscapes from which its formality arose were based on an abundance of land, and attempts to diminish the grand to the small scale have been a recurrent theme in gardening since the nineteenth century. Whilst the Victorian suburban tradition has proved more influential, the vernacular tradition has persisted to the present day, and both have left a clearly identifiable legacy to the modern domestic garden. Consequently, we must explore this legacy before we can begin to understand the twentieth-century garden.

THE ORIGINS OF THE MODERN DOMESTIC GARDEN: THE VERNACULAR GARDENING TRADITION

The nineteenth-century, working-class experience of gardening enabled a genuinely vernacular tradition to survive, and it was particularly well-established in those areas which had experienced the first stage of industrialization in the eighteenth century. The level of expertise was so high that the cultivation of particular plants or produce became associated with specific locations: for example, gooseberries in Manchester, pinks in Glasgow, and pansies among Derbyshire miners (Hoyles, 1991).

The popular tradition of planting vegetables, fruit and flowers in one plot was extended to an urban setting through the allotment garden. Throughout the nineteenth century, and despite the pressure of residential development, the humble allotment became an established feature of urban centres. Some sites had a history going back several hundred years or were established according to local 'Freemens' rights' or Acts of Parliament. Legislation in 1819 and 1845 provided additional plots or 'field gardens' for the labouring poor and local authorities became involved through the 1892 Smallholdings Act. By 1900, allotments marked the fringe of every industrial city and an estimated 700,000 existed in urban and rural locations (Thompson, 1988).

The use of allotments was particularly associated with 'necessity-growing' in order to supplement the income of working-class households. The moral benefits of such activity were also vigorously promoted in the Victorian period. 'Individual gardens were seen as antidotes to the evils of urban life and their cultivation a relief from the associated dangers' – that is, of drink, fecklessness and political radicalism

(Gaskell, 1980, p. 488). *Active* gardening complemented the 'virtues of hard work and industry, of self-reliance and self-improvement' (*Ibid*, 1980, p. 483). It was a 'respectable' and 'rational' recreation which fully accorded with the values of the time.

Housing reformers, and Octavia Hill in particular, were active in the provision of gardens and open spaces. She wrote that all should have access to 'the beauty of earth and sky, trees and flowers' (Bell, 1942, p. 141) and was extremely critical of stark new tenement blocks lacking garden space. Her practical initiatives were, however, eclipsed by George Cadbury's work at Bournville at the end of the nineteenth century. Houses in his model village were not allowed to occupy more than a quarter of the plot, and garden maintenance was a condition of leases and tenancy agreements. The gardens were already dug over and hedges, creepers and fruit trees planted before the houses were occupied (Gaskell, 1980). The rear gardens were divided between areas for flowers, vegetables and fruit trees, a sequence which anticipated common practice in the first half of the twentieth century. Even the pecuniary value of gardening was determined by analysing the value of produce from twenty-five typical plots which averaged 425 yds^2 in size.

Bournville provided a detailed and unique case study of the value of gardens adjacent to houses for manual workers. The garden here was convenient, productive, and a safe place for children to play. However this was exceptional for the time, and the contemporary model village of Port Sunlight provided what was then a more normal arrangement, of houses with small back yards, supplemented by common allotments.

For the majority of the working classes, privately rented, terraced housing made access to garden space almost inconceivable. One exception was Birmingham, where a long tradition of gardening led to the provision of gardens in up to one third of nineteenth-

'Her only garden'. Transformation of a terraced back yard in the centre of Birmingham. (*Source*: Bournville Village Trust, 1941)

century dwellings (Bournville Village Trust, 1941). The ordinary back yard offered little scope for conventional gardening but could, with ingenuity, be transformed. In the East End of London, such practices became legendary and were still thriving in the 1950s; 'Attachment to flowers and pets is almost universal. The back-yards or back-gardens of many old houses are filled with masses of flowers and sometimes with hen-runs, rabbit hutches and aviaries. One old man . . . grew prize dahlias and others had sheds in which they repaired shoes or furniture' (Townsend, 1957, p. 12). The keeping of animals for food, especially pigs, was a long-lasting practice in many regions.

Thus the garden space actually available to the mass of the population is not indicative either of working-class preference for gardens or the widespread belief in the social benefits of gardening. However, it was not until 1919 that the extent of under-provision was addressed, and in the meantime a new set of garden conventions concerning use and design had been developed.

THE ORIGINS OF THE MODERN DOMESTIC GARDEN: THE VICTORIAN SUBURBAN GARDEN

Like many other values embraced by the emerging middle classes, the preference for a home with a garden emulated the pre-industrial landed classes. The Victorian suburban garden drew on the late eighteenth-century practices of landscape and town gardening, and so broke with the vernacular tradition. From about 1800, the country house garden experienced a revival through the practice of landscaping. While this could have little relevance within the rapidly growing city, it established garden design as a fashionable social activity. The fashion for gardening was extended to towns by the same landed classes. 'The town garden as we understand it – the back garden of a terraced house – was an upper-class innovation which probably first appeared in London around 1720' (Burton, 1989, p. 96). Its features are familiar to us today: back yards, window sills, roof parapets and first floor verandahs were decorated with hanging baskets and pots of flowering plants or trees. By the 1780s, glass doors or french windows gave access to small back gardens consisting of gravel walks between decorative flower beds. Tall wooden fences enclosed the new gardens and gave them an intended privacy (*Ibid*, 1989).

The urban garden was also combined with the better known residential square. Humphrey Repton was involved in the design of London's Bloomsbury and Russell Squares in the 1820s, but more significantly, Ladbroke Square and fourteen smaller squares were constructed in the 1840s with the surrounding houses opening directly onto the public street but backing onto private gardens. This pattern was followed elsewhere, helping to encourage the fashion for private back gardens.

The distinction between front and back was reinforced by the location of service functions in the humbler terraced house. The typical concentration of these in a back yard constituted an effective barrier to the creation of a garden here, both because of the negative status of this area, and because such functions used up the available space. One solution was their progressive incorporation into a relatively inconspicuous basement. This freed space at the rear of the dwellings for the development of a private garden.

From the 1840s, there was a clear distinction between the provision of suburban mansions and villas with private back gardens for a middle-class minority, and the relative exclusion of the mass of the population from private garden space. Plot sizes were indicative of social status and the best were large enough to include the much reduced features of the fashionable landscaped garden: flower beds, a lawn, and distinctive trees. These could only be incorporated at the rear of the dwelling and, encouraged by the preference for privacy, the development of the domestic garden became concentrated in this area. Rectangular plots suggested a sequential 'ordering' of garden layout. By the mid-nineteenth century, the typical back garden of a villa began with geometric flower beds which were planted with spring bulbs, followed by bedding plants in summer. Beyond these was a lawn, defined by narrow and winding gravel paths, beyond which Douglas firs or a weeping willow might provide a point of interest (Hadfield, 1960). The lawnmower, which became available in 1831, enabled the regular and close cropping of the lawn. Meanwhile the vegetable, which could now be obtained more easily and cheaply from the shops, was banished from the fashionable garden.

Constraints on the shape and size of plots were more than compensated by the extraordinary proliferation of new plant types. The availability of cheap and durable glass and the creation of an efficient transport system enabled plant nurseries to develop a mass market for seeds and plants. Hybridizing extended the variety of such things as tulips, carnations, and above all the rose (*Ibid*, 1960). Roses suited the suburban soils of London and the Home Counties, and an unlimited supply of stable manure ensured a healthy display. From the 1840s, plant collecting introduced a new range of colourful 'exotics' from South Africa and South America (Wright, 1934). Salvia, French and African marigolds, lobelias and many others provided brilliant colours which could be seen at their best in geometric beds planted in blocks or in ribbon borders (Bisgrove, 1990). Many of the plants could only survive during the summer months and 'bedding out' became common practice in domestic gardens as in the public parks, which vied with each other for the brilliance of their displays (Hoyles, 1991).

The enthusiasm for novelty also extended to trees and shrubs. New varieties of rhododendron from China and the Himalayas gave a new glow of colour to the shrubbery and were particularly suited to the sandy soils of major areas of suburban expansion, Surrey, Sussex and Hampshire. Conifers provided a focus of admiration when planted in small groups or in pineta. Hedging plants provided privacy with formality, and a new function was given to a vernacular shrub, the privet, now supplemented by new varieties from the East. Its rapid growth and exceptional resistance to air pollution made it particularly useful for privacy-giving hedges.

The Victorian garden was also embellished by furniture and 'novelties'. Advances in the production of cast iron added a new material to the typical stone and brick, and emblems of landscaping like the lawn were complemented by new symbols of the suburban garden. Raised beds were edged by broken bricks and decorated with urns and statuary. Trellises, benches and garden seats were located at strategic points and constructed in a rustic style. Interesting objects such as shells and pebbles were displayed and gravel paths were brightened by the addition of coloured minerals.

Throughout the century, the popular rockery was further encouraged by the fashion for mountain walking and climbing. The garden gnome made its first appearance in the 1880s in the rockery of Lamport Hall in Northamptonshire. Imported from Germany as matchbox-holders, gnomes were used by the garden's owner, Sir Charles Isham, to represent 'earth spirits' (Isham, 1890). Water gardening grew in popularity in the latter half of the nineteenth century. It was encouraged by the fashion for Italianate gardens with fountains; by the Japanese influence, which bestowed bamboo and bridges; and by the late Victorian 'Vernacular Revival', using water lilies.

The domestic hothouse and, from 1850, the glasshouse enabled the cultivation of bedding and indoor plants. Preference was given to ferns and plants with strongly coloured leaves, including the ubiquitous aspidistra. The term 'greenhouse' acknowledges the nineteenth-century preference for plants grown for their leaf colour. Whilst glass houses could be used functionally or as a room outside, conservatories were on the boundary between home and garden. The availability and versatility of cast iron and rolled glass gave considerable scope for design. The mid-century structures at Kew Gardens and Crystal Palace were undoubtedly influential in encouraging the fashion for glasshouses and conservatories.

The Victorian suburban garden depended on a coincidence of new ideas and new materials. Carpet bedding would have lacked impact without the newly imported and colourful 'exotics'; the lawn could not have become universal without the lawnmower; rose gardens would have lacked variety without hybridizing. The new element that was injected in the later part of the century was the 'natural' school of gardening led by William Robinson, inspired by the English cottage garden, which donated the herbaceous border of hardy plants (Robinson, 1883). Carried forward into the twentieth century by his most eminent follower, Gertrude Jekyll, this was particularly compatible with the new domestic-style suburban housing of the early garden city settlements (Barrett and Phillips, 1987).

By 1914, the typical middle-class garden owed something to this, as well as the more formal tradition. It was carefully ordered and compact; it was decorative, and above all it was designed for family leisure in a private setting. The recreational use of the garden was dependent on the employment of at least a jobbing gardener, and the control exercised over both man and nature appealed to a class anxious to consolidate its position in society. By 1914, gardening had become an established middle-class activity and a private garden was both a functional and a symbolic addition to the suburban home.

THE FORECOURT AND THE FRONT GARDEN: THE EDWARDIAN HOUSE

Whilst the back garden was largely confined to the middle class, the front garden was less exclusive. By the turn of the century, most new houses were being provided with either a clearly defined forecourt or a front garden (Muthesius, 1982). The primary function of these was to mark the boundary and act as a 'buffer zone' between the private home and the public street. The observance of minimum byelaw street widths and the density of urban development ensured that space at the front of dwellings was minimal. This gave rise to a conflict between public and private zones which was further complicated by the desire to project social status through 'the furnishing of

the front windows [and] the arrangement of the front garden. The idiom in which these acts were performed varied from class to class' (Dyos, 1966, p. 89).

The outcome was a series of compromises in which privacy was combined with decorative enclosure and display. Smog-resistant privet hedging could be trimmed with military precision, iron railings could be defensive but also ornamental. Low walls with railings or fences with hedges could shield the front of the house from both street and side neighbours, and a floral arrangement in the front garden could be enjoyed equally from within or without. Above all, the growing of vegetables in this space was taboo.

Changes in the front area in the Edwardian period came from two directions, the influence of the garden city movement, and the experience of the early LCC estates. The garden city idea influenced the general environment in two ways: the universal provision of gardens, and the 'greening' of urban environments. In particular, the grass verge complemented the front garden and helped to achieve an overall visual unity. This concept was carried further in the LCC's cottage estates, in which the sense of uniformity was increased by the use of less varied house types. In private sector developments, control over the use of the front garden was achieved by a combination of covenants and social pressure, but in the public sector a more direct approach could be taken. In both sectors, the effect was to place greater emphasis on the conspicuous display of the front garden and to heighten the tension between this and the desire to maximize privacy through enclosure.

TIDY AND 'TWEE': THE INTERWAR FRONT GARDEN

The extent of external control over the front garden was a major difference between the public and private sectors in the inter-war years. Whilst the integrity of Howard's garden city principles was increasingly undermined by the practices of speculative developers, the council estate provided an unparalleled opportunity for comprehensive planning. Here, front gardens could be individual but uniform, while in the private sector they could also be individualistic or, more exceptionally, following the precedent of Port Sunlight, they could be incorporated into open-plan landscaping.

Despite a lack of detail, there was an implicit assumption in the Housing Manual of 1919 that individual front gardens should not detract from the visual impact of the council estate. The standardized provision of private hedging, fences and gates was common, and as the Becontree Tenants' Handbook specified, tenants were expected to keep the front garden 'in a neat and cultivated condition' (Young, 1934, p. 373). Its size gave little opportunity for anything more adventurous than a front path, a patch of lawn, and a border of flowers. In an era when the motor car was still unheard of on council estates, the visual unity achieved must have been impressive.

Such uniformity was anathema to private developers and this had a dual effect on the speculative front garden. Firstly it was not allowed to conceal or detract from the face of the dwelling, and secondly, it should be an attraction in its own right. Under such conditions, and in a garden which might differ little in size from that of a council house, the challenge was to achieve individuality within socially acceptable limits. This was also in the interests of developers, and it was not unusual for gardens to be 'dug over, made up, turfed or otherwise rendered presentable' on sale: 'it was almost always the front garden that received attention as this rendered the estate more attractive to later arrivals' (Jackson, 1973, p. 37).

While houses remained on sale, Wimpey, Laing and other developers organized competitions for the best kept front garden, and in 1935 D-C Estates presented a prize of £15 and a challenge cup for the best front garden in Canons Park, Harrow. This would have been clearly defined, compact and manicured, in the best tradition of the Victorian suburban garden. 'In the ribbon development houses of the time . . . the mode was for crazy paving, dwarf conifers, weeping trees, gnomes and other tiny ornaments, sundials, very small ponds and rockeries. To use the word of the time, they were "twee" ' (Fleming and Gore, 1979, p. 226). This 'twee-ness' was achieved by using decorative devices previously restricted to the back garden and, although this was a departure from previous practice, it was hardly more modern. Even the Modern Movement house failed to make its mark on the garden and 'the half sunburst, a favourite motif of the time . . would in fact have been an ideal plan for a front garden' (Ibid, 1979, p. 226).

The emphasis on the decorative function of the front garden led to changes in the marking of boundaries. Rather than impenetrable privet hedging or severe iron railings, there were now low walls 'of bricks or of crazy stones, sometimes topped by wooden posts carrying ornamental chains or low wood palings' (Jackson, 1973, p. 150). These were still symbolic of enclosure, but they reduced domestic privacy. This reduction was further accelerated by an increase in car ownership among owner occupiers from the 1920s onwards, and a consequent need for access to storage space for the car. The addition of a 'drive-way' breached the front boundary of the dwelling, so opening up the prospect from the street. Fortunately the impact of this incursion was moderated by the semi-detached layout, which enabled driveways and garages to be located at the sides and rear of dwellings.

Whilst the need for any such provision was unimaginable in council housing, a further development was to have significant consequences for the public–private relationship. The controlled uniformity of the interwar

Two solutions to the
decorative front garden: from
the 'twee' of the 1920s to the
cement of the 1960s. (*Sources*:
Sedgwick, *c.* 1920;
Cement and Concrete
Association, 1960)

council estate was taken a stage further in
Welwyn Garden City from 1920, when front
gardens were incorporated into open forecourts
(Osborn and Whittick, 1963). Such a novelty,
which compromised the sanctity of the private
front garden, was the subject of widespread
comment at the time. However, it was not until
the postwar years that the open-plan philosophy
was fully to take effect.

In contrast, the growing numbers of flat-
dwellers in both public and private sectors
were denied access to private garden space.
Communal gardens were provided for council
flats in London and Liverpool from the 1920s
onwards, but individual gardening activity was
limited to private balconies or window boxes.
The latter were a long-established tradition in
London, and competitions for the best kept

box were held by the LCC (LCC, 1931). The practice was further encouraged following municipal deputations to model tenement estates throughout central Europe (City of Birmingham, 1930). The floral displays at the Karl Marx Hof in Vienna made a particular impression, and flower boxes were incorporated into the structure of the more progressive developments of flats in London, Liverpool and Leeds. One of the gardener's greatest enemies is a cold wind, and a steady blast from the Mersey would have put paid to the tender bedding plants of Liverpool's Gerard Gardens. By the same token, it is ironic that these most gardenless of environments were given a 'Gardens' suffix, a tribute to the imagery if not the reality of the garden.

THE EROSION OF THE FRONT GARDEN

The practice of providing a semi-private front garden was systematically undermined in the postwar years, first in the public and then in the private sector. The reasons were three: the introduction of landscaping; an increase in densities per acre; and the extension of car ownership. The Dudley Report gave no direct guidance on the design of front gardens but practice was influenced by experimental layouts in New Towns, and Harlow in particular indicated the way forward (Cleeve Barr, 1958). The new towns programme offered an unparalleled opportunity to achieve a totally controlled design, with front gardens incorporated into the overall landscape. This was at first resisted for council housing because of the extra cost, and because of an argument that 'it should be the object of the management of an estate to encourage initiative, and a sense of personal responsibility in the tenant. The care of a garden is one of the ways in which this can be done, and to take the front garden from him would seem more likely to encourage the tendency to expect the local council to do

Image of a Radburn 'greenway': gentle strolls through the new town of Dawley. (*Source: Dawley: A New Town in the Making*, 1964)

everything' (Ministry of Health, 1948, para. 31). However, Radburn planning, with its pedestrian routes, 'greenways' and garage courts brought a new relationship between public and private, in which open-plan fronts were appropriate (Scoffham, 1984). In the context of the early postwar years, with their debate about a more modern and classless society, the open-plan front garden could be interpreted as a symbol of social progress.

The increase in public sector densities after 1951 was largely achieved at the expense of front gardens and was masked by open-plan landscaping (Cleeve Barr, 1958). The individualizing of such space was forbidden by tenancy conditions, thus leading to a generation of complaints about lack of privacy, pedestrian short-cutting, fouling dogs and noisy children. The front area became a prominent estate management issue and, in one recorded conflict, it involved an Afro-Caribbean resident who had the temerity to plant vegetables in his front garden (Andrews, 1979).

Open-plan landscaping was subsequently taken up by private developers. Whilst land use was a major consideration, the modernity of the practice was confirmed by the thirty Span housing schemes built between 1959 and 1969 (Brown, 1986). Mature trees, green spaces and open-plan gardens were intended to contribute to a harmony between landscape and dwellings. The sensitivity of the Span schemes may have been lost in translation elsewhere, but open-plan landscaping became an accepted feature of speculative housing development from the 1960s onwards.

The growth of car ownership in all sections of society has had a major impact on houses of all ages and tenures. From the early 1950s, car space and storage began to be incorporated in council as well as speculative housing (Scoffham, 1984). Where provision was made within the curtilage, it required either a drive-way or hard-standing: either practice effectively 'opened up' the dwelling to the street and strongly compromised any decorative or defensive use for the front garden. The impact of car ownership on earlier housing has since been dramatic. Whilst the forecourts of pre-1914 terraces or the small front gardens of inter-war semis may be just deep enough to accommodate one or two parking spaces, it is at the expense of any decorative or defensive use. Where terraced houses lack any space in the curtilage, the problem of on-street parking is clearly evident.

THE BACK YARD AND ALLOTMENT GARDEN

The history of the domestic garden in the twentieth century is mainly concerned with the back garden. In contrast to the front, the back garden has been premised on the assumption of exclusive use and access. Between 1900 and 1939 there was a steady increase in availability for the expanding middle classes; a delayed increase for the 'respectable' working classes; and only a limited 'trickling up' for the remainder of the population. Throughout the period, allotments continued to provide a surrogate back garden, for produce if not for privacy.

The garden suburb captured the imagination of the upwardly mobile and by 1914 over fifty schemes were completed or in progress (Constantine, 1981). Quite apart from its wider town planning and social motives, it gave the theme of 'rus in urbe' a domestic reality. The use of back gardens continued to be shaped by nineteenth-century ideas concerning decoration, recreation and above all privacy. However, increased availability was not accompanied by an increase in garden size, and in most cases this remained small. The features of the formal landscaped garden were diminished still further, until all that remained was a lawn edged by a paved path and bordered by flower beds. Novelty was added in the form of garden ornaments, garden furniture, or a summer house. Detailing could be provided by using tiled edging to lawns and borders, by creepers on trellises, or a distinctive tree.

For most of the population, with at best a back yard, the opportunities for emulating the suburban garden were severely constrained. In partial compensation, the allotment movement continued to flourish, particularly as a result of the 1908 Small Holdings and Allotments Act (Crouch and Ward, 1988). This consolidated the earlier legislation and obliged all local authorities to provide allotments for the 'labouring population' where they were not available privately.

The allotment's popularity was significantly increased by measures taken during the First World War. As early as 1914, the Board of Agriculture recognized the significance of domestic food production but the German blockade and Allied shipping losses gave greater urgency to the situation. In December 1916, local authorities were given powers to appropriate land suitable for allotments. Common land, parks and playing fields were subdivided, but this was still insufficient and from 1917 horticultural advisers were appointed to seek out more land. Growing produce became a public duty and both the King and Lloyd George became enthusiastic vegetable growers. The campaign exceeded all expectations, and by the end of 1917 the number of allotments had increased threefold, to 1.5 million. By 1918, it could be claimed that, 'for every five occupied houses throughout two kingdoms, there is one allotment' (Ibid, 1988, p. 71).

The significance of this 'active gardening' cannot be overestimated. Not only did it provide a restatement of the genuinely vernacular tradition of gardening but it gave it a mass appeal and a new respectability. The introduction of daylight saving time in 1916 extended the hours available for gardening. The demand for allotments persisted after the First World War, and in 1919 there were an estimated 7,000 new applicants each week, mostly ex-servicemen. 'Allotments fit for heroes' may not

have had the same appeal as 'homes fit for heroes' but allotments played their part in the resettlement of ex-servicemen. Under the Agriculture Act of 1920, allotment tenants were given the right to compensation for disturbance. The Allotments Act of 1922 increased protection from eviction and compelled local authorities to appoint an 'allotment committee' with tenant representation (Ibid, 1988). This support for allotment holders, in the face of demands for the return of requisitioned land, is indicative of the recognition given to gardening in postwar civilian life.

THE 'HOME GARDENER': BACK GARDENS IN THE INTERWAR YEARS

Between 1919 and 1939, nearly four million new houses with gardens were constructed, including over one million in the public sector. The almost universal provision of back gardens constituted a revolution in bringing 'the cultivation of a private garden within reach of a large and previously uninitiated section of society' (Constantine, 1981, p. 397), although flat dwellers were of course excluded from this dimension of home life.

In the public sector, the influence of Bournville and the garden city movement was evident in the Tudor Walters Report's recommended densities of twelve houses to the acre, which provided back gardens of about 400 yds^2. It was now seen to be possible as well as desirable for working-class families to have such gardens.

From the first generation of council houses, it was clear that back gardens were intended to be more than a decorative addition to the home. The size of plots, the gardening advice to tenants, and a steep rise in vegetable prices all encouraged the growing of produce. However, the length of back gardens and tenants' privacy of access also permitted other uses. Children could play in safety, washing could be dried, and relaxation enjoyed in summer. Like the early villa and Bournville gardens, the

The interwar 'home gardener'
hard at work: a productive
plot for the new council tenant.
(*Source*: *Pilot Papers*, 1947)

typical rectangular plot could be 'zoned' to
accommodate a lawn and flowerbeds next to
the house, with a vegetable plot and fruit
bushes beyond.

This compromise between the vernacular
and suburban gardening traditions was also
extended to the new owner-occupied sector.
The experience of wartime 'necessity-growing',
the increasing costs of employing a gardener,
and the universal emphasis on 'fresh air for
health' all encouraged a move towards more
active gardening and the return of fruit and
vegetable growing. Plot sizes showed a marked
increase as suburban house-building moved
outwards in pursuit of cheaper land.

The extent of the shift away from passive
suburban gardening was confirmed by the
finding of a 1939 survey that 'only in three

gardens out of each hundred was the garden work done by a paid gardener' (Wibberley, 1959, p. 121). In the new suburbia, gardening could be undertaken by husband and wife together, and its benefits enjoyed by all the family. However, it should not be too onerous, and the concept of the 'labour-saving' garden went hand in hand with the revival of active gardening. This could be achieved through the easily manageable lawn, rock garden and rosebeds, and by the increased use of garden gadgetry. The suburban middle classes had access to a constantly increasing range of lawn-making equipment, hoses and sprinklers, weed killers, pesticides and fertilizers (Hadfield, 1960). Keeping the lawn in trim was made easier by the manual mower or the petrol 'motor-mower', and the resulting problems of

Give that "velvet" touch to your LAWN

which delights the eye and enhances the beauty of the garden. In every part of the country you will find GREEN'S MOWERS giving the utmost satisfaction to their owners. Choose a GREEN Mower, such as the "SUPREME." There are other types suitable for large and small lawns, as well as the famous Green series of motor mowers.

The "Supreme" & Cutters in Cylinder, Steel sides, Ball bearings.

10", £7 10s.
12", £9 0s.
14", £10 5s.
16", £11 15s.
Grass box included.

If you need a GARDEN ROLLER Green's make them for every purpose.

Please write for List No. 66.

Established nearly 100 years.

THOMAS GREEN & SON, LTD., Smithfield Ironworks, LEEDS. New Surrey Works, Southwark Street, LONDON, S.E.I

GREEN'S MOWERS

The widely available manual mower that could create ideal lawn for the 'Ideal Home'. (*Source*: Advertisement in *Ideal Home*, 1927)

storage could be solved by adding a 'tool-house', located either at the bottom of the garden or at the side of a semi. The heyday of the domestic greenhouse was in this period and 'the small, cheap and practically unheated greenhouse became popular – particularly with the working man with his devotion to the chrysanthemum' (*Ibid*, 1960, p. 384). The home gardener had access to a vast range of pamphlets, books and journals and, from 1934, could listen to the first specialist programme on radio, Mr Middleton's *In Your Garden*.

The suburban back garden both complemented and reinforced a sense of home-centredness, whether among home owners or council tenants. 'The revolution in housing design coupled to a reduction in family size gave many families more space and privacy than they had ever enjoyed before' (Constantine, 1981, p. 399) and this privacy extended to the back garden, which was incorporated into home life with remarkable ease. Unfortunately, exclusive access and use did not necessarily mean visual or aural privacy, and commentators of the period could be scathing about the peculiarly English and illusory nature of 'privacy' in the back garden. ' "As for privacy – its absence is the most outstanding drawback in these (so highly respectable) suburbs. If I start to sing, my wife has to remind me that the neighbours will think we are quarrelling . . . And, of course, to sit in the garden and converse intimately is a sheer impossibility" ' (Boumphrey, 1940, pp. 53–54). The close proximity of gardens, the limitations of screening by fence or hedge, and the ability of neighbours to overlook gardens from bedroom windows, all undermined outdoor domestic privacy.

THE INTERWAR GARDEN: PREFERENCE AND POPULARITY

It was estimated that approximately two thirds of houses in England and Wales possessed

'Privacy in a garden suburb'!
A scathing comment from the
interwar years. (*Source*:
Boumphrey, 1940)

gardens by 1939 (Wibberley, 1959). The Mass Observation sample of working-class housing found that the overwhelming majority of garden city and housing estate dwellings had gardens, while less than a quarter of pre-1914 houses were entirely without one. All but two per cent of its home owners had gardens, compared to 22 per cent of its renters, and owners on the whole had larger gardens than renters. The movement of substantial numbers of the middle classes to the outer suburbs created an opportunity for others to 'filter up' into inner suburban, pre-war houses and so acquire 'second-hand' gardens. Although the amount of allotment land was reduced by over eighteen per cent between 1929 and 1939 (owing to the return of land to its owners, in addition to suburban expansion), it was more than compensated by the increase in gardens for many people.

There is limited knowledge of how gardens were used, particularly in the private sector. Patterns evidently varied regionally (*Ibid*, 1959) and according to the age and type of housing. In the 753 gardens assessed in detail by Mass Observation, only 37 per cent in districts of old houses were classified as 'well-kept', compared to 76 per cent in Garden Cities and 49 per cent

on (council) housing estates. Larger gardens in owner-occupied suburbia were considered to be better maintained than the medium to small gardens of council estates. According to another observer, 'if the gardens of an average suburban housing estate are examined, it will be found that out of every ten, two or three are neglected, four or five are laid out so as to require as little gardening as possible, and of the remainder, not more than one or two will be showing much in the way of fruit and vegetables' (Boumphrey, 1940, p. 48).

More is reported of the state of gardens on council estates. The Central Housing Advisory Committee found that most gardens were admirably kept, and 'to some the garden was a new toy of which they were obviously proud' (Ministry of Health, 1938, para. 59); and in York in the summer of 1936 gardens were 'ablaze with colour. It is indeed amazing how soon families, most of whom have never had a garden before, turn the rough land surrounding their new homes into beautiful gardens' (Rowntree, 1941, p. 234). At a slightly later date it was suggested that, in general, 'two-thirds of the gardens are well cultivated; one-third partially cultivated; and only about seven per cent neglected though valued as private space' (McAllister and McAllister, 1945, p. 113).

Mass Observation found that 'the great majority' of people in all its seven sample areas wanted a garden, and that 'many people . . . had a very strong attachment to their garden, the care of which formed their principal leisure time occupation' (Mass Observation, 1943, pp. 162, 163). 'The urge to grow things is clearly a very deep seated one . . . In practically every garden we have surveyed . . . there was something growing other than grass even if it was only a few straggly shrubs or a "chaos of chrysanthemums" ' (*Ibid*, 1943, p. 165). In practice, people used their gardens to grow vegetables and flowers, for drying washing, keeping chickens, rabbits and dogs, children's play, relaxation, and 'nothing'. The only other thing that a sample of gardenless north Londoners would have added to this list, if they had had a chance, was 'keeping pigs' (*Ibid*, 1943, p. 164).

THE WAR YEARS: 'DIG FOR VICTORY'

At the outbreak of war in 1939, domestic food production was again an important issue. Within a month, the Minister of Agriculture announced an immediate target of half a million new allotments and proclaimed, 'Let's get going and let "Dig for Victory" be the matter for everyone with a garden or allotment' (Crouch and Ward, 1988, p. 75). The outcome was even more impressive than in the First World War, and by 1943 it was estimated that over half of all manual workers kept either an allotment or a garden. These were located on any available strip of land from grass verges to railway embankments, and between 1939 and 1944 the number of allotments increased from 815,000 to 1.5 million.

A 1939 survey showed that one in eight town houses and one in three rural houses kept small livestock: hens, rabbits, and sometimes pigs (Wibberley, 1959). The domestic production of

poultry and pork in fact made a significant contribution to the war effort. The Domestic Poultry Keepers' Council had over one and a quarter million members by 1943, and nearly seven thousand 'Pig Clubs' reared their animals mainly on kitchen waste. By the end of the war it was estimated that domestic food production was meeting ten per cent of all Britain's needs (Crouch and Ward, 1988).

The war had a disruptive effect on decorative gardening (Hadfield, 1960). On council estates, in particular, standards of back gardens deteriorated because of the absence of men at war, and the effects were still noticeable several years after the war ended (Ministry of Health, 1948). One important use was found for the back garden, however, as the site of the Anderson shelter, which saved many lives. The shelter was originally intended for erection inside the house and its relocation outside, it was noticed, excluded people without gardens. By the outbreak of war, 1.5 million shelters had been distributed free to working-class families, and by the time the programme ended, in June 1940, they formed an important part of the entire civilian shelter programme. 'A masterpiece of cheap and simple engineering', the shelter consisted of two curved walls of corrugated steel which were sunk three feet into the ground, bolted together, and covered over with eighteen inches of earth (Calder, 1969, p. 179). Inside, though they were subject to flooding, they were often made as domestic as possible, with bunks, floor coverings and decorated walls. Patriotic gardeners did not hesitate to plant vegetables on top of them, and the 'Andersons' became a fixture in many gardens for long years to come, often put to use as garden sheds.

The war affected the front garden in two ways. For a period a taboo was broken, and it was dug up for vegetables. Of more lasting effect was the technically unproductive but briefly morale-boosting campaign to collect scrap metal as part of the civilian war effort.

The wholesale shearing of metal railings and gates transformed the terraced streets which had had them, giving their defensive forecourts a wholly unintended and deceptive openness. Subsequently, they were scarcely ever re-instated, and this was in itself a testimony to the changed relationship between private dwelling and public street.

THE POSTWAR YEARS: FROM THE 'MINIMUM' TO THE 'PATIO' GARDEN

While the wartime achievements of necessity-growing were not soon forgotten – they seem reflected, for instance, in the good-sized plots of the temporary 'prefabs' – garden size in new, postwar developments was governed by the prescriptions for population densities of town and country planning. These were variable, depending on and decreasing with distance from the urban centre, and only in the outer ring would they be low enough to permit gardens large enough for the conventional sequence of decorative gardening, recreation and produce growing. In council housing, the Tudor Walters norm of twelve houses to the acre was abandoned, and plot size in future would depend on location and layout. The mixed developments prescribed for inner areas, for instance, would contain a range of houses, flats and maisonettes with and without gardens, and with gardens of different sizes, but none of them large.

On the face of it, this ran counter to people's strongly expressed wish for gardens and the functions now generally thought desirable for them, including ornamental gardening and vegetable growing. The minimum size these would require was a plot of 800 yd^2 which was regarded as 'still easily within the range of one person's spare time maintenance' (EAW, 1946), p. 36). The desire to recreate a home-centred family life after the disruption of war was overwhelming at this time, and in this connection it was emphasized that the back garden was an

French windows opening on to a 'sun terrace' create an 'outdoor room': a prophetic view from the 1940s. (*Source*: Yerbury, 1947)

extension of the home. It was a place 'where the children can play, father can dig and baby can sleep' (Halton, 1943, p. 270). 'There should be a close relationship between the garden and the house, with French windows and folding door transforming the living room in the summer' (McAllister and McAllister, 1945, p. 113). The garden now began to be described as 'the outdoor room' (EAW, 1946, p. 38) and trade literature and the press were not slow to exploit and develop this concept (*Modern Homes Illustrated*, 1947). It was essential, in this connection, that however much the front garden changed, the principle of private access to the back should remain sacrosanct.

At the same time the demands of large, pre-war back gardens were perhaps beginning to be onerous. A 1951 study reported that eleven per cent of council house plots were now 'derelict' and fruit and vegetable growing were in decline

(MacKintosh and Wibberley, 1952). A solution was offered by a reworking of the idea of the 'labour-saving' garden (Streeter, 1956). This could be achieved in three ways: by the use of plants which did not require replacement each season; by taking advantage of garden chemicals, aids and gadgets, and, more fundamentally, by changes in garden design. The overall direction of these changes was indicated by Geoffrey Jellicoe's 'minimum garden', laid out at the rear of a terraced house in Lansbury for the Festival of Britain in 1951. Its features included a 'flower box', pots of plants, a bamboo trellis and the extensive use of concrete paving. Despite its small size (20 ft^2) beds were included for growing flowers and vegetables (Shepheard, 1953).

This initiative laid the basis for a radical rethinking of the functions of the 'modern garden' and led to the emergence of a distinctive as opposed to a derivative style of small-scale English gardening (Allen, 1956; Bisgrove, 1990). Whilst this process was slow to take effect, the need for it was increased by the

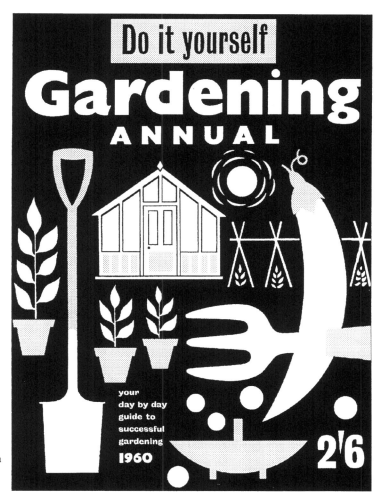

The postwar gardener was bombarded with advice from a wide range of popular books and journals.

general contraction in plot size which resulted
from subsidy reductions in the public sector
and increases in land prices in the private
sector. Whilst open-plan landscaping could
compensate for the loss of space in the front
garden, the impact on the back garden was a
progressive reduction.

The new emphasis on the labour-saving or
'leisure garden' (Genders, 1959), meant that
'necessity-growing' had to be sacrificed, those
who wanted a larger plot having to use allotments. Back gardens could still incorporate
decorative flower growing but increasingly
their main use was that of an 'open-air room'
(Whittick, 1957, p. 158). Thus within thirty
years of making back gardens large enough to

grow produce available to most families, the
practice was abandoned. By the 1960s the
perceived affluence of British society had
taken the necessity out of 'necessity-growing'.
These changes were reflected in contemporary
user studies and acknowledged in the Parker
Morris Report: 'the postwar improvements in
the standard of living mean that few families
now rely on the garden to keep properly fed. It
is now used for outdoor living, for children's
play and the baby's sleep. With the tendency
for densities to increase at the same time as
space has to be provided for more cars to be
kept, it will be a temptation to squeeze garden
sizes to a point where they will no longer cater
for these things. The evidence we received

The versatility of the terraced
yard is demonstrated at
Deeplish: new uses are grafted
on to an old territory. (*Source*:
MHLG, 1966*b*)

suggests that any call for large gardens is declining as other interests, such as the car, come to take up more of people's leisure time' (Parker Morris, 1961, para. 169).

Whilst growing produce was sacrificed, pressure was increasing from the new paraphernalia of leisure, including 'caravans, boats, racing cars, trailers, &c' (Cook, 1968, p. 233). The subsequent adoption of high-density housing, and of high-rise flats in particular, focused attention on the adequacy of garden space and on the user's experience and preferences. A study of seven postwar local authority estates of different densities confirmed the desire for a private garden, but for most tenants, the issue was one of screening rather than space (*Ibid*, 1968). Frequently, 'demarcation from side neighbours is by chain-link fencing only, supplemented on some layouts by anti-gossip fences, coal stores, or single storey back additions which might offer a modicum of privacy' (*Ibid*, 1968, p. 229).

By the late 1960s, a consistent view of adequate garden size can be found, but it had been largely overtaken by events. The implication of the survey mentioned was that gardens of less than 800 ft^2 were 'too small' and a 1968 National Opinion Poll survey found that '88 per cent of respondents preferred a private garden of some 900 ft^2' rather than a smaller garden with a communal addition (Edwards, 1981, p. 243). However, a study of twelve high-density Radburn schemes revealed that 'the average area of the private garden was 680 ft^2, substantially less than that of the gardens in the outer-ring development schemes illustrated in the Housing Manual of 1949' (MHLG, 1968*b*, p. 240).

User studies of council estates of the 1960s and 1970s reported problems of privacy and noise, and of inadequate space for drying clothes and children's play (MHLG, 1967*b*; 1969*a*; 1969*b*; 1970*a*). Play areas had been provided around municipal blocks of flats since the 1920s, and children in flats had been the

subject of investigation since the early 1950s (White, 1953; RIBA, 1957). However, the extension of high-density housing revived concern over the relationship between child development and the built environment (Scoffham, 1984). The addition of purpose-built play areas on conventional housing estates could partly compensate for the loss of garden space, but it was no solution for family dwellers in high-rise flats. Problems of child safety and supervision were often compounded by the sacrifice of public amenities on economic grounds, and as we have seen in Chapter 3, above, the problem of children living in tall flats was never satisfactorily resolved.

By the mid-1960s, changes in plot size and garden use had overtaken the interwar concept of the 'zoned' garden. In new homes, space for drying clothes, growing flowers, children's play and 'sitting out' had to be integrated into one well-used area. As Jellicoe had shown in 1951,

A maisonette tenant colonizes some public space on a high-density and high-rise estate.

the ideal material for this was concrete, which was durable, versatile and, from 1960, available in a number of forms (Cement and Concrete Association, 1960). Provided in the form of stepping stones or slabs it overcame the problem of the 'dewy lawn' (Bisgrove, 1990, p. 271), and as patterned blocks, it could be used in screens and walls. This new material confirmed the direction of changes to garden design. The outcome was the 'patio', a style of garden introduced from Spain and clearly influenced by the new 'package holiday' experience. The 'patio' marked the clearest break with the traditional English domestic garden and encapsulated the new relationship between home and garden. The classic statement of the perspective this entailed was provided in 1969: 'gardens are now for people, even for people who do not always enjoy gardening. The small garden could function as an extension of the too-small house as a room outside, and the small useful garden should be designed as one might design a room' (Brookes, 1969, p. 5).

This outside room could incorporate a sand-pit, a barbecue and a drying area; it could be 'instantly planted' with pots and containers containing 'Mediterranean' plants, and made private by the use of fence panels and the rapidly growing Leyland cypress. The very boundary between it and the house could be minimalized by use of the patio door, while the new enthusiasm for indoor plants enabled greening within as well as outside the house.

The final stage in this process of transformation was the emergence of the 'garden centre', from which all the ingredients of the patio garden could be obtained. It came about through two major changes, the application of new technologies, and the growth in car ownership. Cheap plastics, which became widely available during the 1960s, were ideally suited to use in the garden. The durable plant pot and plastic seats and tables were the most important of the resulting products. Cheap electric motors, when combined with plastic, gave new, light-weight mowing machines. The development of micropropagation enabled the production of millions of plants from one piece of stem or bud, and the 1964 Plant Varieties and Seeds Act gave encouragement to plant breeders by allowing them to patent new varieties. The opportunity to make direct sales of cheap plants to the car-owning public could be supplemented by an ever-increasing range of sundries, and during the 1960s almost all plant nurseries added a 'garden centre'. Within twenty years, the exclusively plant-growing nursery was almost entirely displaced by outlets buying in imported stock.

Small and 'patio-style' back gardens were thus sustained by a constantly growing range of garden-centre products. 'Grow-bags', hanging baskets and the Flymo all made gardening more manageable, and garden chairs, sun loungers and the barbecue confirmed the primacy of their leisure function. The new, small size of garden was adequate for these, and only the addition of a conservatory or a swimming pool might require a larger plot. The 'patio style' proved so popular that its influence has since spread beyond the type of housing in which it originated, and many English back gardens have now been provided with a defined area for sitting out. One of its main attractions must undoubtedly have been that it offered a new solution to the deeply rooted desire for back-garden privacy.

The popular shift towards leisure gardening has also had an impact on another vestige of the nineteenth century, the allotment. Between 1950 and 1970 its total numbers halved, to just over half a million (Crouch and Ward, 1988). The return of land to its owners and the 'Beeching' rationalization of railway-owned plots provide a partial explanation, but there is also evidence of a decline in demand. The number of empty plots reached a peak of twenty per cent by the mid-1960s, although current trends are less clear-cut. There have been significant increases in demand in some localities, and the growing popularity of home-grown and organic produce must have contributed to this, as well as the wish of ethnic minorities to grow their own special produce, as at Birmingham's Ashram Acres. Some local authorities have sought to encourage such demand (*Independent*, 1993), but at the same time others are being constrained by central government to sell off their allotment land. The continued existence of over half a million plots, however, demonstrates that the vernacular tradition of 'necessity growing' is still alive and productive.

THE SIDE OF THE HOUSE

Until the introduction of the semi-detached house, space at the side of the home was available only to those living in detached or end-of-terrace houses. The detached villas of the late nineteenth century were often closely spaced. Where plots were more spacious or were not rectangular, the sides could be used as gardens and often provided convenient sites for conservatories or greenhouses. In the case of terraced housing, the function of any space at the end of the row was mainly to mark its limit. No particular significance was assigned to it and normally it was part of the public street. In exceptional cases, it was incorporated into the curtilage and enclosed, to create a stronger sense of detachment from the public domain.

By 1914, the side of the home had a primarily utilitarian function which was reinforced by the general adoption of the semi and the extension of car ownership. The layout of semi-detached housing 'provided a ready solution to the problem of access to garden, back-door, coal-shed and dustbin' (Edwards, 1981, p. 103). Side space marked the boundary between adjacent pairs of semis and could be used to tidy away external plumbing from the front. The place of bathrooms and WCs within the house can only have strengthened its

negative status and, although it had a semi-privacy similar to the front garden, it was seldom ornamented. The main exception to this pattern was on council and better quality private estates where houses were laid out diagonally at road junctions in order to achieve a more open view. In this case the conspicuousness of the sides was reduced by enclosing them in garden space.

Unregulated by any byelaw requirements, the space provided at the side of typical semis was often minimal. Even when small, however, it was useful for storage and it was usually possible to squeeze in a car. The need for this was acknowledged by speculative developers as early as 1906, when houses on the Hale Brook Estate, Edgware, were advertised as having 'room for a motor' (Jackson, 1973, p. 150). 'Motor houses' or 'motor sheds' were provided from 1912, but the demand for garage space did not become significant until the 1920s, by which time, 'whilst not, strictly speaking, a portion of the "home", the garage especially for those living outside a town, has now become a sine qua non' (A Layman, 1927, p. 39).

Fortunately, rising car ownership coincided with the near universal adoption of the semi-detached house in speculative suburbia. Here, the obvious solution was to locate garages between pairs of semis, a practice which became common from the mid-1920s. By the end of the decade, builders were providing brick 'garages' at between £30 and £60, and within a few years an increasing number of semi-detached houses were being designed with integral garages (Jackson, 1973). Perhaps the most common practice, however, was merely to provide a garage space so that people could erect their own garages at their leisure. Frequently these were 'temporary', prefabricated, often asbestos sheet constructions which remained in situ for the next half century or more.

Although it was often only just large enough

1st September, 1927

MOTOR HOUSES

HANDSOME
- STAUNCH -
FIRE-RESISTING

MORRIS MOTORS (1926) LTD., COWLEY, OXON

The prefabricated asbestos garage makes its appearance in the 1920s. (*Source*: Morris Motors, 1927)

for a small car, the garage potentially provided additional storage space, so reinforcing the utilitarian nature of the side of dwellings. As early as the 1930s, it was 'frequently used for games or as a workshop for hobbies . . . A properly constructed brick garage attached to the house sometimes had its doors replaced by a window to become an extra living-room, playroom or even bedroom' (Burnett, 1986, p. 276). This set a precedent for a practice that became increasingly common in the postwar period, the building on of an extra bedroom over the garage. It is clear from user studies of the 1960s that garages continued to perform a range of functions. All households on a new

Radburn estate in Coventry used their garages for storing such items as scooters, deckchairs, washing machines and prams; two-thirds used them for children's play and some as workshops (MHLG, 1967*b*). Similarly, London households reported garages used for storage, drying clothes, children's play and workrooms (MHLG, 1969*b*). As time went on, the spread of 'patio-type' gardening, home decorating and DIY added to the paraphernalia needing to be stored. Not uncommonly the car was actually the last item to be put in the garage, and instead it was left standing on the drive.

Whilst garage provision was limited to the private sector in the interwar years, side spaces of council houses were similarly utilitarian. They were used for coal stores and second entrances, and in blocks of cottage and tenement flats for staircases and pram stores (Liverpool Corporation, 1951). After 1945, provision of car storage was extended to council estates. However, it was assumed that car ownership here was unlikely to exceed 25 per cent, so that provision for every house was considered unnecessary (Cleeve Barr, 1958). The solution recommended in the 1949 Housing Manual was garage blocks, with sufficient space to make additions if the level of car ownership increased. This advice was frequently ignored and many early postwar council estates, like those dating from before the war, have a legacy of inadequate parking provision.

Building on the experience of the first generation of new towns, Radburn planning located service courts or garage blocks at a distance from dwellings. The Parker Morris Report also advocated 'the Radburn system of layout' but on the basis of drastically revised figures for car ownership (Parker Morris, 1961). It projected an average of one car per household by 1980, an increase which could only be accommodated by provision 'on the basis of one car per dwelling, and with provision for visitors'; its only advice on the form of provision was that 'the car should be kept as near as possible to the owner's home' (*Ibid*, 1961, p. 54). The outcome was a drastic increase in both garage and hard-standing provisions on council estates, either within the curtilage or more commonly in nearby blocks.

Pressure on housing densities since the 1960s has led to a dramatic reduction in the space provided at the side of dwellings, irrespective of tenure. The close proximity of pairs of semis and smaller detached houses is a conspicuous feature of recent housing estates, where garages are squeezed out and replaced by hard-standing at the side or front of the house, or in shared courts of 'mews' layouts. This has been at the expense of side space that, as we have seen, serves a variety of useful functions, and, ironically, a higher status is now attributed to it. In particular, the detached house with a double garage behind the sight-line, approached by a generous-sized drive, is now one of the most exclusive types of dwelling.

THE GARDEN AND EXTERNAL SPACE IN THE TWENTIETH-CENTURY HOME

As with rooms, the history of the garden is a history of continuity, conservatism and change. The Victorian suburban tradition proved remarkably durable, and much of the twentieth-century development has been concerned with the diminution and reworking of its suburban garden. The legacy is all around us, from the manicured lawn and the cupressus, to bedding plants and the gnome in the rockery. The traditions of the pre-industrial vernacular plot also endure. Prize chrysanthemums, pigeons and potatoes can still be found in the municipal allotment, especially in established industrial areas. The National Society of Allotment and Leisure Gardeners has over 100,000 members in 1,400 societies, and prize leeks and dahlias continue to excite local passion. Concern over pollution and food additives and a demand for organic produce seem likely to perpetuate

The gardening tradition has endured if not revived in the second half of the twentieth century. (*Source*: MHLG, 1966*b*)

this 'necessity-growing' into the next century.

The main period of change was the 1960s, when these practices were challenged and partly superseded by the open-plan front garden and the low-maintenance, 'patio-style' back garden. The latter has proved popular, not least because it is intended for intensive leisure use and can be accommodated within a small area. It is also a style which can readily be applied to 'second-hand' gardens at relatively low expense, and the 'room outside' seems likely to dominate the use of private external space for the foreseeable future.

There are very few exceptions to these main traditions. The exploitation of flat roofs for gardens (for instance in blocks of flats) is very exceptional; and any attempt to create the bizarre, as in the case of the man who erected an upended Vauxhall car in his front garden, tends to be met with ridicule and hostility (McGhie, 1993). Gardens purposely designed by users of housing co-operatives and self-build schemes follow the conventions of their time, although those created on Merseyside are striking for the quality and individuality of their defensive planting. Gardening and small-holding are central to the lifestyles of some

alternative communities (Michèle and Kevin, 1983) and certain ethnic minorities have different concepts of planting, for instance using front gardens as vegetable plots (NFHA, 1993); but the impact of these is likely to remain very localized.

What, clearly, was accomplished in the twentieth century was the almost universal attachment of the garden to the home, with the very concept of 'home and garden'. Not far short of half the adult population now seem to be fairly frequent gardeners, but men are more active gardeners than women, with a participation rate of 52 per cent (GHS, 1992). Gardening activity is also age specific, and as many as 59 per cent of men aged sixty to sixty-nine do gardening, and they continue to keep up high levels of activity even above the age of seventy. The commonest age for women gardeners is forty-five to fifty-nine, but gardening activity is low among all people under thirty.

What historical and social constructions should be put on this are not entirely clear. Time available for gardening increases with age, so all may eventually give more time to it; but the habits and expectations of people who are now elderly were formed through their housing experience of fifty years ago, and may

In the late twentieth century the patio garden has inspired an architecture of its own. (*Source*: Gardening magazine advertisement, 1993)

be specific to this particular generation. There is an obvious connection between gardening and affluence. In general, the acquisition of gardens was a great leap forward in housing standards, and tending the garden became part of the joint conjugal enterprise of improving the home. It is not, therefore, surprising to find that gardening activity is associated with social class, as well as age and gender. In 1986, for instance, over sixty per cent of professional men but under 40 per cent of unskilled men reported doing some gardening in the previous four weeks (GHS, 1989). It seems clear that in future the domestic garden will continue to serve the interests of the electronic home, where quite possibly it will become even more private and defended. It will also be an essential part of any energy-saving and self-sufficient home. It is less clear what its role will be among the poorest members of society. The peripheral council estate has seen it put to good use for an adventure playground and for taking old cars apart; but for its upkeep in the conventionally approved manner, the money and skills may be lacking.

10

THE CHANGING EXPERIENCE OF HOME

HOUSE AND HOME: HOUSING PROGRESS AND HOUSING USERS

The evolution of the house is not, as the well known phrase suggests, synonymous with the evolution of the home – even though the two work in close counterpoint, as the preceding chapters have been at pains to show. The story must be completed, therefore, by some attempt to determine how houses and dwellings of all kinds are turned into homes and what changes of significance have taken place in this transformation during our period of concern. The range of dwellings available at any time is the product of past choices and actions: land development, finance, building construction and governmental policy-making, with architectural design and various technologies making an essential contribution. The process is cumulative and, while yearly additions to the stock are small, they are directed to certain targeted groups who get, as it were, privileged access to the most up-do-date and therefore supposedly the 'best' dwellings.

The first task of users is to get access to some part of the housing stock. If they fall outside one of the targeted groups this may be difficult and their options lie within surviving, pre-1914 houses or unpopular dwelling types like flats, in institutional housing of one kind or another, or in the range of unconventional, self-help remedies discussed in Chapter 6, above. While the last were used in a small minority of cases to serve a different culture, like the gypsies, or

to develop an alternative society or lifestyle, they were for the most part *ad hoc* strategies for obtaining homes of a conventional kind.

The housing stock thus appears in a sense to move forward under its own momentum, leaving individuals and households to fit into it and adapt it to their needs and desires as best they can. The arenas for user action are, in the first place, to gain access to the available stock, moving around within it as far as choice dictates and opportunity offers. Secondly, there is a range of domestic usage and behaviour, including decisions as to room use, decorating and furnishing, and housework of various kinds. With other and less well documented aspects of people's relationships to their most intimate environments, these combine to create the unfolding history of the home. It has been suggested that 'being "at home" means something quite different in the 1980s from what was understood by the term forty or fifty years ago' (Crow, 1989, p. 14). The purpose of this final chapter is to put this proposition to the test and to consider how far attitudes towards the home, the range of tasks performed in it, and users' contributions to its operation have in fact changed in the course of this century.

RESIDENTIAL MOVEMENT

The engine of housing change, determining both additions to and changing use of the stock, was residential movement. After 1945, newly formed households setting up home for the first time and the movement of established households, with a relatively small number of immigrating households in various periods, combined to create a national residential movement rate of some 7–8 per cent a year. The rate remained remarkably steady from this time, but little is known of general residential mobility prior to this, although much interest was taken in movement from the then new council estates, as will appear below. Prior to 1914, residential movement had to take place in a housing system where private renting dominated. There is abundant documentation of the acute awareness people of that time had of the subtle social nuances of streets and neighbourhoods (p. 4, above), and it was possible to protect or enhance one's social status by changing tenancies, which was reported as relatively easy to do. Home buyers of that and later periods acted on the same principle, using the mechanism of price to ensure compatible neighbours. Thus Chapman found that in their selection of houses purchasers 'chose the class to which they felt they rightfully belonged' (Chapman, 1955, p. 159).

An inevitable consequence was the tendency of residential environments to become single-class or socially homogeneous. When gentrifiers invaded lower-class areas it provided a diversion but did not really challenge this general pattern. The greatest hazard to the self-protective home owner was the parvenu, the new neighbour who was able to produce enough money to buy, but who did not come from the right background. This accounts for the panic that often occurred in owner-occupied neighbourhoods, after mid-century, at the merest prospect of 'the blacks moving in', although in fact the wholesale settlement of ethnic minorities in English suburbia was an almost unheard-of occurrence.

Council tenants were in a different position from home owners. Their quest for respectability was no less serious: on the contrary, it might be more important to them since they were closer to real poverty. But their movement was regulated by bureaucracy rather than price. They were 'allocated' to a dwelling rather than choosing one, and they lacked any formal control over the selection of their neighbours. They were vulnerable to the placing of people perceived as undesirable – most particularly 'rough' people from slums or the homeless, and one natural reaction, though not exclusive to tenants, was to make use of the deeply rooted domestic custom of 'keeping oneself to oneself' (Mass Observation, 1943; Young and Willmott, 1957).

Once installed in a tenancy, the only way for council tenants to improve their housing status, apart from buying a house, was to obtain a transfer to another tenancy or to exchange with another tenant. Not surprisingly, these became critical issues in the management of council housing, although local authority landlords did allow for their tenants' social preferences in certain ways. It was a standard practice to grade all applicants for the purpose of deciding which dwellings and estates best corresponded to their social level and placing them with compatible neighbours, but it was customary for housing managers to recognize the existence of local patterns of residential settlement which could not reasonably be flouted. It would be accepted, for instance, that people would want to stay in their own urban territories, as for instance on one side or another of a river. In addition, managers habitually reserved a proportion of lettings on new and superior estates for favoured tenants of long standing. But individual requests for transfers and exchanges were often obstructed and some authorities banned exchanges altogether (MHLG, 1953).

The parochial way in which council housing operated made removal from one local authority to another particularly difficult. This brake upon mobility did not begin formally to be addressed until the GLC pioneered an exchange scheme which was followed in 1981 by the government financed National Mobility Scheme. This, however, remained discretionary and even where it was adopted it applied to only a tiny minority of all lettings. It did not therefore in any real sense confer on council tenants the right to move.

There was no such restraint on the mobility of home owners. On the contrary, 'trading up' to a better house was strongly encouraged by estate agents, developers, building societies and the press, and over certain periods it was largely subsidized by inflation of house prices and consequently of the equity people had built up in their homes. There was no suggestion, here, that mobility was detrimental to the community life of suburbs but on the contrary, as appeared in Chapter 2 above, it was supposed that new arrivals generally settled quickly into their surroundings.

These differences, however, were evidently too slight to register in the global figures of residential movement, presumably because they were very localized, and also because in both cases they resulted from the main underlying cause of mobility, which was family formation and growth. Thus although a council tenancy was a recognized stepping stone to home ownership (Greenslade, 1976) the mobility patterns of home owners and council tenants in general were similar. The evidence was that the majority of moves made took place within rather than across tenures. Amongst other things this meant that those living in the least desirable part of the system, privately rented, furnished accommodation, had little chance of escaping from it, although within it the movement rates were higher than in any other tenure (GHS, 1971; 1980).

RESIDENTIAL MOVEMENT AND 'COMMUNITY'

The residential movement of council tenants continued to be scrutinized throughout the century, largely because of its supposed connection to the vexed question of 'community'. From its origins, council housing adhered to the principle that tenants would be lifelong residents, and that they would not be required to move on if their incomes rose (as was the case, for instance, in subsidized housing 'projects' of the United States). Deriving from garden city philosophy, the principle was clearly humane in intent, but it was imperceptibly translated into a fixed assumption that council estates were 'communities' for which the tenants were individually responsible. Hence it was argued that the desire of some tenants to use transfers as a housing ladder endangered 'the stability of estates which had often only existed for a generation'; such transfers 'undermined among residents the commitment to improve conditions. It has left a constant vacuum at the bottom of the scale since families only ever want to transfer upwards' (Power, 1987b, p. 98). Such reasoning laid different sets of expectations on council tenants and home owners, in which tenants were expected to be more immobile and to take more responsibility for the other people around them.

This assumption was contradicted by many of the realities of the situation. Allocation procedures, as we have seen, allowed only limited scope for personal choice. Councils were at liberty to adopt their own particular system but the usual pattern was, after the initial social grading, to take applicants in strict order of priority, allotting them the precise number of bedrooms that they required, according to the principle of 'tight fit'. While medical and a few other priorities might be considered valid reasons for an applicant to ask for one location rather than another, mere preference for a particular place, or a plea to be in surroundings or with people one liked, did not normally carry any weight. This was so much so, in fact, that when the innovative Newcastle estate of Byker adopted 'advance allocation' which allowed people to relocate in new houses beside their former friends and neighbours, this was regarded as a small revolution in housing management (Ravetz, 1976).

This was one of a number of contradictions highlighting the gap between the ideal of the council estate as a settled community and the actual wishes and behaviours of its tenants. While housing managers worked towards the ideal by encouraging the formation of community associations, architects believed themselves to be designing for 'community' through the garden-city derived cul-de-sac or the Radburn layout, although neither of these, as we have seen, corresponded to any real social patterns and indeed often inhibited them. At the same time, contradictory attitudes were not confined to officials. For instance, it was a frequently aired grievance of council tenants that their adult sons and daughters did not automatically become eligible for vacancies on the estates they had grown up in, but had to compete with 'outsiders' on the general waiting lists. In this respect, therefore, they chose to behave as members of rooted communities with rights to continuity of settlement – so much so that on some estates, when outsiders were seen filling vacancies, and particularly if the people in question were black, feelings were inflamed to the extent of physical violence or extreme political action.

As social experiments, early council estates were closely scrutinized and their annual turnover of tenancies was one of the more obvious things to note, becoming the subject of much concern when it seemed abnormally high. On both council and new town estates or parts of estates that were very unpopular, and particularly when other rented housing was available to movers, annual removal rates could indeed rise far above the norm (White, 1946; Kuper, 1953; Jennings, 1962; Morton, 1994). An outstanding and frequently quoted example was the LCC's inter-war Becontree-Dagenham estate where up to 17 per cent of households moved out in some years (Young, 1934). Such

a high turnover of population challenged the ideal of the estate as a static community, and it must also have evoked in planners' minds the sinister 'zone of transition' which figured large in the Chicago School of urban theory (Ravetz, 1986). This was an unstable inner ring round city centres which served as a reception area for immigrants, and was notorious for its social problems.

A sinister interpretation was put on these occasionally high removal rates, therefore; but it was also linked to a misapprehension concerning the normal turnover rates that were found. Interpretation of the data came to be based on the practice of making a distinction, on any particular estate, between tenancies of under and over five years duration. The division was an entirely arbitrary one, but on it was based a belief that 'there were two distinct groups of people, those who were very mobile, and only stayed in any one place for a few years or even months, and those who picked on a place to live and stayed there for as long as they could' (Mass Observation, 1943, p. 183). The fallacy lay in supposing that the future length of tenancies could be predicted from their observed length to date. Implicitly, it rested on the old assumption that the ideal rate of population turnover among council tenants would in fact be nil.

A more exact analysis, based on a complete set of records for a thirty-year old estate, showed that the structure repeatedly found in estate populations was the product of quite normal rates of residential movement (Ravetz, 1974b). That is, a normal annual rate of around 8 per cent could not do other than yield a population where some 35–40 per cent of households had been present not more than five years, and the balance of 60–65 per cent for six years and more (Cullingworth, 1965; MHLG, 1970b; GHS, 1971; 1977; 1991). There was no need, therefore, to suggest that tenants who moved out fairly quickly were undermining an otherwise stable 'community' or were evid-

ence of serious estate failure. While the occasional excessive rates of turnover required
some special explanation, some of the early
council estates were in fact found to have less
rather than more residential movement than
other sectors, with many of their tenancies
lasting twenty-five years or longer. Indeed, the
passing down of tenancies from parent to child
made possible tenancies of fifty or sixty years
duration, which were not infrequent. In this
respect the more undisturbed council estates
came to resemble those most sedentary areas
of all, old working-class inner urban neighbourhoods where some families might live for
generations (MHLG, 1970a; GHS, 1971; 1977;
1980).

The assumptions based on mobility rates of
council tenants, therefore, are reflections of a
special emphasis on council housing and its
problems rather than a reliable guide to general
patterns. In taking the idea of 'the less movement
the better' as axiomatic, they overlooked the
extent to which residential movement might be
beneficial as well as detrimental and what it
might or might not do for the home. Not only
did it, presumably, provide movers with homes
that they preferred but it was often associated
with improvement of the dwelling. New home
owners would normally carry out redecoration
and other improvements on moving in, and
their building societies sometimes made repairs
a condition of loans. In councils and housing
associations, it was customary to carry out
redecoration on change of tenancy or, alternatively, to give new tenants cash grants to carry
out work themselves, on the grounds that 'a
council house becomes more of a home when it
is decorated to the tenants' individual taste . . .
and far more care is taken of a house when the
tenant has spent a good deal of time and
trouble on it' (MHLG, 1959, para. 89). In such
ways, therefore, residential mobility promoted
the improvement and updating of the housing
stock.

The personal experience of moving house

was a significant part of people's housing
experience, and is too large a subject to be
fully covered here. For some, the act of moving
appeared to be easy: with or without specialist
help they contrived to pack up and unpack all
their belongings and have the new home in
functioning order in a matter of days. But in
general, moving was recognized as an ordeal
and was high on the list of traumatic life
events, although for different reasons in different times and contexts. Some of the earliest
council tenants, for example, trundling a few
poor belongings on handcarts, had to run the
gauntlet of their new neighbours. The space
and emptiness of their new homes, with the
sometimes deathly quiet of their surroundings,
came as a terrible shock, particularly to women
used to the hustle and bustle of the old streets
(Durant, 1939; Allaun, 1972). A similar experience occurred to the 'captive housewife' of the
postwar new town who was prey to the newly
named disease of 'new town blues'. 'Marooned
in her kitchen' she looked out of her windows
'only to see blank expanses of landscape,
devoid of familiar landmarks or human activity'
(Attfield, 1989, p. 218).

Greater affluence, with a higher degree of
choice, should have made moving house easier;
but under English law the process of selling
and buying dwellings was long drawn out and
often agonizing. Purchasers could go back on
their word or be 'gazumped' (edged out by
higher bidders) until a very late stage in the
process. When the market was slow, long
'chains' of interdependent sellers and buyers
developed, while the constraints of borrowing
and interest rates meant that both sale and
purchase completions were required to take
place simultaneously, with all parties moving
house on the same day. With the huge sums of
money involved, such things made moving a
very stressful event. When, as was often the
case, it was associated with a personal bereavement or the break-up of a family after separation, divorce, or children leaving home, it was

bound up with many painful and conflicting emotions.

WHY PEOPLE MOVED

Although mobility data were repeatedly worked on and referred to through the later half of the century, the real implications were not always clear. It was not of course difficult to discern a relationship between mobility (actual or potential), people's satisfaction with their homes, and house type and quality, for all these were closely interwoven; but in the last resort it was impossible to distinguish cause and effect because the very fact of moving denoted a purpose of bettering one's conditions. Thus there was an obvious correlation with technical factors: housing satisfaction increased as dwellings increased in size, number of bedrooms, and exclusive use of amenities (Cullingworth, 1965; GHS, 1976, 1990). People were more satisfied with detached houses than with semis, with semis than terraced houses or flats, and least of all with converted flats, 'rooms' and maisonettes. There were obvious tenure implications in this. The key variable, however, was the family or household type, for the most frequent movers were young families in search of more bedroom accommodation, who frequently used the occasion to move into the catchment area of a desirable school. In most cases the actual distances moved were very small, and it was perhaps surprising to find this perpetuation of local patterns of settlement in the supposedly mobile twentieth century. House builders and estate agents naturally exploited this in the targeting of their publicity and there is a further history waiting to be written on how people searched out the districts and housing developments that they might move to.

Among those who were parents, moving tended to be justified by its presumed benefits for children, although the latter might well be ignorant of these. People living in older districts of terraced housing, for instance, thought it

particularly desirable to remove their children from the streets where they played, and to give them gardens instead. 'As children you don't miss a garden, but as parents you know they're missing it' (Allaun, 1972, p. 61). In satisfying the children's interests, grandparents and other relatives were left behind in the old neighbourhood, and this was a sacrifice that was noticed but felt to be justified (Young and Willmott, 1957; Vereker et al., 1961). With the social mobility that movement to the suburbs also implied, this accentuated a growing gap between the generations (Willmott and Young, 1960). Once families had met their needs by moving into larger and better homes, their rate of movement slowed, and older people moved significantly less often (GHS, 1970; 1977). The gross national mobility rate, therefore, was brought up to its normal level by younger home-makers and young people making multiple moves before forming new and settled households.

As home ownership rose to dominate the housing system, it seemed increasingly self-evident that home owners enjoyed and took pride in their homes to an extent impossible for tenants, particularly council tenants. As early as 1943 Mass Observation noted that home ownership 'clearly correlated with a more intense feeling about the home' (Mass Observation, 1943, p. 177), and much the same observation was repeated throughout the century (Zweig, 1961; Hall, 1976; GHS, 1978; Saunders, 1990). With the rise of home ownership went a corresponding decline in public esteem of council housing. It comes as no surprise, therefore, that council tenants who bought their homes under the 'right to buy' in the 1980s felt 'more secure', as if 'the house was "more mine, somehow" ' (Stubbs, 1988, p. 153). As time went on, home improvements were increasingly related to ownership. It was not that council housing did not lend itself to schemes of interior improvement, as was made clear in Chapter 8, above, but that as the status of council tenancy fell it seemed less and less worthwhile to invest the time and money, even if this was possible, so the freedom of home owners to remodel their homes was something that tenants came to envy (Holme, 1985).

These, however, were trends pertaining to the later part of the century. In its earlier decades the recent legacy of the pre-1914 housing system meant that 'a home of one's own' meant, not a dwelling that one owned, but one not shared with another family, with its own front door (Mass Observation, 1943) – and this was, in fact, what council housing delivered, to the evident satisfaction of its early beneficiaries. About three-quarters of the people canvassed by Mass Observation were doubtful of the wisdom of buying their own homes, owing to the blitz and general uncertainties of the time. In the 1960s there were still some who regarded renting a council house as superior to owning their own: 'You have it for life, it's like your own, cheaper, nothing to worry about, when out of work you get consideration, no responsibility anyhow' (Zweig, 1961, p. 125; Gray and Russell, 1960). But given the growing constraints and stresses of the tenure after its peak in the mid-1970s, it is not surprising that owner occupation was increasingly seen as necessary self protection, as well as something on which all resources and creativity could be lavished. Thus housing tenure came to usurp even location as the criterion of residential and social status – that of design and quality had, of course, long since ceased to be operative.

ATTITUDES TO THE HOME

In the last resort analysis of mobility data can only yield limited information about people's feelings and inner motivations, and the reason for this must lie in the subtle but crucial difference between house and home. At various stages of people's lives, particularly in their earlier years, there was no alternative to

moving round the housing system, and their attitudes and decisions about homes and moving were in essence rational responses to this, and to the houses or dwellings that were available. Feelings about the home, however, wherever and whatever this was at any time of life, were internalized and so less amenable to objective measurement. A clue seems to be provided in the innumerable surveys of council and housing association estates – as in official Design Bulletins of the 1960s and 1970s and academic or consultancy studies to the 1990s – which found, invariably, that people were much more contented with their homes than with their estates. The difference was found to be particularly related to 'feelings about the appearance of the approach to the front door' (Burbidge, 1975, p. 159), which in turn was related to several other issues 'which all impinge particularly on the feelings of pride and identification which residents may or may not have in relation to their estate' (Ibid, 1975, p. 161).

What is of interest in the present context is that people were able, consciously or unconsciously, to make such a distinction, and the close bond with the home that was felt. This may be connected to something observed at various points in this history, that people contrived to be 'at home' in the most surprising circumstances, which included, for instance, the generally stigmatized and unpopular high-rise flat, the derelict squatted house, or the flimsy shack. It also helps to elucidate the paradox of the housing of old people, whose housing standards were among the worst, objectively speaking, but whose expressed levels of satisfaction were consistently higher than other age groups (GHS, 1978; 1990). What from an external view was seen as inconvenient and substandard housing was for them a home, perhaps hallowed by longstanding and precious associations, which provided a secluded and private environment where they could use well worked out practical coping strategies. Here and in numerous similar cases it was apparent that objective and measurable standards could weigh less than personal and subjective considerations. As Mass Observation noticed: 'People became sentimentally attached to houses that medical officers of health would condemn at first glance' (Mass Observation, 1943, pp. 68–69). More than a generation later it still held true that for many people 'the meaning they attached to home did not appear to be affected by the standard of their accommodation nor how they regarded this' (Holme, 1985, p. 135).

This was consistent with other evidence that people made the best of what housing they had, however others might view this. It appears, for instance, among the residents of old people's Homes who made a point of being satisfied when there was no alternative (Allen *et al.*, 1992), and that surprising majority in bed-and-breakfast accommodation and hostels who expressed themselves content with where they lived (Thomas and Niner, 1989). A technical measure of housing satisfaction, while appearing to have the merit of objectivity, could easily overlook such subjective responses. In attempting to make some allowance for this, one official report surmized that people's attitudes were 'a combination of realism and wish fulfilment, of resignation and resentment' (GHS, 1978, p. 58). With stricter accuracy it might be said that people's feelings were conditioned by the functions that particular dwellings or accommodation performed in their lives. The point was dealt with in the 'freedom to build' debate, where it was used as the rationale for self-build housing. Although the debate almost certainly overestimated the likely public enthusiasm for this (p. 118, above), its distinction between 'housing as a noun', imposed by authority, and 'housing as a verb' as utilized by people, conveyed the essence of the matter (Turner, 1972).

However, the causes of subjective responses are for obvious reasons difficult to find. One clue is the relationship found between satisfac-tion with the home and the extent to which its inhabitants felt they had exercised choice in its selection. Thus people rehoused after slum clearance and council tenants generally were demonstrably more settled when they felt they had chosen their new homes (Ravetz, 1974*b*; Goodchild and Furbey, 1986). Perhaps the most outstanding case of this principle at work was among those squatters who made a positive virtue of their chosen housing conditions because these liberated them 'from the mystery and tyranny of the workings of a house', so allowing them to develop a 'unique' relationship with their homes (Ingham, 1980, p. 173).

Another determinant of feelings about the home was people's previous housing experience (Mass Observation, 1943; Vereker *et al.*, 1961; Allaun, 1972). To people renting slum property, their first council house seemed 'a dream come true' (Stubbs, 1988, p. 151). But once higher standards were experienced, people became more discriminating and their own standards rose (Spring Rice, 1939; Mogey, 1956; Allaun, 1972).

The most recently proposed variable in attitudes to the home is that of gender. Perhaps surprisingly, this is difficult to substantiate from the historical evidence. Since women always spent more time in the home and contributed far more of their own labour to it than men, it would be surprising if their feelings were not significantly different from men's, as recent feminist critiques assume to be the case (pp. 174 above; 220 ff.). Some support for the idea comes from Mass Observation's finding that women were more favourably inclined towards flats than men because of their reluctance to move away from city centres, and the same thing evidently still applied a generation later (Mass Observation, 1943; GHS, 1978). In general, women appeared to be less eager to move house than men (Allaun, 1972). But such suggestions are on the whole insubstantial when compared with a large bulk of evidence showing that married women strongly identified with the marital home, which they were eager to embellish (Holme, 1985; Saunders, 1990; Partington, 1989; Attfield, 1989; Hunt, 1989). Some of the very poorest women limited their families so that they could go out to work to pay for a better family home (White, 1986), while the great majority evidently concurred with a conventional domestic ideal that was 'cosy, individualist, home-loving, materialist' (Pugh, 1992, p. 292).

USERS' CONTRIBUTIONS TO THE HOME: HOUSEKEEPING

'The home, what it is, what it means, and how it is experienced, does not just happen, or get structurally determined, but it is the product of negotiations by people who operate within certain constraints' (Mason, 1989, p. 104). The housewives who looked after the houses and created the home must surely be the first among such people. For the most part their contribution, even the fact that they made a contribution, was taken for granted by the rest of society. The only exception was in time of war, when governments appealed to housewives to keep the nation well fed and in good morale. Their assumed needs and wishes were addressed by architects and manufacturers – in the case of architects often mistakenly, as we have seen. But the real content and development of their role received little serious attention outside feminist circles.

Housekeeping in the sense that the twentieth century came to understand it evolved with industrialism, in which the domestic economy became physically and functionally separate from 'real' economy of production and commerce. The care of the home, with or without domestic servants, became the responsibility of wives and other female family members, who were expected to treat it as a fulltime responsibility (Oakley, 1974a; Davidoff, 1976). In

reality, the housewife role was neither irrelevant to the main economy, nor static. As a manager of servants and budgets, the middle-class housewife learnt new skills, and began early to develop importance as a consumer (Branca, 1975). The lot of the working-class housewife depended on the income coming into the home. If this was low, or uncertain, her main task was to survive from week to week, combating dirt, drink, disease and death. When there was an assured and reasonable income, her skills were crucial to her family's comfort and social status. If, as was often the case, she had worked in domestic service before marriage, she was likely to introduce some middle or upper-class domestic routines and standards into her own home.

There are many contemporary descriptions, from both before and after 1914, of poor working-class women living in shared houses, enslaved to yearly pregnancies and weakened by poor diet and frequent miscarriages (Pember Reeves, 1913; Spring Rice, 1939). This made it seem obvious to social reformers, as well as to the women themselves, that decent housing (but not, as we have seen, co-operative housekeeping) would remedy their situation. In the upper middle classes the main preoccupation was the very different one of how to cope with housework once domestic servants became unobtainable. Middle-class housewives, therefore, were likely to set more store on household appliances than better houses. Developed in the first place to lighten the work of servants, appliances were increasingly looked to as aids for the housewife herself.

Housekeeping encompasses the dual functions of home making and housework: care of people and care of the house itself, each of which has a complex history to which class differences, rising incomes, house design, the manufacturing and food industries have all contributed. Both the content of the two functions and their weighting relative to one another changed significantly after 1914.

The task of the working-class housewife. (*Source*: Town and Country Planning Association)

Shrinking of household size meant that, as well as fewer people to care for, there were fewer to share the work of the home. In past history, quite far down the social scale there had been servants on hand. The domestic servant was the survivor of a time when house servants were inferior and subordinate members of the main family, analogous in some respects to children, bearing their owners' names, perhaps wearing their owners' livery, and expected to merge their fortunes and identities with those of their masters. Their own housing needs were invisible since they were tucked away in the family's home without being allowed to create families of their own. By 1900, domestic service had become overwhelmingly female and youthful, staffed largely by young country girls for whom it acted as a stepping stone to marriage.

In 1914 'the servant problem' was already of long standing, but the draining away of servants during the First World War and the growing independence of those that remained prompted the Ministry of Reconstruction to set up a committee to discuss the renewal of the industry, among other things through state-supported training centres (Butler, 1916). The absolute numbers of servants were maintained between the wars, and 'going into service' remained the main occupational option for women; but the body of servants was shrinking relative to the numbers of households, while those able to afford a servant were diminishing. They did not, for instance, include the new wave of suburbans, whose only domestic help was a daily 'char' (Chapman, 1955).

Domestic service did not survive the Second World War, in spite of the Labour government's

 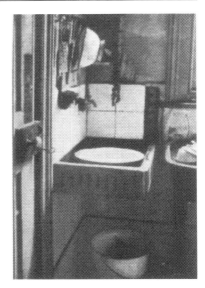

THE SORT OF SINK THE HOUSEWIFE WANTS.   THE SORT OF SINK SHE OFTEN GETS.

What had long been good enough for servants did not suit the twentieth-century housewife. (Randall Phillips, 1923)

support for a national Institute of Houseworkers set up in 1947. By 1951, it had shrunk to a third of its prewar size. Those who wanted live-in help – particularly the rising but impoverished professional classes – resorted to foreign au pairs. Typically young girls fresh from school, these worked long, unspecified hours with little reward other than pocket money and perhaps time off to attend language classes. In many ways they were in the same dependent position as the Victorian 'maid-of-all-work', except that their main task was child care rather than housework and that, typically, they shared the same social class as their employers.

The demise of domestic service left the care of the home and the people in it entirely to the housewife, apart from any help that other family members chose to give her. In larger families, now mainly confined to the working class, help was expected from older daughters, who might well be of an age to mother their younger siblings. The fall in numbers of children per family, together with suburbanization,

brought into being a new housewife role which seems captured in the anonymous woman who was one of the two hundred or so people who kept a detailed one-day diary on March 12th, 1937, for Mass Observation. She passes the day in the company of her only child, a boy of five. After a morning spent on housework and sending off an item for the 'This England' column of the *New Statesman*, she goes to the shops (walking to save the bus fare) where an elegant young woman emerging from the hair-dresser makes her feel like a charwoman with her heavy basket. This gives her 'a sense of despair because I am never likely to be in a much better position, not at any rate until M is grown up' (Jennings, Madge *et al.*, 1937, p. 370). Back home, she works on a handmade rug, puts out bread for the birds, and dances to the gramophone with her boy. In the course of her day, five tradesmen come to her door, in addition to the postman and a neighbour who has taken in her laundry.

Neighbours potentially performed a very

important role, especially in the poorer classes. They could be counted on when need arose for 'care of each other's children, help in illness, small loans of food and money and equipment, and on occasion help with domestic work' (Chapman, 1955, p. 69). Among the poorest, neighbouring was mainly carried on outside the home, and between women rather than men. The reasons for this were clear: there was no space and little to share inside the home while, above all, the husband's privacy and relations between husband and wife, were to be protected. Only emergencies and the special allowance that was always made for the needs of the aged, overrode a taboo against socializing in the home. This, as much as anything, was based on the fear of getting a reputation as a 'nosey-Parker'. Both helpers and helped, therefore, drew as far apart as ever once the need

The context, object and sharing of child care were transformed after suburbanization. (*Source*: *Pilot Papers*, 1947)

for help had passed (Ravetz, 1974*b*). Neighbours knew too much about one another's affairs for the relationship to be allowed easily to slide into friendship.

Relocation in the suburbs naturally disrupted established patterns of neighbouring. They were sometimes transferred to or recreated on new council estates (Kuper, 1953; Mogey, 1956; Jennings, 1962; Allaun, 1972); but for the most part the move encouraged the family to withdraw defensively into itself: 'the estate family in its bureaucratic landscape was more inturned on itself and can be said to be family-centred' (Mogey, 1956, p. 75). This then gave rise to a new role for neighbours: that of mutual admiration of the new possessions and status objects of the home which, though it applied equally to home owners and council tenants, could be seen as part of the transformation 'from a people-centred to a house-centred existence' (Young and Willmott, 1957, p. 154; Kuper, 1953; Zweig, 1961). While this could give new meaning to the neighbour role, the increasing technical autonomy of the home threatened to make it irrelevant. As early as the 1950s it was noticed that television and the telephone were starting to displace social interactions between neighbours (Kuper, 1953; Chapman, 1955). Late in the century, the completely self-servicing and self-sufficient house would need to call on the services of neighbours even less than its Victorian and Edwardian predecessors that had been fully staffed with servants.

CARE OF PEOPLE IN THE HOME: MEALS AND HOSPITALITY

Besides fewer people to care for, the nature of personal care in the home changed through the century. The Victorian housewife was intimately concerned with life and death, and her household manuals took it for granted that they needed to give her advice on illness, convalescence, childbirth and its following month of 'lying in', all of which took place at home, as did the education of very young children and much of the education of girls. Education became a state responsibility from early in the century so that, above the age of five, twentieth-century parents had to get special dispensation if they wished to educate their children at home. Some thought was still given to home nursing of the sick in the Parker Morris Report, although mainly in relation to small children. After the advent of the National Health Service in 1948 and with changing medical practices, people were strongly discouraged if not outright prevented from giving birth or caring for the seriously and terminally ill at home, even when they wanted to. Changes in hospital practices in the 1990s threatened to bring these activities back into the home, although by this time it was not necessarily well equipped nor family members prepared to take them on.

The most important daily care that was given in the home was the provision of meals. While there were wide class and regional variations, general standards of nutrition rose between the wars, when the growth of prepared foods and of eating out by the more affluent began to lighten the housewife's load (Burnett, 1966). National catering services were set up in each World War, the 'British Restaurants' of the second being a particularly popular network surviving in some places, as civic restaurants under the 1947 Civic Restaurants Act, down the 1960s (Roberts, 1984). But despite the hopes of many women and housing reformers both in the 1920s and the 1940s that such services would survive on a permanent basis, and notwithstanding continuing growth of factory canteens, the great majority of meals continued to be provided at home well into the second half of the century (Burnett, 1966; Chapman, 1955).

Traditionally the most important meal of the week in all social classes was the midday Sunday dinner: ideally a family meal built around a roast joint of meat, which was often followed by a special tea with delicacies like tinned fish or fruit and home made cake. Weekday meals were a succession of leftovers from this, enlivened by cheap easy dishes like sausages and kippers towards the end of the week. In households with resident servants these, and often also children, ate in separate rooms at special times, often with inferior bills of fare.

One of the functions of meals was to reinforce family solidarity, hierarchy and discipline. Among the comfortable working classes, before and after 1914, a plentiful supply of tasty and preferably home-baked food was as essential to the sense of home as a good blazing fire (Hoggart, 1957). There was a strong and enduring pattern of giving the best of anything going to the breadwinner. In poorer families, females fared worse than males for food, and worst of all fared the mother, who would plead lack of appetite while waiting on the rest, to make do with little more than a cup of tea later. Children admitted to family meals were often placed under a ban of silence or even forbidden to sit down (Roberts, 1971). Perhaps the basis for this was a widespread view throughout all social classes that it was improper to indulge in conversation at meals.

It is difficult to gauge the work involved in cooking for a family when incomes and housing conditions were so varied and when, for lack of storage, women in slums had to do daily or more than daily shopping. According to a survey of the mid-1930s, around three hours a day were spent on cooking and washing up (PEP, 1945), the burden of work depending partly on family timetables. It was the common pattern for the men as well as the children of the family to come home for midday dinner, which was then complemented by 'high tea' rather than another cooked meal in the evening. Towards 1960, this was still the case in 60 per cent of families (Burnett, 1966), but meanwhile suburbanization was forcing a change which

'One of the functions of meals was to reinforce family solidarity, hierarchy and discipline': the Sunday roast in a postwar setting. (*Source*: McAllister and McAllister, 1945)

had already been noticed twenty years before (Bournville Village Trust, 1941; *Our Towns*, 1944). This was the shift of the main meal from midday to the evening, a culinary 'embourgeoisement' which was strongly related to house types. Thus in mid-1950s Liverpool, the meal patterns in council houses were halfway between those in small byelaw houses and semis: 72 per cent of council tenants had their dinner in the evening, in contrast to 45 per cent in small byelaw houses and 86 per cent in semis; and 38 per cent of council tenants had afternoon tea, in contrast to 13 per cent in small byelaw houses and 68 per cent in semis (Chapman, 1955).

In 1944, the Dudley Report thought it reasonable to suppose that most husbands would not come home at midday and concluded that they and the children of the family would require two different programmes of meals. Seventeen years later, the Parker Morris Report envisaged meals being taken in relays and families eating together, if at all, only at weekends. The freeing up of meal times was given still more impetus with the postwar spread of 'pizza parlours', Indian and Chinese 'takeaways', which were usually open longer hours than traditional English fish and chip shops. Within the home, impetus was also given by the introduction of ready-made, quick-frozen meals and microwave ovens. By the 1990s, the family meal had disappeared from many households and the various family members 'grazed' as they felt inclined from refrigerators and freezers. By this time home baking had become much more rare – so much so, in fact, that traditional English puddings and pies were being offered as gourmet fare in restaurants and sold in easy-to-make 'kits' in supermarkets.

Another aspect of personal care through food and drink was the giving of hospitality, to which suburbanization also brought new patterns. In small, pre-1914 houses in Liverpool, hospitality consisted mainly of informal 'dropping in' and cups of tea between women and children, but people in larger terraced houses also used more formal arrangements (Chapman, 1955). In early postwar council houses there was seen 'the beginning of entertaining with a social, religious or political purpose' (*Ibid*, 1955, p. 69); while people in semis entertained invited guests with coffee, wines and spirits. It was customary to celebrate special occasions like funerals, weddings, and christenings in all grades and conditions of home, but by the 1980s and 1990s they were increasingly being catered for commercially outside the home. This applied even to the birthday tea of small children, which could now be moved to the local branch of McDonalds.

Christmas had long made its own special contribution to the home. Before the Second World War it was for most families a short and simple festival, starting not long before Christmas Eve and ending with Boxing Day, the day after Christmas. In the later part of the century it became progressively longer and more elaborate, as (for most people) the religious content diminished but the associated present-giving and hospitality increased. It became, for practical purposes, a festival of goodwill and material consumption which was practised by people of any or no religion. Augmented by New Year bank holidays and 'days in lieu', the festival eventually stretched over several days, the management of which needed to be planned and prepared for by housewives over many months. The first outward sign was the decoration of the home with coloured lights and baubles from a date early in December – and the display of these was often as much for the benefit of the passer-by in the street as for the inmates themselves. The central ritual of the secularized festival was the Christmas family dinner, but the labour of this, and the difficulties posed for people whose families were grown up or who had no families to be with, encouraged a trend of transferring it to a hotel or restaurant. For those with the money to spend, it became an increasingly attractive option to pass the whole festival in a hotel, which laid on all the festivities once provided in the home.

OTHER FORMS OF CARE GIVING IN THE HOME

The care of clothing was another important element of personal care. The evolution of domestic laundry was a complex one, influenced by the rise of commercial laundry services, public wash houses, and the technical development of washing machines, which caused it alternately to leave and return to the home at different periods (PEP, 1945). The taking in of other people's washing was one of the last surviving home industries and one that remained important for poor women, at least to 1939. The ordinary weekly family wash was counted as 'one of the most arduous and unpopular household duties', involving as it did not only washing but wringing, hanging out, ironing and airing, which together dominated several days of the week (*Ibid*, 1945, p. xiii). The almost universal washday was Monday, and the dislocation then caused was habitually blamed for driving working men to drink: 'fortunate the men who [then] receives a welcoming smile and a hot meal' (Bournville Village Trust, 1941, p. 76).

The time that had to be spent on the family wash was, of course, a function of household size, the clothes owned, and the number of times these were changed. In poor working-class families, for instance, sole sets of underwear, working clothes or school uniforms had to be washed and dried overnight if they were to be worn the next day. For a five-person household in 1918, an estimate of time taken was between eight and nine hours; but for larger numbers this might rise to over twelve hours. When an electric machine was available, however, the whole task from start to finish, including drying and folding, might be done by teatime of the same day, while other tasks could be accomplished meanwhile (PEP, 1945; see pp. 153–154, above).

Sewing, mending and knitting were habitually classed as 'leisure' activities of the housewife (*Ibid*, 1945), but in some respects they can be regarded as late survivals of traditional home-based production, as well as a strategy obligatory for the poor, who had no option but to recycle their clothing. The sewing machine in its modern (lockstitch) form began its domestic diffusion in the 1860s, and besides being the earliest, it was often said to be the most valuable of all the housewife's mechanical aids. If it was a treadle machine it was a substantial piece of furniture in its own right, and as such needed to be allotted space in the home.

Cutting down clothes for children, unpicking and turning cloth, unravelling and rewinding wool, were tasks that many housewives had to resort to during times of war. Towards the end of the century, the activity of dressmaking had contracted, surviving mainly for the purpose of making clothes for small children, while mending, patching and darning were fast becoming obsolete, rendered unnecessary by the spread of synthetic textiles and cheap, discardable clothing. Knitting, however, appeared as though it would survive indefinitely, not only because hand knitted garments remained competitive with factory made ones but because many knitters did it for enjoyment as much as utility, liking to have something to occupy their hands while listening to the radio or watching TV.

While the physical care of people became less onerous, the nature of care went through a qualitative change. Suburbanization again made a large contribution to this, by plucking children from the rough and tumble of the common street to play in their own back gardens. Parents noticed immediate returns in better sleeping and eating patterns, which made children easier to nurture. At the same time, mothers were deprived of the casual oversight that next door neighbours and others on the street had given, and there was a case for saying that being immured in back gardens was detrimental to children's social development (Newson, 1968).

Ideas about child care were in any case changing. In Victorian families and among the early twentieth-century poor, to rear a child through the hazards of birth and infancy, to clothe and feed it adequately and educate it as far as practically possible, were sufficient testimonials of maternal love. In a tough world, a gentler upbringing would not necessarily be a kindness. As families became smaller, children became, not necessarily more precious, but individuals on whom a subtler kind of care might be bestowed. The change in emphasis placed different demands on mothers, and fathers were also affected, for it entailed a shift in the balance of care provided within the family circle. Thus it became less automatic for the breadwinner to be given the best food, the biggest share of the fire, and to have his peace and leisure protected from all disturbance. Ultimately, he responded by contributing to child care himself, even if not equally or to the extent that his wife might have wished.

Two further important demographic changes had implications for child care. One was a doubling of the proportion of one-parent families in the twenty years to 1981, and a nearly as large increase over the next decade. The lone parent – in the vast majority of cases the mother – obviously carried an extra burden of care. The other change came from the new types of family that arose from divorce and remarriage, which could contain children of more than one marriage, as well as children who divided their time between the separate

Even Debonair magic won't dry babies!

but it will dry everything else you wash

The father's role in child care in the postwar era. (*Source*: *House Beautiful*, April 1959.

households of different parents. This had a number of possible consequences, as yet little understood, stemming from an increase in the number of dependents within a household, fluctuating numbers of dependents at different stages of the family cycle or in different parts of the week or year, and new patterns of apportioning child care and other work within the home.

Lastly, a thought may be given to the household pet as a recipient of care. As we have seen in the previous chapter, the keeping of livestock for food was an important part of many homes before and during the Second World War. Slum clearance threatened to eradicate this, together with pigeon fancying, greyhound breeding and similar customs. In particular, they were terminated when people moved into flats, although the Central Housing Advisory Committee recommended that councils should adopt liberal policies towards flat dwellers in this respect (MHLG, 1956). The keeping of racing pigeons and rabbits were hobbies often found on council estates, where also there developed a serious problem of undisciplined and semi-feral packs of dogs which terrorized other residents and for which official dog catchers had to be appointed.

Records indicated that pet ownership was slightly commoner among men than women. Around a quarter of adults kept a dog in 1981: a slight increase over 1959; but cats and other pets declined in numbers after the latter date. Having a pet was recognized as good for health, and it also brought people into social contact with neighbours, whether through walking the dog or asking them to feed the cat or the goldfish when owners were away – this being a favour that was legitimate to ask of a neighbour (Zweig, 1961). The overall increase in numbers of people without pets after 1959 was attributed to the rise of consumer goods, which provided people with an alternative 'outlet for their energies' (Abrams, 1983, p. 15). A more convenient kind of pet for the future, it was suggested, might come back in the form of a robot (Miles, 1988).

THE CONTRIBUTIONS OF HOUSEWORK TO THE HOME

As the home became separated from the

Today's cat with privileged entry. Leeds, 1995.

workplace of the formal economy, it became the subject of work routines and rituals whose daily and weekly rhythms were added to the annual rhythms of earlier times (Davidoff, 1976). Deriving in part from the organization of great houses with hierarchies of servants, they also represented an extension of factory routines and timekeeping to the home, as well as being practical responses to a polluted external environment and the need for care of a growing number of furnishings and possessions. In the middle-class home the work of looking after the house was divided: the dirty work apportioned to servants and management to the mistress. In lower social strata there was a variety of patterns, but often the housewife struggled to keep up elaborate routines with little or no domestic help. Among the poor, cleaning was a gauge of social respectability,

extending beyond the home into the public street, which might itself be swept and scrubbed (see p. 4, above). To a late date, the polishing of a neighbour's doorstep was one of the greatest services that could be rendered (Kuper, 1953). Such was the importance of cleanliness that women became obsessed, even mad, through it (Roberts, 1971).

In assessing the development of housework, the role of domestic appliances has perhaps been emphasized at the expense of other and more fundamental things such as the internal layout of the dwelling, the amount of space available to each person, water supply, and the lighting and heating systems. Another important influence was the composition of various items, including cleaning and decorating materials, and the extent to which people were able to acquire appropriate utensils or 'sets' of things like bedlinen and crockery, or were rich enough to discard things that were worn out without struggling to mend them. It could plausibly be argued that the biggest contribution of all to housework was made by synthetic textiles, plastics and detergents. Although plastics of various types went back to the previous century, the full impact of these on housework was not felt until after 1945.

Eventually certain tasks of housework which had once been routine were rendered obsolete. They included the carrying of water and slops; all coal-related tasks (apart from the open hearths that were kept by choice); most scouring, scrubbing and metal cleaning; most if not all vermin-related tasks; most sewing and mending; and much of the ironing. Spring cleaning, once the main annual ritual, eventually became redundant, very largely replaced by annual or less frequent interior redecoration. Towards the end of the century it may be said that the 'dirty' home of earlier years has more or less disappeared, notwithstanding the huge amounts of TV advertising time that continue to be devoted to cleaning and laundry preparations. Regular daily or even weekly cleaning and routines for maintaining hygiene are now no longer essential for a healthy, warm and reasonably comfortable home, although levels of untidiness and mess are a direct function of the number of people at home, and in particular the presence of young children.

A historical overview of the century suggests that the manifestation of poverty in the home has gone through a qualitative as well as a quantitative change, with many implications for housework. There is a big contrast between the poor housewife of the 1930s struggling to keep her slum home clean and orderly, or the early council tenant with empty rooms and newspaper-covered windows, and the low-income householder of today. This is not to say that the last's relative deprivation may be any easier, and indeed it may be harder to bear given the higher standards of the majority; but even those living on social security usually manage before too long to acquire what are now regarded as the essentials of automatic cooker, refrigerator and TV. A washing machine may be less essential owing to the availability of commercial launderettes, which are concentrated in poorer districts. The home will be likely to contain many of the items of contemporary domestic comfort such as the three-piece lounge suite, picked up from charities or second-hand dealers, but few if any of the ingenious makeshifts of earlier poor house-wives (Waplington, n.d.).

While much significant change took place independently of domestic appliances, the role of these was undeniably important. The three which took precedence, the vacuum cleaner, refrigerator and washing machine, each had a technical history predating this century (in the case of the last two, even predating the industrial revolution) and they had been developed initially for households with servants. They could not realize their full potential until they were fitted with small electric motors, but their diffusion was also constrained by other factors. The vacuum cleaner, for instance, was

of limited use until people had enough rooms and carpets for it to be worthwhile, and the washing machine had to compete at different times and places with commercial laundries and public wash houses. Refrigerators could be run from gas as well as electricity, but their general diffusion, like that of a host of lesser kitchen and laundry appliances, effectively depended upon an electrical power circuit. For the majority of homes, as we have seen, this meant the 1950s at the earliest.

Electricity was seen as the great liberating force for women. Besides the Electrical Association for Women (p. 123, above) which disseminated the gospel through its journal, *Electrical Age for Women*, the 'new feminism' of the inter-war years, now that the Vote was won, espoused the modernization and electrification of the home, promoting the cause of women as mothers and home-makers so that they could become active citizens (Pugh, 1992). Through electricity, 'the work of woman could be dignified, demanding intelligence rather than physical labour' (Davidson, 1982, p. 40). This fitted well with the long-established American and English traditions of home economics, and of women in public welfare who, as housing managers, teachers, demonstrators, charity workers and politicians, sought to dignify and professionalize the housewife role.

The first mass diffusion of electrical appliances took place in the inter-war semis, whose housewives were blandished by manufacturers into seeing them as substitutes for the servants they no longer and in many cases had never had. They were thus made devotees of the new 'religion' of labour-saving (Crittall, 1934, p. 111). These new and 'ideal' homes then became an inexhaustible market for new tools and devices, and this was constantly reinforced by the women's magazines, not new at this time but now greatly augmented by many new weeklies and monthlies. Three of their main functions were to glamourize the housewife role, to give serious consumer advice, and to provide stereotyped patterns for the making of a large range of soft furnishings and other items for the home (White, 1970). A still greater expansion of the market for appliances was anticipated after the war, and this prompted PEP's survey and report (PEP, 1945). Postwar magazines became glossier and more seductive, presenting showers of toasters, irons, kettles, food mixers, cutlery, as virtually synonymous with romance and marriage. With the help of such goods, women were led to understand, they could effortlessly combine the roles of mistress, servant, wife, mother, and hostess (Winship, 1980).

The working-class housewife, although doubtless also influenced by such devices, was meanwhile following a different path. Appliances were of little use to her until she had a proper home to use them in, and no amount of gadgets could overcome slum conditions. In her case, therefore, better housing took priority, and although it was recognized that a new home might cause her financial hardship – among other things forcing her to cut back on her own diet – it could be argued that a better home would confer 'a far keener *sense* of well-being than she dreamt was possible before. Over and over again the women of this investigation have expressed this feeling of comparative ease and comfort when they speak of having recently moved from a bad to a good house' (Spring Rice, 1939, p. 154).

THE POSTWAR HOUSEWIFE AND THE DIVISION OF HOUSEHOLD LABOUR

Perhaps the most important change brought about by postwar council housing was a transformation of the husband's attitude towards the home and a consequent change in the relationship of husband and wife (Mogey, 1956; Willmott and Young, 1960; Zweig, 1961). The traditional working-class pattern had been strict gender division in virtually all activities.

Men willing to help with child care or domestic labour had to do so in secret, for fear of losing their manhood in the eyes of neighbours. Apart from shoe mending and cleaning, therefore, men behaved like paying guests in their own homes (Eyles, 1922). This pattern began to change in the higher social classes, as George Orwell observed: 'In a working-class home it is the man who is the master and not, as in a middle-class home, the woman or the baby' (Orwell, 1937, pp. 72–3). As families moved out to the suburbs husbands were severed from their old habitats and associates, while they were struck by the rise in status that the move entailed: 'When I moved to a council house I became more house-proud and stopped at home more frequently. First because the house was more comfortable, then because the public house was further away' (Zweig, 1961, p. 6).

The 'almost universal' task undertaken by husbands on moving in was painting and wallpapering (Mogey, 1956, p. 25; see pp. 169–170, above). Improving the home became a joint project of husband and wife, taking up most of their combined leisure time (Zweig, 1976); but decorating, repairs, care of the car (if any) and much of the gardening became the husband's particular responsibility: 'I never saw my father handling a brush, now it seems I have a use for my brush the whole year round' (Zweig, 1961, p. 207). Male participation in these – the more technical and external household tasks – eventually spread to all social classes and age groups. The proportion of men doing some DIY in the home rose from 55 per cent in 1959 to over 80 per cent in 1981–82 (*Social Trends*, 1984, 1990) and, as we have seen (p. 198, above), older men in particular work their gardens.

This active conjugal work on the home accelerated during the 1970s, when 'DIY', in which women now increasingly participated, was held to be the fastest growing sector of the building industry. The cheapening of domestic tools and appliances relative to services encouraged a new domestic culture of 'self-provisioning' where husbands and wives used their own labour 'to produce goods and services for themselves' rather than paying specialists (Pahl, 1984, p. 315). This they felt to be not so much an imposition as something creative, an opportunity to express themselves and their values. Inevitably, the fact that money was needed for goods and materials meant that it was a path taken by those with more rather than less choice.

'WOMEN'S LIBERATION' AND THE TIME SPENT ON HOUSEWORK

There is, however, another and contradictory body of evidence to consider, arising from the rebirth of feminism after its apparent disappearance in the immediate postwar years. The public debate was opened by the American journalist, Betty Friedan, who described a number of affluent and (by English standards) lavishly housed, fulltime American housewives, always tired and depressed, who needlessly expanded their housework 'to fill the time available' (Friedan, 1963, p. 205). Her conclusion was that they magnified what was essentially trivial work in order to justify a meaningless role in society, sometimes with the hidden motive of dominating their families.

In spite of differences in housing standards and other cultural distinctions, Friedan's message found immediate response in England, where it was reprinted many times, to become one of the foundation texts of 'women's liberation' with its ideological attack on the patriarchal structure of society. The earliest serious English contribution to the critique of housework and domestic culture was in the tradition of urban sociology, taking cognisance of housing conditions and noting that bad housing dominated the lives of over half its working-class subjects

From *House Beautiful*, April 1958.

(Gavron, 1966). As the argument was further developed, housing conditions and quality ceased to be regarded as important (Comer, 1974; Oakley, 1974*a*; 1974*b*). Women's day-dreams about the sort of house they might one day own were dismissed as spurious, on the grounds that it was an illusion to suppose that 'owning the floors one cleans' would make the work more palatable (Oakley, 1974*a*, p. 83). This was connected to a suggestion that sub-urban housing and home ownership were inimical to the interests of women (McDowell, 1983; Watson and Austerberry, 1986); for, among other things, 'the ideal of "each woman in her own house" is certainly one fostered by advertising, and . . . it may be, in part, a stereotyped response to the boredom of house-work' (McDowell, 1983, p. 83).

This body of ideas presents something of a historical conundrum, for in effect it took no cognisance of the housing progress that English-women of the working class, at least, felt themselves to be making at this time, nor of the earlier campaigns on their behalf of different kinds of feminist. Far from regarding the family home, and the kitchen in particular, as a workshop where the housewife's tasks could be performed with dignity, the new feminist dis-course represented it as her prison (Comer, 1974; Francis, 1984). It made no reference to any emerging conjugal interest and enjoyment in the home but on the contrary excoriated husbands for the insignificance of their con-tributions to the work of the home. Leading protagonists in the debate no longer took any interest in the content or future improvement of housework: 'the inherent deprivations of housework as work cannot be banished by the mere improvement of housework conditions: better and nicer houses, more machines, more coffee mornings, or housewife's clubs' (Oakley, 1974*b*, p. 224): the only real solution would be abolition of the role itself.

The heat of the debate was such that, with a still stronger stream of American feminist polemic, it became a force in itself, very possibly provoking – or inspiring – an increase in men's participation in housework that was apparent in younger age groups and middle-class households (*Social Trends*, 1985). The debate raised the question what, if conventional homes and marriages were incapable of change, should replace them. 'Wages for housework' were canvassed at one extreme, but the question was more usually answered in abstract terms (Oakley, 1974*a* and *b*). Apart from child care, co-operative housekeeping solutions were seldom advanced, and then not in realistically achievable terms (Williams *et al.*, 1969; Comer, 1974). Only occasionally, and then in an American rather than a British context, was the logic of the argument carried to proposals

The new mother's help is —father!

'Anne Blythe begs mothers of small boys not to bring them up to despise housework.' (*Source*: *Housewife*, March 1943)

for communal households, which might be accompanied by technologies to eliminate biological reproduction (Firestone, 1979). It was, once again, left to the squatter communards to give practical expression to their own radicalism, and they maintained that the lower housekeeping standards which they voluntarily adopted provided a release for women who learned 'how to tolerate dirt and disorder' (Osborn, 1980, p. 188; Moan, 1980).

What, then, does the stream of postwar feminist debate contribute to the history of the twentieth-century home? Clearly it does not provide evidence of contemporary working-class domestic life or the general experience of conventionally domesticated women, whose expressed liking for housework was so summarily dismissed as irrelevant to issues of gender inequality (Oakley, 1974a and b). Rather, it must be considered as an expression of the experience, and the passionate rejection of the housewife role, of a generation of young women, whose very formulation of the problem places them in the middle rather than the working class. Among a range of issues that can be abstracted from the debate, three are particularly salient. One is childcare, which was found to be totally demanding, unshared and isolating, its great and acknowledged psychological importance conflicting with innumerable other demands that were made on the mother's time (Oakley, 1974a; Gardiner et al., 1976). The point was made that until they had their own first child, many of the women in question had never seen or handled a newborn baby (Gavron, 1966).

The second theme was a strong sense of betrayal and disillusionment with domestic appliances: 'efficient design and household appliances have not reduced the time spent on housework. Housewives have not acquired vast amounts of leisure time. Housework is not significantly more pleasant to do. Indeed the experience of many indicates that housewives have become more isolated and more desperate

as these changes have occurred' (Craik, 1989, p. 48). In spite of her sophisticated gadgets, the housewife's working day and week seemed mysteriously to have lengthened rather than shortened. The explanation usually adduced for this was that higher standards and more tasks were imposed, or self-imposed, on her: appliances, in fact, 'freed' her to perform ever more tasks. If this was true, it gave the dictum that 'housework expands to fill the time available' a different meaning from the one intended by its author.

In consequence, the third theme concentrated on the shortcomings of the husband – now, in most households, the only other available adult – for not giving more help, and for lacking understanding of his wife's exhaustion and depression. Evidence for the length of the housewife's working day was in fact scattered and inadequate, culled from many different times, locations and nationalities, and unsystematic in its inclusion or exclusion of certain tasks. In drawing from it, Ann Oakley worked with two separate conclusions: one that the housewife's average working week was 77 hours ('among the longest in contemporary society' – Oakley, 1974a, p. 92), and the other that it was between 51 and 82 hours (*Ibid*, 1974b). The first estimate was taken over and used uncritically in a succession of contributions to feminist debate (Francis, 1984; Roberts, 1984), to the extent that it continued to be assumed to be 'well known that the introduction of "labour-saving" equipment has coincided with an increase in the average amount of time women spend on housework' (Partington, 1989, p. 213).

There is now, however, a more carefully worked out estimate based on sets of consistent English data of 1961 and 1974–75, which presents a very different picture. It shows, for instance, that between 1930 and 1960 there was a steep rise in the weekly hours of middle-class housewives, with a much shallower rise in the hours of working-class housewives between

1930 and 1950. The time spent on housework by the former peaked at around 50, and by the latter around 58 hours per week. The two classes reached parity in the later 1960s, after which the hours worked by each declined. By 1975, the middle-class housewife devoted on average some 44 hours, and her working-class counterpart less than 40 hours per week to housework (Gershuny, 1983). The hours were fewer when there were no children or when women had fulltime jobs; but taken over time, the general patterns are consistent with other known phenomena: the decline of domestic service in middle-class homes, the boost given to standards and productivity by the first wave of electrified machines, and a predictable fall in time spent once machinery was used to rationalize labour.

There remains no doubt that the wife continued 'to do most of the work in and around the household' (Pahl, 1984, p. 327). In 1987, she rather than her husband was still overwhelmingly responsible for laundry, ironing, cooking, cleaning, shopping and care of children (Halsey, 1987). This remained the case even when she had a 'dual role', that is a paid job, which made her total working week several hours longer than her husband's, particularly when there were children (Gershuny, 1983). With children, husbands' contribution to household labour was lower rather than higher, and it did not significantly increase even when wives had fulltime paid jobs (*Ibid*, 1983). The home, therefore, remained the woman's workplace, and according to feminist dicta this should have been widely resented by them. Doubtless it was, at a grumbling level, in many homes; but in the main the evidence does not support the thesis that the majority of housewives were resentful. On the contrary, like some of the subjects of Oakley's sample of forty women at an earlier date, a thousand housewives of the later twentieth century seemed on the whole contented with their role. They appeared to have purposely chosen it and

to be able to discuss its pros and cons with objectivity, while giving it their 'basic endorsement' (Bonney and Reinach, 1993, p. 626).

It seems likely, therefore, that the postwar feminist critique of the housewife role was specific to a particular generation and class of women. Their mothers' generation was that of the innovative suburban housewife between the wars and, while this had established a model that was still percolating down the social scale, some at least of their daughters were challenging the role altogether and in doing so creating a new chapter in the ever-changing history of housekeeping and home making. The main outcome may have been in the area of inter-personal relationships within the home, rather than the practicalities of housework.

While this had long-term effects on the division of domestic labour, it had little to do with the rise of either the self-provisioning or the electronic home towards the end of the century. In these, the paramount issues would be not only income, but degrees of information and skills, and these were predominantly issues of social class rather than gender. Thus in his 1981 study of over 500 households in the Isle of Sheppey, R.E. Pahl noticed the crucial role of income in domestic self-provisioning or the productive use of the home to replace commercial goods and services: 'the contrast between households with money being productive and busy and the households without money being unproductive and idle is the overwhelming conclusion of the empirical part of this book' (Pahl, 1984, p. 336).

This was not, of course, without implications for women. Under this new domestic order they might yet again be handicapped by their traditionally lesser access than men to technical skills, while their inherited responsibility for housework and personal care would presumably become heavier with the presence at home of the unemployed, the self-employed or home-based, 'telecottaging' workers (Wajcman, 1992). But in future the crucial distinction might be not so much between men and women as between the mainstream and the marginalized. The former would include all who are well and securely housed, with sufficient income to participate in technological change, and having fulfilling relationships with family members or others within the home. The latter would largely consist of the socially and economically deprived who have long been marginalized within the housing system. They would thus include those on low incomes, notably low-income single people, poor pensioners, lone parents, and the long-term sick: all those, in fact, who might have need of institutional housing or who, living alone, are likely to call on 'care in the community' and so are potential victims of inadequately resourced policies.

THE FURTHER REACHES OF THE HOME IN THE TWENTIETH CENTURY

All our attempts to reach the essence of people's experience of the home, with the whole lengthy history of twentieth-century housing itself, yet leave a territory to which we cannot readily gain access. Inevitably what the historical record opens up is what can be reached from outside, by objective techniques. This permits an adequate representation of that large range of domestic behaviour that is social and cultural: the home as an index of social status, an arena of intimate relationships, a refuge, a container of possessions and icons, and even the carrier of one's self-image. There remains something still more intensely internal and subjective which can be only glimpsed and guessed. It is seen, for instance, in the sense of personal violation known to be felt after break-ins and burglaries, even when these are comparatively trivial; in the common bereavement reaction to moving house; and in an inner sense, often unshared with the closest of intimates, of all that one has invested in a home of love, creativity, daydreams, spiritual striving and sense of being. All such experience is by definition impossible to arrive at through objective data: it must be reached, if at all, through diaries, biography, literature, or psychological awareness (Forster, 1910; Cooper, 1971). We leave the story at a time of great economic, social and technical as well as personal changes which present as well as closing many options for the century to come.

BIBLIOGRAPHY

Abrams, Mark (1983) Changes in the life-styles of the elderly, 1959–1982. *Social Trends*, No. 14.

A Layman and His Wife (1927) *Planning a Home*. London: Arrowsmith.

Allaun, Frank (1972) *No Place Like Home: Britain's housing tragedy (from the victim's view) and how to overcome it*. London: Deutsch.

Allen, Graham (1989) Insiders and outsiders: boundaries around the home, in Allen, Graham and Crow, Graham (eds.).

Allen, Graham and Crow, Graham (eds.) (1989) Home and Family: creating the domestic sphere. London: Macmillan.

Allen, Isobel, Hogg, Debra and Peace, Sheila (1992) *Elderly People: choice, participation and satisfaction*. London: Policy Studies Institute.

Allen, Marjory (Lady Allen of Hurtwood) (1956) *The New Small Garden*. London: Architectural Press.

Allied Iron Founders Ltd (*c.* 1954) The Stockton Test.

Ambrose, Peter (1974) *The Quiet Revolution: social change in a Sussex village, 1871–1971*. London: Chatto & Windus.

Andrews, C. Lesley (1979) *Tenants and Town Hall* (DoE Social Research Division). London: HMSO.

Anning, Nick and Simpson, Jill (1980) Victory Villa. Challenging the planners in South London, Villa Road, in Wates, Nick and Wolmar, Christian (eds.).

Architects' Journal (1989) Studies in practice: Coin Street Design Team, 7 June, pp. 93–96.

Architectural Press (1924) *Garden City Houses and Domestic Interior Details*, 4th ed. London: Architectural Press.

Armor, Murray (1978) *Building Your Own Home*. Dorchester: Prism Press.

Armor, Murray (1991) *Plans for Dream Homes*, 3rd ed. Dorchester: Prism Press.

Ascot (1938) *Flats: municipal and private enterprise*. London: Ascot Gas Water Heaters Ltd.

Atherton, James S. (1989) *Interpreting Residential Life: values to practise*. London: Tavistock/Routledge.

Attfield, Judy (1989) Inside pram town: a case study of Harlow house interiors, 1951–61, in Attfield, Judy and Kirkham, Pat (eds.).

Attfield, Judy and Kirkham, Pat (eds.) (1989) *A View from the Interior. Feminism, Women and Design*. London: The Women's Press.

Bailey, Ron (1973) *The Squatters*. Harmondsworth: Penguin.

Banham, Reyner (1976) *Megastructures: urban futures of the recent past*. London: Thames & Hudson.

Barker, Diana Leonard and Allen, Sheila (1976) *Dependence and Exploitation in Work and Marriage*. London: Longman.

Barrett, Helena and Phillips, John (1987) *Suburban Style. The British Home, 1840–1960*. Boston: Little Brown.

BBC 2 (1992) Signs of the Times. Broadcast August–September.

Bell, E. Moberly (1942) *Octavia Hill: a biography*. London: Constable.

Benson, John (1989) *The Working Class in Britain, 1850–1939*. London: Longman.

Bereano, Philip, Bose, Christine and Arnold, Erik (1985) Kitchen technology and the liberation of women from housework, in Faulkner, Wendy and Arnold, Erik (eds.).

Berridge, David (1985) *Children's Homes*. Oxford: Blackwell.

Berthoud, Richard and Casey, Bernard (1988) *The Cost of Care in Hostels*. London: Policy Studies Institute.

Betham, Ernest (ed.) (n.d. presumed 1936) *House Building 1934–1936*. London: Federated Employers' Press.

Birchall, Johnston (1988) *Building Communities the Co-operative Way*. London: Routledge & Kegan Paul.

Bisgrove, Richard (1990) *The National Trust Book of the English Garden*. London: Viking.

Bonney, Norman and Reinach, Elizabeth (1993) Housework reconsidered; the Oakley thesis twenty years later. *Work, Employment & Society*, **7**(4), December, pp. 615–627.

Boseley, Sarah (1988) Home is where the developer wants to make it. *The Guardian*, 24 February, p. 4.

Boumphrey, Gerald (1940) *Town and Country Tomorrow*. London: Nelson.

Bournville Village Trust (1941) *When We Build Again: a study based on research into conditions of living and working in Birmingham*. London: Allen & Unwin.

Bournville Village Trust (*c.* 1946) *Our Birmingham*. Birmingham: Bournville Village Trust.

Bowley, Marian (1945) *Housing and the State, 1919–1944*. London: Allen & Unwin.

Boyd Orr, Sir John (1943) *Food and the People*. London: Pilot Press.

Branca, Patricia (1975) *Silent Sisterhood. Middle-class women in the Victorian home*. London: Croom Helm.

Branson, Noreen (ed.) (1989) London Squatters 1946. Proceedings of a conference held by the Communist Party History Group, May 1984. *Our History* Pamphlet 80.

Brent Community Law Centre (n.d.) *Making an Entrance*. [Gloucester House, Brent]. London: Brent Community Law Centre.

British Way and Purpose (1944) *The Home of the Citizen*.

Brookes, John (1969) *Room Outside. A new approach to garden design*. London: Thames & Hudson.

Broome, Jon (1986) The Segal method. *Architects' Journal*, 5 November, pp. 31–66.

Brown, Jane (1986) *The English Garden in Our Time: from Gertrude Jekyll to Geoffrey Jellicoe*. London: Antique Collectors' Club.

Bumby, Arthur (1976) To a grand old couple it's home sweet hut. *Yorkshire Evening Press*, 12 March.

Burbidge, Michael (1975) The standards tenants want. *Housing Review*, **24**(6), pp. 159–161.

Burke, Gill (1981) *Housing and Social Justice. The role of policy in British housing*. London/New York: Longman.

Burnett, John (1966) *Plenty and Want. A social history of diet in England from 1815 to the present day*. London: Nelson.

Burnett, John (1986) *A Social History of Housing 1815–1985*, 2nd ed. London: Methuen.

Burton, Neil (1989) Georgian gardens. *Architectural Review*, No. 186, September, pp. 93–97.

Butler, Alan, Oldman, Christine and Wright, Richard (1979) *Sheltered Housing for the Elderly: a critical review*. Leeds: University of Leeds, Department of Social Policy and Administration.

Butler, C.V. (1916) *Domestic Service. An enquiry by the Women's Industrial Council*. London: Bell.

Calder, Angus (1969) *The People's War. Britain 1939–45*. London: Cape.

Campbell, Beatrix (1993) *Goliath. Britain's Dangerous Places*. London: Methuen.

Campbell, Duncan (1994) Police track travellers by computer. *The Guardian*, 25 February, p. 6.

Carpenter, (Peter) (1993) Ten Years of Earth Shelter. *Eco Design*, **11**(2).

Cement & Concrete Association (1960) *Concrete in Garden Making*. London: Cement & Concrete Association.

Census (1935) *Census of England and Wales 1931: Housing Report*. London: HMSO.

Census (1956) *Census of England and Wales 1951: Housing Report*, London: HMSO.

Chapman, Dennis (1948) *A Survey of Noise in British Homes*. National Building Studies Technical Paper No. 2 (Department of Scientific and Industrial Research). London: HMSO.

Chapman, Dennis (1955) *The Home and Social Status*. London: Routledge & Kegan Paul.

City of Birmingham (1930) Report to the Public Works and Town Planning Committees of the deputation visiting Germany, Czechoslovakia and Austria in August 1930. Birmingham City Council.

City of Coventry (1952) *Coventry Development Plan 1951*. Coventry.

City of Leicester (*c.* 1946) *Leicester of the Future*. Leicester.

City of Sheffield (1955) *Multi-Storey Housing in Some European Countries*. Sheffield.

Cleeve Barr, A.W. (1958) *Public Authority Housing*. London: Batsford.

Coal Utilisation Council (n.d.) *Survey and Recommendations*. London: CUC.

Coleman, Alice (1985) *Utopia on Trial. Vision and Reality in Planned Housing*. London: Shipman.

Coleman, Alice (n.d.) *The DICE Project, High Rise Housing,* Housing & Planning Review special issue. London: National Housing & Town Planning Council.

Coleman, David (1988) Population, in Halsey, A.H. (ed).

Collison, Peter (1963) *The Cutteslowe Walls: a study in social class*. London: Faber & Faber.

Comer, Lee (1974) *Wedlocked Women*. Leeds: Feminist Books.

Community Action (1990) Coin Street community plan in action. No. 83, Spring, pp. 15–19.

Community Links (1988–) *The View: the National Tower Blocks Bulletin. 1988–*. London: Community Links.

Constable, Moira (1975) *Factory Built Houses. A Shelter Report on the present and future use of caravans, mobile homes and prefabricated houses*. London: Shelter.

Constantine, Stephen (1981) Amateur gardening and popular recreation in the 19th and 20th centuries. *Journal of Social History*, **14**(3), pp. 387–406.

Cook, J.A. (1968) Gardens on housing estates. A survey of user attitudes and behaviour on seven layouts. *Town Planning Review*, **39**, pp. 217–234.

Cook, Stephen (1991) Bedsit fire checks urged. *The Guardian*, 26 September.

Cooney, E.W. (1974) High flats in local authority housing in England and Wales since 1945: in Sutcliffe, Anthony (ed.).

Cooper, Clare (1971) The House as Symbol of Self. Working Paper 120. Institute of Urban & Regional Development. University of California.

CoSMITH (Council for Scientific Management in the Home) (1951) Report of an Inquiry into the Effects of the Temporary Prefab Bungalow on Household Routines. *Social Review*, Section 2.

CoSMITH (Council for Scientific Management in the Home) (1955) *Meals in Modern Homes: A study made . . . amongst housewives living in houses and flats built 1945–52 in various parts of the UK*. London: CoSMITH.

Council for Research on Housing Construction (1934) *Slum Clearance and Rehousing*. London: P.S. King.

Country Life (1947) *Recent English Architecture 1925–1940*. London Country Life.

Cowan, Robert, Hannay, Patrick and Owens, Ruth (1988) Community-led regeneration by the Eldonians. *Architects' Journal*, 23 March, pp. 37–63.

Craik, Jennifer (1989) The making of mother: the role of the kitchen in the home, in Allen, Graham and Crow, Graham (eds.).

Crawford, David (ed.) (1973) *A Decade of British Housing, 1963–1973*. London: Architectural Press.

Crittall, Mr and Mrs F.H. (1934) *Fifty Years of Work and Play*. London: Constable.

Crouch, David and Ward, Colin (1988) *The Allot-ment, its Landscape and Culture*. London: Faber & Faber.

Crow, Graham (1989) The post-war development of the modern domestic ideal, in Allen, Graham and Crow, Graham (eds.).

Cullingworth, J.B. (1965) *English Housing Trends. A Report on the Rowntree Trust Housing Study*. London: Bell.

Cullingworth, J.B. (1966) *Housing and Local Government in England and Wales*. London: Allen & Unwin.

Cullingworth, J.B. (1979) *Essays on Housing Policy: the British Scene*. London: Allen & Unwin.

Cullingworth, J.B. (1985) *Town and Country Planning In Britain*, 9th ed. London: Allen & Unwin.

Dagenham Borough Council (1949, 1956) *Municipal Tenants' Handbook*. London: Dagenham Borough Council.

Dagenham Digest (1959) No. 43.

Daunton, M.J. (1983) *House and Home in the Victorian City. Working-class housing 1850–1914*. London: Arnold.

Daunton, M.J. (ed.) (1984) *Councillors and Tenants: local-authority housing in English cities, 1919–1939*. Leicester: Leicester University Press.

Daunton, M.J. (1987) *A Property-Owning Democracy? Housing in Britain*. London: Faber & Faber.

Daunton, M.J. (1990) Housing, in Thompson, F.M.L. (ed.) Vol. 2.

Davidoff, Leonore (1976) The rationalisation of housework, in Barker, Diana Leonard and Allen, Sheila (eds.).

Davidoff, Leonore and Hall, Catherine (1983) The architecture of public and private life. English middle-class society in a provincial town 1780 to 1850, in Fraser, Derek and Sutcliffe, Anthony (eds.).

Davidson, Caroline (1982) *A Woman's Work is Never Done. A history of housework in the British Isles 1650–1950*. London: Chatto & Windus.

Davis, Leonard (1982) *Residential Care: a community resource*. London: Heinemann.

Department of Health (1989) *Homes are for Living In* (Social Services Inspectorate). London: HMSO

Devine, Fiona (1989) Privatised families and their homes, in Allen, Graham and Crow, Graham (eds.).

DoE (Department of the Environment (1971) *Housing Single People: 1. How they live at present*, Design Bulletin 23. London: HMSO.

DoE (1972) *Development and Compensation: putting people first*, Cmnd. 5124. London: HMSO.

DoE (1974) *Housing Single People: 2. A design guide with a description of a scheme at Leicester*, Design Bulletin 29. London: HMSO.

DoE (1975) *Housing Act 1974: Renewal Strategies*, Circular 13/75. London: HMSO.

DoE (1978) *Housing Single People: 3. An appraisal of a purpose-built scheme*, Design Bulletin 33. London: HMSO.

DoE (1982) *Regional Distribution of Gypsy Caravans*, Report 1/82. London: HMSO.

DoE (1993) *English House Condition Survey 1991*. London: HMSO.

DoE (Department of the Environment) and Department of Transport (1977) *Residential Roads and Footpaths*, Design Bulletin 32. London: HMSO.

Department of Health (1989) *Homes are for Living In*. London: HMSO.

Donnison, D.V. (1961) The movement of households in England. *Journal of the Royal Statistical Society*, Series A. **124**, pp. 60–80.

Dresser, Madge (1984) Housing policy in Bristol, 1919–30, in Daunton, M.J. (ed.).

Drew, Ruth (1960) Life with the telephone. *Home*, May, pp. 59–63.

Dudley Report (1944) *Design of Dwellings* (Central Housing Advisory Committee). London: HMSO.

Dunleavy, Patrick (1981) *The Politics of Mass Housing in Britain, 1945–75. A study of corporate power and professional influence in the Welfare State*. Oxford: Clarendon Press.

Durant, Ruth (1939) *Watling: a survey of social life on a new housing estate*. London: P.S. King.

Dyos, H.J. (1966) *Victorian Suburb. A study of the growth of Camberwell*. Leicester: Leicester University Press.

EAW (Electrical Association for Women) (1946) *Housing Digest. An analysis of housing reports 1941–1945*. (Prepared by the Association for Planning and Regional Reconstruction). London/Glasgow: Art & Educational Publishers.

Edwards, Arthur M. (1981) *The Design of Suburbia: a critical study in environmental history*. London: Pembridge Press.

Elek, Paul (1946) *Homes for the People*. London: Paul Elek.

Essex County Council (1973) *A Design Guide for Residential Areas*. Essex County Council.

Eyles, Margaret Leonora (1922) *The Woman in the Little House*. London: Grant Richards.

Faegre, Torvald (1979) *Tents: architecture of the nomads*. London: Murray.

Fanfare (1939) Women's Gas Council. No. 4.

Faulkner, Wendy and Arnold, Erik (eds.) (1985) *Smothered by Invention. Technology in Women's Lives*. London/Sydney. Pluto Press.

Fenter, F. Margaret (n.d. but 1960) *Copec Adventure*. Birmingham: Copec House Improvement Ltd.

Ferguson, Alan and Sim, Duncan (eds.) (1992) *System Building: making it work*. Stirling: Housing Policy and Practice Unit, University of Stirling.

Ferris, J. (1972) *Participation in Urban Planning. The Barnsbury Case: a study of environmental improvement in London*. London: Bell.

Fichter, Robert, Turner, John F.C. and Grenell, Peter (1972) Increasing autonomy in housing: review and conclusions, in Turner, John F.C. and Fichter, Robert (eds.).

Finnegan, Robert (1984) Council housing in Leeds, 1919–1939: social policy and urban change, in Daunton, M.J. (ed.).

Firestone, Shulamith (1979) *The Dialectic of Sex: the case for feminist revolution*. London: The Women's Press.

Fitzgerald, Mike and Sim, Joe (1979) *British Prisons*. Oxford: Blackwell.

Fleming, Laurence and Gore, Alan (1979) *The English Garden*. London: Michael Joseph.

Foo, Benedicte (1984) House ahd home, in Matrix (ed.).

Forrest, Ray and Murie, Alan (1990) *Moving the Housing Market: council estates, social change and privatization*. Aldershot: Avebury.

Forster, E.M. (1910) *Howards End*. London: Arnold.

Forty, Adrian (1975) *The Electric Home. A case study of the domestic revolution of the inter-war years*. A305. 19–20. History of Architecture & Design 1890–1939. Milton Keynes: Open University Press.

Francis, Sue (1984) Housing the family, in Matrix (ed.).

Francis Report. 1971. Report of the Committee on the Rent Acts. Cmnd. 4609. London: HMSO.

Frankenberg, Ronald (1966) *Communities in Britain. Social life in town and country*. Harmondsworth: Penguin.

Fraser, Derek and Sutcliffe, Anthony (eds.) (1983) *The Pursuit of Urban History*. London: Arnold.

Friedan, Betty (1963) *The Feminine Mystique*. London: Gollancz.

Fuller, R. Buckminster and Marks, Robert (1973) *The Dymaxion World of Buckminster Fuller*. Garden City NY: Anchor/Doubleday.

Gardiner, Jean, Himmelweit, Susan and Mackintosh,

Maureen (1976) Women's domestic labour: in Malos, Ellen (ed.) (1980).

Garside, P.L. (1990) London and the Home Counties, in Thompson, F.M.L. (ed.).

Garside, P.L., Grimshaw, R.W. and Ward, F.J. (1990) No Place Like Home: the hostels experience (DoE). London: HMSO.

Gaskell, S. Martin (1980) Gardens for the working class: Victorian practical pleasure. Victorian Studies, 23(4), pp. 479–501.

Gaskell, S. Martin (1987) Model Housing: from the Great Exhibition to the Festival of Britain. London: Mansell.

Gavron, Hannah (1966) The Captive Wife. Conflicts of housebound mothers. London: Routledge & Kegan Paul.

Genders, R. (1959) The Leisure Garden. London: Garden Book Club.

Gerlach, Lynne, Hillier, Stella, Bermott, Julia and Hearty, Danny (n.d.) Moving On. A Photopack on Travellers in Britain. MRG Education.

Gershuny, Jonathan (1983) Social Innovation and the Division of Labour. Oxford: Oxford University Press.

GHS (General Household Survey) (1971–) Nos. 1–. (Office of Population Censuses and Surveys, Social Survey Division). London: HMSO.

Gibson, M.S. and Langstaff, M.J. (1982) An Introduction to Urban Renewal. London: Hutchinson.

Gililan, Lesley (1990) Absolutely prefabulous. Guardian Weekend. 5 December, p. 37.

Gimson, Mark (1980) Everybody's doing it, in Wates, Nick and Wolmar, Christian (eds.).

GLC (1967) Housing and the GLC. London: GLC.

Goodchild, Barry (1981) The Application of Self Help to Housing: a critique of self-build and urban homesteading, Working Paper 1. Sheffield City Polytechnic Department of Urban & Regional Studies.

Goodchild, Barry and Furbey, Robert (1986) Standards in housing design: a review of the main changes since the Parker Morris Report (1961). Land Development Studies, 3, pp. 79–99.

Grant, Carol (ed.) (1992) Built to Last? Reflections on British Housing Policy. London: ROOF Magazine, Shelter.

Gray, Edmund (1994) The British House: a concise architectural history. London: Barrie & Jenkins.

Gray, Percy G. and Russell, R. (1962) The Housing Situation in 1960. An inquiry covering England & Wales carried out for the Ministry of Housing and Local Government, SS319. (Central Office of Information). London: HMSO.

Greenslade, Roy (1976) Goodbye to the Working Class. London: Boyars.

Greve, John and Currie, Elizabeth (1990) Homelessness in Britain. York: Joseph Rowntree Memorial Trust.

Habraken, N.J. (1972) Supports: an alternative to mass housing. London: Architectural Press.

Hadfield, Miles (1960) A History of British Gardening. London: Spring Books.

Hall, Catherine (1982) The Butcher, the Baker, the Candlestickmaker: the shop and the family in the Industrial Revolution, in Open University (ed.).

Hall, John (1976) Subjective measures of the quality of life in Britain: 1971–1975. Social Trends, No. 7.

Hall, Peter (1963) London 2000. London: Faber & Faber.

Hall, Peter, Gracey, H, Drewett, R and Thomas, R. (eds.) (1973) The Containment of Urban England, 2 vols. London: Allen & Unwin.

Halsey, A.H. (ed.) (1972) Trends in British Society since 1900. A guide to the changing social structure of Britain. London: Macmillan.

Halsey, A.H. (1987) Social trends since World War II. Social Trends, No. 17.

Halsey, A.H. (ed.) (1988) British Social Trends since 1900. A guide to the changing social structure of Britain. London: Macmillan.

Halton, Elizabeth (1943) The Home of the Citizen. The British Way and Purpose (Directorate of Army Education). July. (Consolidated Edition of Booklets 1–18, 1944).

Handy, Charles (1984) The Future of Work: a guide to a changing society. Oxford: Blackwell.

Hannah, Lesley (1979) Electricity before Nationalisation: a study of the electricity supply industry in Britain to 1968 (The Electricity Council). London: Macmillan.

Hansard (1923) The Parliamentary Debates, Cols. 310, 335, 352. London: HMSO.

Hansard (1947) The Parliamentary Debates, Col. 1607. London: HMSO.

Hardoy, Michael (1989) Lone Parents and the Home: in Allen & Crow (eds.).

Hardy, Dennis and Ward, Colin (1984) Arcadia for All. The legacy of a makeshift landscape. London: Mansell.

Harrisson, Tom and Madge, Charles (1939) Britain by Mass Observation. Harmondsworth: Penguin.

Hayden, Dolores (1981) The Grand Domestic Revolution: a history of feminist designs for American homes, neighborhoods, and cities. Cambridge, Mass: MIT Press.

Heath, Robinson (c. 1930) *How to Live in a Flat*. London: Hutchinson.

Hencke, David (1993) Hepatitis cases rise as water is cut. *Guardian*, 27 April.

Henry, Jane (1950) A caravan home, in Sherman, Margaret (ed.).

Higgins, Joan (1989) Homes and institutions, in Allen, Graham and Crow, Graham (eds.).

Hillier, Bill (1988) Against enclosure, in Teymur, Necdet *et al.* (eds.).

Hoggart, Richard (1957) *The Uses of Literacy: aspects of working-class life, with special reference to publications and entertainments*. London: Chatto & Windus.

Hole, W.V. and Attenburrow, J.J. (1966) *Houses and People: a review of user studies at the Building Research Station* (Ministry of Technology). London: HMSO.

Holmans, A.E. (1987) *Housing Policy in Britain: a history*. London: Croom Helm.

Holme, Anthea (1985) *Housing and Young Families in East London,* London: Routledge & Kegan Paul.

Home, Robert (1994) The planner and the gypsy, in Thomas, Huw and Krishnarayan, Vijay (eds.).

Home Life (1984) *A Code of Practice for Residential Care*. Report of a Working Party sponsored by the Department of Health & Social Security. London: Centre for Policy on Ageing.

House Beautiful (1957) New Background to Living. February, pp. 66–7.

House Beautiful (1959) A Home grows in your house. February, pp. 8–9.

House Beautiful (1961) Bathroom luxury: the twenty year plan. July–August, pp. 54–57.

Housing Act (1957) 5&6 Eliz.2. London: HMSO.

Housing Manual (1949) (Ministry of Health). London: HMSO.

Hoyles, Martin (1991) *The Story of Gardening*. London: Journeyman.

Hulme Study (1990) Stage One: initial action plan commissioned by the Department of Environment and prepared by Capita *et al.*

Hunt, Pauline (1989) Gender and the construction of home life, in Allen, Graham and Crow, Graham (eds.).

Ideal Homes (n.d.) *Book of Plans*. London: Ideal Home Magazine.

Independent (1993) 6 December, p. 4.

Ingham, Andrew (1980) Using the space, in Wates, Nick and Wolmar, Christian (eds.).

Innes Wilkin, Ainsley, Gommon, with Krajewska,

Sophy (1984) Co-op dividends. *Architects' Journal*, 18 July, pp. 35–59.

Institute of Housing (1983) *Trends in High Places*. London: IoH.

Isham, Sir Charles (1890) Remarks on rock gardens, also notes on gnomes, quoted in Barrett, Helena and Phillips, John, 1987, p. 177.

Jackson, Alan A. (1973) *Semi-detached London. Suburban Development, Life and Transport, 1900–39*. London: Allen & Unwin.

Jacobs, Jane (1961) *The Death and Life of Great American Cities: the failure of town planning*. New York: Random House.

Jennings, Hilda (1962) *Societies in the Making. A study of development and redevelopment within a county borough*. London: Routledge & Kegan Paul.

Jennings, Humphrey, Madge, Charles, *et al.* (eds.) (1937) *May the Twelfth. Mass Observation Day-Surveys 1937 by over two hundred observers*. London: Faber & Faber.

Jones, D. Caradog (ed.) (1934) *The Social Survey of Merseyside*, Vol. 1. London: Hodder & Stoughton.

Jones, Francis M. (1988) Technology and social needs, in Teymur, Necdet *et al.* (eds.).

Karn, Valerie (1977) *Retiring to the Seaside*. London: Routledge & Kegan Paul.

Keegan, Victor (1994) Fibre firepower. *The Guardian*, 25 February, pp. 2–3.

Kemp, Peter (1992) *The Ghost of Rachman*, in Grant, Carol (ed.).

King, Anthony D. (1984) *The Bungalow. The production of a global culture*. London: Routledge & Kegan Paul.

King, Michael (1992) *Cold Shouldered*. London: Winter Action on Cold Homes.

Kirby, David A. (1971) The Inter-war council dwelling: a study of residential obsolescence and decay. *Town Planning Review*, **42**(3), pp. 250–268.

Kirkup, Gill and Keller, Laurie Smith (eds.) (1992) *Inventing Women: Science, Technology and Gender*. London: Polity Press/Open University.

Kuper, Leo (ed.) (1953) *Living in Towns*. London: Cresset Press.

Lancaster, Osbert (1960) *Here, of all Places: the pocket lamp of architecture*. London: Murray.

Larkham, Peter J. (1991) Gentrification, Renewal and the Urban Landscape. School of Geography, Working Paper Series No. 59. University of Birmingham.

Larkham, Peter J. (1992) The Redevelopment of the Suburban Estates. Paper presented to a conference of the Urban History Group, University of Leicester, April.

Lawrence, Hanna (1987–) Lightmoor diary. *Town and Country Planning*, July 1987 and *passim*.

Lawson, Marcia (1976) The sad plight of Caddy Cates. *Newmarket Journal*, 8 April, pp. 1–3.

LCC (London County Council) (1931) *Housing, 1928–1930*. London: LCC.

LCC (1933) *Becontree Tenants' Handbook*. London: LCC.

Leat, Diana (1988) Younger physically disabled adults, in Sinclair, Ian (ed.).

Liverpool Corporation (1951) *Housing Progress, 1864–1951*. Liverpool: City of Liverpool.

Loney, Martin, Bocock, Robert *et al.* (eds.) (1987) The State or the Market: politics and welfare in contemporary Britain: a Reader/London. Sage/Open University.

McAllister, Gilbert and McAllister, Elizabeth Glen (1945) *Homes, Towns and Countryside. A practical plan for Britain*. London: Batsford.

McDonald, Alan (1986) *The Weller Way. The Story of the Weller Streets Housing Co-operative*. London: Faber & Faber.

McDowell, Linda (1983) Towards an understanding of the gender division of urban space. *Environment & Planning D*, **1**, pp. 59–72.

McGhie, Caroline (1993) Driven up the wall by him next door. *Independent on Sunday*, 30 May, pp. 72–73.

McKay, David H. and Cox, Andrew W. (1979) *The Politics of Urban Change*. London: Croom Helm.

McKenna, Madeline (1991) The suburbanization of the working-class population of Liverpool between the wars. *Social History*, **16**(2), pp. 173–189.

McKie, Robert (1971) *Housing and the Whitehall Bulldozer. A study of the maintenance of demand and a proposal for the cellular renewal of twilight zones*. London: Institute of Economic Affairs.

McKie, Robert (1974) Cellular renewal: a policy for the older housing areas. Town Planning Review, **45**(3), pp. 274–290.

McKie, Robert (1975) Gradual renewal. *Architects' Journal*. 19 February, p. 392.

MacKintosh, P. and Wibberley, G.P. (1952) The use of gardens for food production. *Journal of the Town Planning Institute*, **38**, pp. 54–58.

Madigan, Ruth, Munro, Moira and Smith, Susan J. (1990) Gender and the meaning of the home. *International Journal of Urban & Regional Research*, **14**, pp. 625–647.

Malos, Ellen (ed.) (1980) *The Politics of Housework*. London: Allison & Busby.

Manchester University Settlement (1932) Some Social Aspects of Pre-war Tenements and of Post-war Flats. Manchester & District Regional Survey Society No. 12.

Manchester & Salford Council of Social Service (1960) *Setting up House: furnishing problems on new housing estates*. London: National Council of Social Service.

Mang, Karl (1978) *History of Modern Furniture*. London: Academy Editions.

Martin, C.R.A. (1935) *Slums and Slummers. A sociological treatise on the housing problem.*. London: John Bale.

Marwick, Arthur (1968) *Britain in the Century of Total War: war, peace and social change, 1900–1967*. London: Bodley Head.

Marwick, Arthur (1982) *British Society since 1945*. London: Allen Lane.

Mason, Jennifer (1989) Reconstructing the public and private: the home and marriage in later life, in Allen & Crow (eds.).

Mass Observation (1943) *An Enquiry into People's Homes*. London: Murray.

Matrix (ed.) (1984) *Making Space: women and the man-made environment*. London: Pluto Press.

Meacham, Standish (1977) *A Life Apart: the English working class, 1890–1914*. London: Thames & Hudson.

MHLG (Ministry of Housing & Local Government) (1952) *Living in Flats. Central Housing Advisory Committee*. London: HMSO.

MHLG (1953) *Transfers, Exchanges and Rents* (Central Housing Advisory Committee). London: HMSO.

MHLG (1956) *Moving from the Slums* (Central Housing Advisory Committee). London: HMSO.

MHLG (1959) *Councils and their Houses: management of estates* (Central Housing Advisory Committee). London: HMSO.

MHLG (1966a) *Old People's Flatlets at Stevenage. Report on an experimental joint scheme*. Design Bulletin 11. London: HMSO.

MHLG (1966b) *The Deeplish Study*. London: HMSO.

MHLG (1967a) *Refuse Storage and Collection. Report of the working party on refuse collection*. London: HMSO.

MHLG (1967b) *Housing at Coventry: a user reaction study* (Social Research Section). 30. 12. London: HMSO.

MHLG (1968a) *Space in the Home*. Design Bulletin 6. London: HMSO.

MHLG (1968b) *Land Use and Densities in Traffic*

Separated Housing Layouts. Urban Planning Directorate Technical Study. London: HMSO.

MHLG (1968c) *Grouped Flatlets for Old People: a sociological study.* Design Bulletin 2. London: HMSO.

MHLG (1969a) *Family Houses at West Ham: an account of a project with an appraisal.* Design Bulletin 15. London: HMSO.

MHLG (1969b) *The Family at Home: a study of households in Sheffield.* Design Bulletin 17. London: HMSO.

MHLG (1970a) *Living in a Slum. A study of St. Mary's, Oldham.* Design Bulletin 19. London: HMSO.

MHLG (1970b) *Moving out of a Slum. A study of people moving from St. Mary's, Oldham.* Design Bulletin 20. London: HMSO.

MHLG (1970c) *Families Living at High Density. A study of estates in Leeds, Liverpool and London.* Design Bulletin 21. London: HMSO.

Michèle and Kevin (of The Teachers) (1983) *Directory of Alternative Communities in the British Isles,* 4th ed. Bangor: The Teachers.

Miles, Ian (1988) *Home Informatics. Information technology and the transformation of everyday life.* London: Pinter.

Miller, E.J. and Gwynne, G.V. (1972) *A Life Apart: a pilot study of residential institutions for the physically handicapped and the young chronic sick.* London: Tavistock.

Milner Holland (1965) *Report of the Committee on Housing in Greater London,* Cmnd. 2605. London: HMSO.

Ministry of Health (1938) *The Management of Municipal Housing Estates* (Central Housing Advisory Committee). London: HMSO.

Ministry of Health (1946) *Report of the Standards of Fitness for Habitation Sub-committee of the Central Housing Advisory Committee.* London: HMSO.

Ministry of Health (1948) *The Appearance of Council Estates. Central Housing Advisory Committee.* London: HMSO.

Ministry of Reconstruction (1918a) *Women's Housing Sub-committee First Interim Report,* Cd. 9166. London: HMSO.

Ministry of Reconstruction (1918b) *Final Report,* Cd. 9232. London: HMSO.

Ministry of War Transport (1946) *Design and Layout of Roads in Built-up Areas.* London: HMSO.

Moan, Pat (1980) Learning to learn: confessions of a layabout, hippie, anarchist, woman squatter, in Wates, Nick and Wolmar, Christian (eds.).

Modern Homes Illustrated (1947) London: Odhams Press.

Mogey, J.M. (1956) *Family and Neighbourhood: two studies in Oxford.* Oxford: Oxford University Press.

Morris, R.N. and Mogey, John (1965) *The Sociology of Housing: studies at Berinsfield.* London: Routledge & Kegan Paul.

Morton, Jane (1994) *From Southgate to Hallwood Park – 25 years in the life of a Runcorn community.* Liverpool: Merseyside Improved Houses.

Mowat, C.L. *(1955) Britain between the Wars 1918– 1940.* London: Methuen.

Murdoch, O. (1986) What your home says about you. *Good Housekeeping,* October, pp. 88–91.

Muthesius, Hermann (1979) *The English House* (1st English edition edited by Dennis Sharp, translated Janet Seligman). London: Crosby, Lockwood, Staples. (First published as *Das englische Haus,* 3 vols. 1904–5).

Muthesius, Stefan (1982) *The English Terraced House.* New Haven, CT: Yale University Press.

NAB (National Assistance Board) (1966) *Homeless Single Persons.* Report of a survey carried out between October 1965 and March 1966. London: HMSO.

Nairn, Ian (1956) Counter-attack. Against subtopia. *Architectural Review,* special edition. December.

NCWGB (National Council of Women of Great Britain) (n.d. [1971]) *Domestic Interior Planning* (Housing Sectional Committee). London: NCWGB.

Newman, Oscar (1972) *Defensible Space. People and Design in the Violent City.* New York: Macmillan.

News of the World (c. 1950) *Better Homes Book.* London: News of the World.

Newson, John and Elizabeth (1968) *Four Years Old in an Urban Community.* London: Allen & Unwin.

NFHA (National Federation of Housing Associations) (1988) *Building Your Future: self-build housing initiatives for the unemployed.* London: NFHA.

NFHA (With North Housing Trust) (1993) *Accommodating Diversity: the design of housing for minority ethnic, religious and cultural groups.* London: NFHA.

NHTPC (National Housing & Town Planning Council) (1987) High Rise Living. A *Housing and Planning Review* special. **42**(1).

Niner, Pat with Hedges, Alan (1992) *Mobile Homes*

Survey, Final Report of the Department of Environment. London: HMSO.

Noble, John (1982) *Activities and Spaces: dimensional data for housing design*. London: Architectural Press.

Nuffield Foundation (1947) *Old People*. Report of a Survey Committee on the Problems of Ageing and the Care of Old People. London: Nuffield Foundation.

Oakley, Ann (1974a) *The Sociology of Housework*. Oxford: Robertson. (Edition used is 1985. Oxford: Blackwell).

Oakley, Ann (1974b) *Housewife*. London: Allen Lane. (Edition used is 1976. Harmondsworth: Penguin).

Oliver, Paul, Davis, Ian and Bentley, Ian (1982) *Dunroamin: the suburban semi and its enemies*. London: Barrie & Jenkins.

Omar Park Homes (1992) Advertisement. *Mobile and Holiday Homes*, October, End page.

Open University (1982) *The Changing Experience of Women*. Milton Keynes: Open University Press.

Orwell, George (1937) *The Road to Wigan Pier*. London: Gollancz. (Edition used is 1962. Harmondsworth: Penguin).

Osborn, Frederic J. and Whittick, Arnold (1963) *The New Towns. The Answer to Megalopolis*. London: Leonard Hill.

Osborn, Tom (1980) Outpost of a new culture. Squatting communities as an alternative way of life, in Wates, Nick and Wolmar, Christian (eds.).

Our Towns (1944) *Our Towns: a Close-up. A study made in 1939-42*, 2nd ed. (Women's Group on Public Welfare & National Council of Social Service). London: Oxford University Press.

Owens, Ruth (1984) Parker Morris in the pub. *Architects' Journal*, 29 June, pp. 52-61.

Owens, Ruth (1987a) Born again. *Architects' Journal*, 18 March, pp. 48-57.

Owens, Ruth (1987b) Bramley Housing Co-op, Freston Road, London W.11: Appraisal. *Architects' Journal*, 29 April, pp. 37-46.

Pahl, R.E. (1984) *Divisions of Labour*. Oxford: Blackwell.

Pankhurst, E. Sylvia (1914) How to meet hardship. *Woman's Dreadnought*, No. 23, 22 August, p. 90.

Parker, R.A (1988) An historical background to residential care, in Sinclair, Ian (ed.).

Parker, Tony (1983) *The People of Providence. A housing estate and some of its inhabitants*. London: Hutchinson.

Parker, Barry and Unwin, Raymond (1901) *The Art of Building a Home. A collection of lectures and illustrations*. London: Longmans.

Parker, Julia and Mirrlees, Catriona (1988a) Housing, in Halsey, A.H. (ed.).

Parker, Julia and Mirrlees, Catriona (1988b) Welfare, in Halsey, A.H. (ed.).

Parker Morris (1961) *Home for Today and Tomorrow* (Ministry of Housing & Local Government). London: HMSO.

Partington, Angela (1989) The Designer housewife in the 1950s, in Attfield, Judy and Kirkham, Pat (eds.).

Pawley, Martin (1971) *Architecture versus Housing*. New York: Praeger.

Pearce, David (1983) Population in communal establishments. *Population Trends*, **33**, pp. 18-21.

Pearson, Lynn F. (1988) *The Architectural and Social History of Co-operative Living*. London: Macmillan.

Pember Reeves, Maud (1913) *Round about a Pound a Week*. London: Bell. (Edition used is 1979. London: Virago).

PEP (Political & Economic Planning) (1945) *The Market for Household Appliances*. London: PEP.

Pepper, Simon (1977) The people's house. *Architectural Review*, **162**, pp. 269-73.

Pepper, Simon (1981) Ossulston Street: early LCC experiments in high-rise housing, 1925-29. *The London Journal*, **7**(1), pp. 45-64.

Phillips, R. Randal (1923) *The House You Want. Some practical data about the building, equipment, and furnishing of it in a series of dialogues*. London: Country Life.

Platt, Steve (1980) A decade of squatting. The story of squatting in Britain since 1968, in Wates, Nick and Wolmar, Christian (eds.).

Pleydell-Bouverie (n.d.) *Daily Mail Book of Post-war Homes, based on the ideas and opinions of the women of Britain*. London: Daily Mail Ideal Home Exhibition Department.

Power, Anne (1987a) *The PEP Guide to Local Housing Management and Estate Action. 1. The PEP Model. 2. The PEP Experience*. London: DoE & Welsh Office.

Power, Anne (1987b) *Property Before People. The management of twentieth-century council housing*. London: Allen & Unwin.

Pugh, Martin (1992) *Women and the Women's Movement in Britain 1914-1959*. London: Macmillan.

Purkiss, Peter (1982) A Survey of Self Build in Great Britain. Diploma Dissertation. Portsmouth Polytechnic School of Architecture.

Raper, Martin (1974) Housing for Single Young People. Research Paper 7. Institute of Advanced Architectural Studies, York University.

Rapoport, Amos (1968) The personal element in housing: an argument for open-ended design. *RIBA Journal*, July, pp. 300–307.

Ravetz, Alison (1968) The Victorian coal kitchen and its reformers. *Victorian Studies*, **XI**(4), June, pp. 435–60.

Ravetz, Alison (1971) Tenancy patterns and turnover at Quarry Hill Flats, Leeds. *Urban Studies*, **8**(2), pp. 181–205.

Ravetz, Alison (1974a) From working-class tenement to modern flat: local authorities and multi-storey housing between the wars: in Sutcliffe, Anthony (ed.).

Ravetz, Alison (1974b) *Model Estate. Planned housing at Quarry Hill, Leeds.* London: Croom Helm.

Ravetz, Alison (1976) Housing at Byker, Newcastle upon Tyne: Appraisal. *Architect's Journal*, 14 April.

Ravetz, Alison (1986) *The Government of Space: town planning in modern society.* London: Faber & Faber.

Ravetz, Alison (1989) A view from the interior, in Attfield, Judy and Kirkham, Pat (eds.).

Ravetz, Alison (1992) Factors contributing to estate write-offs and their relevance to current theory and practice: Quarry Hill Flats and Hunslet Grange, Leeds, in Ferguson, Alan and Sim, Duncan (eds.).

Ravetz, Alison and Low, Jim (1980) PSSHAK 18 months on. *Architects' Journal*, 27 February, pp. 425–440.

RECO I. (1918) Correspondence with the Leeds Women Citizens' League (unpublished). File 623. Public Record Office, London.

Regional Trends (1975) Volume 11. (Central Statistical Office) London: HMSO.

Regional Trends (1993) Volume 28. (Central Statistical Office) London: HMSO.

RIBA (Royal Institute of British Architects) (1957) *Family Life in High Density Housing.* Report of a symposium held on 24 May. London: RIBA.

Richards, J.M. (1946) *The Castles on the Ground.* London: Architectural Press.

Richards, J.M. (1973) *The Castles on the Ground. The anatomy of suburbia*, 2nd ed. London: Murray.

Rigby, Andrew (1974) *Communes in Britain.* London: Routledge & Kegan Paul.

Roberts, Marion (1984) Private kitchens, public cooking, in Matrix (ed.).

Roberts, Robert (1971) *The Classic Slum. Salford life in the first quarter of the century.* Manchester: University of Manchester Press.

Robinson, W. (1883) *The English Flower Garden.* London: Murray.

Rollett, Constance (1972) Housing: in Halsey (ed.).

Rowntree, B. Seebohm (1941) *Poverty and Progress. A second social survey of York.* London: Longmans.

Roy, Robin and Cross, Nigel (1975) Technology and Society. Man-made Futures: Design and Technology. T262, 2–3. Milton Keynes. Open University Press.

Royal Commission (1909) *Report of the Royal Commission on the Poor Laws and Relief of Distress.* London: HMSO.

Saunders, Peter (1990) *A Nation of Home Owners.* London: Unwin and Hyman.

Scoffham, E.R. (1984) *The Shape of British Housing.* London: George Godwin.

Seabrook, Jeremy (1990) Cornwall gone west. *New Statesman and New Society*, 7 August, pp. 12–14.

Sedgwick, H.D. (c. 1920) *What Shall I Do with my Garden.* London: Collingridge.

Sharp, Thomas (1932) *Town and Countryside. Some aspects of urban and rural development.* Oxford: Oxford University Press.

Shaw, Frederick (1985) *The Homes and Homeless of Postwar Britain.* London: Parthenon.

Shepheard, Peter (1953) *Modern Gardens.* London: Architectural Press.

Sherman, Margaret (ed.) (1950) *Daily Mail Ideal Home Book, 1950–51.* London: Daily Mail.

Sinclair, Ian (ed.) (1988) *Residential Care: the research reviewed.* London: HMSO.

Sinha, Sumita (1992) Home is a little mud hut in Dagenham. *Independent*, 12 August.

Smithells, Roger (ed.) n.d. *News of the World Better Homes Book.* London: News of the World.

Smithson, Alison and Peter (1967) *Urban Structuring. Studies of Alison & Peter Smithson.* London: Studio Vista.

Social Trends (1970–) (Central Statistical Office). London: HMSO.

Sociological Review (1951) *The Effect of the Design of the Temporary Prefabricated Bungalow on Household Routines*, The Sociological Review, XLIII Section 2. Ledbury: Le Play House Press.

Spring, Martin (1991) Starting Blocks. *Building*, 29 November, 52–6.

Spring, Martin (1994) Hulme brew. *Building*, 28 January, pp. 41–46.

Spring Rice, Margery (1939) *Working-class Wives, their Health and Conditions*. Harmondsworth: Penguin Books. (Edition used in 1981. London: Virago).

Stearn, Jonathan (1992) Can't pay, won't pay. *New Statesman & Society*, 26 June, p. 16.

Stedman-Jones, Gareth (1974) Working-class culture and working-class politics in London, 1870–1900: notes on the remaking of a working class. *Journal of Social History*, 7, pp. 460–508.

Stephenson, H. and L. (1964) *Eating, Sleeping, Living*. London: Cooperative United Ltd.

Stevenson, John (1984) *British Society 1914–45. Pelican Social History of Britain*. Harmondsworth: Penguin Books.

Stewart, W.F.R. (1970) *Children in Flats: a family study*. London: NSPCC.

Streeter, Fred (1956) *The Labour-saving Garden*. London: Odhams Press.

Stubbs, Cherrie (1988) Property rights and relations: the purchase of council housing. *Housing Studies*, 3(3), pp. 145–158.

Sumner, Greta and Smith, Randall (1969) *Planning Local Authority Services for the Elderly*. London: Allen & Unwin.

Sutcliffe, Anthony (1974) *Multi-storey Living: the British working-class experience*. London: Croom Helm.

Swenarton, Mark (1981) *Homes Fit for Heroes. The politics and architecture of early state housing in Britain*. London: Heinemann.

Swingler, Nicholas (1969) Move on, gypsy. *New Society*, 26 June, pp. 985–987.

Tarn, J.N. (1971) Working-class Housing in 19th-century Britain. Paper No. 7. London: Architectural Association.

Tarn, J.N. (1973) *Five Per Cent Philanthropy: an account of housing in urban areas between 1840 and 1914*. Cambridge: Cambridge University Press.

Teymur, Necdet, Markus, Thomas A. and Woolley, Tom (eds.). (1988) *Rehumanizing Housing*. London: Butterworths.

Thomas, Andrew and Niner, Pat (1989) *Living in Temporary Accommodation: a survey of homeless people* (DoE). London: HMSO.

Thomas, Huw and Krishnarayan, Vijay (eds.) (1994) *Race, Equality and Planning: policies and procedures*. Avebury: Aldershot.

Thomas, Ivor (1935) *Housing Principles*. Fabian Tract 242. London: Fabian Society.

Thompson, F.M.L. (1988) *The Rise of Respectable Society: a social history of Victorian Britain, 1830–1900*. London: Fontana.

Thompson, F.M.L. (ed.) (1990) *The Cambridge Social History of Britain, 1750–1950*. 1. *Regions and communities*. 2. *People and their environment*. 3. *Social agencies and institutions*. Cambridge: Cambridge University Press.

Thompson, John (1985) *Community Architecture: the story of Lea View House, Hackney*. London: RIBA Community Architecture Group.

Toland, Sue (1980) Changes in living standards since the 1950s. *Social Trends*, No. 10.

Town and Country Planning Association (1939) *Houses, Towns and Countryside*. London: TCPA.

Townsend, Peter (1957) *The Family Life of Old People*. London: Routledge & Kegan Paul.

Townsend, Peter (1962) *The Last Refuge. A survey of residential institutions and homes for the aged in England & Wales*. London: Routledge & Kegan Paul.

Tudor Walters (1918) *Report of the Committee . . . to consider questions of building construction in connection with dwellings for the working classes*, Cd. 9191. London: HMSO.

Turner, John F.C. (1972) Housing as a verb, in Turner, John F.C. and Fichter, Robert (eds.).

Turner, John F.C. (1976) *Housing by People. Towards Autonomy in Building Environments*. London: Boyars.

Turner, John F.C. and Fichter, Robert (eds.) (1972) *Freedom to Build. Dweller Control of the Housing Process*. New York: Macmillan.

Unwin, Raymond (1902) *Cottage Plans and Common Sense*. Fabian Society Tract No. 109.

Vale, Brenda and Robert (1975) *The Autonomous House: design and planning for self-sufficiency*. London: Thames & Hudson.

Vereker, Charles, Mays, John Barron, Gittus, Elizabeth and Broady, Maurice (1961) *Urban Redevelopment and Social Change. A study of social conditions in central Liverpool, 1955–56*. Liverpool: University of Liverpool.

WACSF (The Women's Advisory Council on Solid Fuel) (1951) *Heating, Cooking, and Hot Water Supplies for the Small House*. London: WACSF.

Wagner, Gillian (Chair) (1988) *Residential Care: A Positive Choice*. Report of the Independent Review of Residential Care. London: National Institute for Social Work.

Wajcman, Judy (1992) Domestic technology: labour-saving or enslaving? in Kirkup, Gill and Keller, Laurie Smith (eds.).

Walley, Joan E. (1960) The Kitchen, London, Constable.

Walter Segal Self Build Trust (1988) Newsletter, Issue No. 1. May.

Waplington, Nick (n.d.) Living Room, Cornerhouse Publications.

Ward, Colin (1976) Housing: an anarchist approach. London: Freedom Press.

Ward, Colin (1980) The early squatters: squatting from the middle ages to the Second World War: in Wates, Nick and Wolmar, Christian (eds.).

Ward-Jackson, C.H. and Harvey, Denis E. (1972) The English Gypsy Caravan: its origins, builders, technology and conservation. Newton Abbot: David & Charles.

Wates, Nick (1976) The Battle for Tolmers Square. London: Routledge & Kegan Paul.

Wates, Nick (1982) The Liverpool breakthrough or public sector housing phase 2. Architects Journal, 8 September, pp. 51–58.

Wates, Nick and Wolmar, Christian (eds.) (1980) Squatting: the Real Story. London: Bayleaf Books.

Watson, Sophie (1987) Ideas of the family in the development of housing forms, in Loney, Martin et al. (eds.).

Watson, Sophie, with Austerberry, Helen (1986) Housing and Homelessness: a feminist perspective. London: Routledge & Kegan Paul.

Weihs, Anke and Tallo, Joan (eds.) (1988) Camphill Villages, 2nd ed. Gloucester: Camphill Press.

Wheatcroft, Muriel (ed.) (1960) Housework with Satisfaction. London: National Council of Social Service.

White, Cynthia L. (1970) Women's Magazines 1693–1968. London: Michael Joseph.

White, Jerry (1986) The Worst Street in North London: Campbell Bunk, Islington, between the wars. London: Routledge & Kegan Paul.

White, L.E. (1946) Tenement Town. London: Jason Press.

White, L.E. (1953) The outdoor play of children living in flats, in Kuper, Leo (ed.).

Whitehead, Christine and Kleinman, Mark (1989) The private rented sector and the Housing Act, 1988. Social Policy Review 1988–9, pp. 67–84.

Whittick, Arnold, with Schreiner, Johannes (1957) The Small House Today and Tomorrow, 2nd ed. London: Leonard Hill.

Wibberley, G.P. (1959) Agriculture and Urban Growth. London: Michael Joseph.

Willcocks, Dianne, Peace, Sheila and Kalleher, Leonie (1987) Private Lives in Public Places. A research-based critique of residential life in local authority old people's homes. London: Tavistock.

Williams, Jan, Twort, Hazel and Bachelli, Ann (1969) Women and the family, in Malos, Ellen (ed.) (1980).

Willmott, Peter (1963) The Evolution of a Community. A study of Dagenham after forty years. London: Routledge & Kegan Paul.

Willmott, Peter and Young, Michael (1960) Family and Class in a London Suburb. London: Routledge & Kegan Paul.

Wilson, Sir Arton (1959) Caravans as Homes, Cmnd. 872. London: HMSO.

Wingfield Digby Peter (1976) Hostels and Lodgings for Single People (Office of Population Censuses & Surveys). London: HMSO.

Winship, Janice (1980) Advertising in Women's Magazines 1956–74. CCCS Woman Series SP No. 59. University of Birmingham.

Wood, Andrew (1988) Greentown: a case study of a proposed alternative community. Energy & Environment Research Unit 057. Open University, Milton Keynes.

Woolf, Myra (1967) The Housing Survey in England & Wales. Government Social Survey SS372. London: HMSO.

Worden, Suzette (1989) Powerful women: electricity in the home, 1919–40, in Attfield, Judy and Kirkham, Pat (eds.).

Wright, Richardson Little (1934) The Story of Gardening. From the hanging gardens of Babylon to the hanging gardens of New York. London: Routledge & Sons.

Yerbury, F.R. (n.d. c. 1947) Modern Homes. Illustrated. London: Odhams Press.

Yorke, F.R.S. (1937) The Modern House in England. London: Architectural Press.

Yorke, F.R.S and Whiting, Penelope (1953) The New Small House. London: Architectural Press.

Young, Michael and Willmott, Peter (1957) Family and Kinship in East London. London: Routledge & Kegan Paul.

Young, Terence (1934) Becontree and Dagenham: a report made for the Pilgrim Trust. London: Sidders.

Zweig, Ferdynand (1961) The Worker in an Affluent Society: family life and industry. London: Heinemann.

Zweig, Ferdynand (1976) The New Acquisitive Society (Centre for Policy Studies). Chichester: Barry Rose.

ABBREVIATIONS AND MEASUREMENTS

ABBREVIATIONS

CoSMITH	Council of Scientific Management in the Home
DoE	Department of the Environment
EAW	Electrical Association for Women
GHS	General Household Survey
GLC	Greater London Council
LCC	London County Council
MHLG	Ministry of Housing and Local Government
NAB	National Assistance Board
NCWGB	National Council of Women of Great Britain
NFHA	National Federation of Housing Associations
NHTPC	National Housing and Town Planning Council
PEP	Political and Economic Planning
RIBA	Royal Institute of British Architects
WACSF	Women's Advisory Council on Solid Fuel
WHTPC	Women's Housing and Town Planning Council
YMCA	Young Men's Christian Association
YWCA	Young Women's Christian Association

MEASUREMENTS CONVERSION

Measurements of houses and other spaces are given throughout in imperial rather than metric, for three particular reasons: this is how they appear in most of the documentary sources used, for England did not begin to 'go metric' until the 1960s; a straight conversion of feet and inches results in some extremely irregular numbers; and most of the readers of this book are likely still to think in feet and inches, particularly in anything relating to the home and its furnishings (at the time of writing English carpeting is still sold by the square yard, while curtain fabric is sold by the linear metre). For the benefit of those readers who do think in metric terms the following conversions are given.

6 inches	= 0.15 metre
1 foot	= 0.30 metre
4 feet	= 1.22 metres
7ft 6 in	= 2.29 metres
8ft 6 in	= 2.59 metres
9 feet	= 2.74 metres
15 feet	= 4.57 metres
20 feet	= 6.10 metres
1 mile	= 1.61 kilometres
1 square foot	= 0.09 square metres
15 square feet	= 1.39 square metres
20 square feet	= 1.86 square metres
100 square feet	= 9.29 square metres
1 square yard	= 0.84 square metres
400 square yards	= 336 square metres
1 acre	= 0.4 hectare

12 houses per acre is equal to approximately 30 houses per hectare

20 houses per acre is equal to approximately 49 houses per hectare

INDEX

Printed in Great Britain
by Amazon

16224100R00145